STEVE CAUTHEN
ENGLISH ODYSSEY

Also by Michael Tanner

Non Fiction
Crime & Murder in Victorian Leicestershire
My Friend Spanish Steps
The King George VI Steeplechase
Teleprompter & Co
The Champion Hurdle
Pretty Polly: An Edwardian Heroine
Great Racing Partnerships
Dessie: A Year in the Life of Desert Orchid
The Major: The Biography of Dick Hern
Great Jockeys of the Flat
Michael Roberts: A Champion's Story
Lester Piggott: Return to the Saddle
Ali in Britain
Branston Abby: Record Breaker
A Season in Stripes: Life with the Leicester Tigers
In Your Face: A Rugby Odyssey
The Champion Hurdle: From Blaris to Istabraq
Troubled Epic: On Location With *Ryan's Daughter*
The Legend of Mick the Miller
Gentleman George? The Contradictory Life of George Duffield
The Suffragette Derby
The Spotted Wonder
The Oxford Murder
The Demon: The Life of George Fordham
From PoW Camp to Oxford University

Fiction
The Tinman's Farewell
The Black Bridge
Red Hand: Secret of the Suffragette Derby

STEVE CAUTHEN
ENGLISH ODYSSEY

MICHAEL TANNER

Foreword by Steve Cauthen

RACING POST

First published by Pitch Publishing on behalf of Racing Post, 2021

Pitch Publishing
A2 Yeoman Gate
Yeoman Way
Worthing
Sussex
BN13 3QZ

www.pitchpublishing.co.uk
info@pitchpublishing.co.uk
www.racingpost.com/shop

© 2021, Michael Tanner

Every effort has been made to trace the copyright. Any oversight will be rectified in future editions at the earliest opportunity by the publisher.

All rights reserved. No part of this book may be reproduced, sold or utilised in any form or transmitted in any form or by any means, electronic or mechanical, including photocopying, recording or by any information storage and retrieval system, without prior permission in writing from the Publisher.

A CIP catalogue record is available for this book
from the British Library.

ISBN 9781839500725

Typesetting and origination by Pitch Publishing

Printed and bound in India by Replika Press Pvt. Ltd.

CONTENTS

Foreword	*vii*
Introduction	*ix*
Prologue	*xix*
One The Rise and Fall of 'Stevie Wonder'	23
Two Adaptation & Redemption	58
Three The Warren Place Harem	117
Four Pace makes the Race	151
Five 'Is Steve Available?'	210
Six The Cadillac Colt	242
Seven Valete	258
Appendix I: Winners By Season	*273*
Appendix II: English Classics	*274*
Appendix III: Other Classics Won	*276*
Appendix IV: Selected Other Major Races Won	*277*
Appendix V: Best Horses	*281*
Acknowledgements	*283*

FOREWORD

IT CAME as quite a surprise to learn that someone wished to write a book devoted to my English-based career so many years after it ended. But it's kinda cool to know my impact on English racing was thought worthy of being recorded for posterity. And also to learn that the book had been inspired by someone's interest in sectional timing. I wasn't aware the subject was being written about back in England in the 1980s and 90s. Hopefully, people learnt something from watching me ride and judge pace by using the 'clock-in-the-head'.

I feel honoured to think I left something behind in my adopted country: not just the incentive to ride and win races from the front, but also by popularising the 'toe-in-the-iron' riding style that has become so commonplace.

My English career would never have got off the ground without the help of numerous people. This is an opportunity to pay tribute and extend my gratitude to a few of them. Barry and Penny Hills treated me like a son, and I love them both; Jimmy Lindley opened so many doors and educated me in the ways of English racing, without which I'd have been lost; jockeys' agents were novelties in England back in the 1980s, but without the priceless assistance of John Hanmer I'd never have become champion jockey; my drivers John Naughton and John Barnes gave me great company and got me where I needed to go in good order. And I remember fondly absent friends: Robert Sangster put his faith in me to bring me over to England; Pat Eddery and Walter Swinburn were tough but fair opponents to ride against and brilliant jockeys both. And there's little I can add about Henry Cecil other than remind everybody what a genius he was with horses and what a loyal supporter he was of me.

Michael's well-researched telling of my 14 seasons in England is informative and entertaining; and he's demonstrated its importance to me by setting it beside the American career I left behind.

I hope readers will enjoy re-living the old days as much as I have being reminded of them.

INTRODUCTION

WHEN CAESAR boasted 'veni, vidi, vici,' he left us one of the most familiar Latin phrases. 'I came, I saw, I conquered' celebrated his subjugation of the Bosporan Kingdom of northern Turkey at the Battle of Zela in 47BC. One hopes the dictator won't take umbrage from beyond the funeral pyre, however, if his declaration is put into the third person singular to salute Steve Cauthen's conquest of the English Turf in the last quarter of the 20th century.

For not since Tod Sloan revolutionised race-riding in England 100 years earlier had an American jockey carved out an imperishable legacy like Cauthen. Sloan brought with him a new style of riding and racing that exposed flaws in our jockeys. Not for him a policeman's seat: he crouched and hid behind his horse's neck, a low and streamlined seat promoting greater speed. And he caught our riders napping by forcing the pace from the gate instead of joining them in the English fashion of dawdling and coming with a late rush. However, fashions changed and, though not so exaggerated as of old, English races again became characterised by lack of early pace during the passage of the 20th century. The eye-catching foreign input came from Australians such as Scobie Breasley and Ron Hutchinson; but nobody tried to replicate their quiet 'bobbing' finesse. Steve Cauthen's arrival in 1979, however, was akin to the second coming of Tod Sloan. Cauthen's back was so low and flat one could barely spot him from head-on: his legs and trunk angled like a human paper clip. And confident in his ability to judge pace to his benefit and the detriment of others, he revived the art of winning from the front. By the time he retired in 1992 his trademark seat and his willingness to employ forcing tactics had been adopted in one way or another by virtually every leading jockey in the country. Truly: he came, he saw, he conquered.

Any fan of the Turf had heard of Steve Cauthen before his arrival. He was 'Stevie Wonder'; 'The Six Million Dollar Man'; 'The Kentucky Kid', who'd taken American racing by storm as a teenager; for two years he was hotter than the hinges of Hell until a 110-ride streak of losers plunged him to the brink of a professional abyss. But in my case a deep interest in his talents developed once I began clocking and writing about sectional times in the mid-1980s. One came to appreciate more fully the uncanny gifts of this supremely talented jockey. The clock became the prism through which Cauthen's talents might be assessed as objectively as the smoothness of his riding style pleased the naked eye. Sectional times were our magnifying glass.

Clocking the component sections of a race was virtually unheard of in England BC – 'Before Cauthen'. In fact, race times overall were not accorded much respect: the only 'time' that matters, suggested one Turf sage, is 'time spent in jail'. Time comparisons of any kind were perceived next to useless owing to the disparate topography – the cambers, switchbacks and undulations – that lent so much character to English tracks. That more enlightened Turf nations – France, Australia, Hong Kong, Japan et al – flashed electronically clocked sectional times onto television screens and trackside teletimers during races to enable spectators and viewers to judge how fast or slow a race was unfolding, and how their wager might cope with either, cut no ice in England. These times would then be printed in the following day's trade papers, such as America's *Daily Racing Form* or France's *Paris Turf*, for more leisurely analysis. But in England it was as if such information didn't exist or didn't matter. That is, until the deeds of Steve Cauthen shook up the English Turf media and made it pay attention.

INTRODUCTION

Nowhere was sectional timing more part and parcel of the racing game than across the Atlantic where American horse-players – on and off track – paid heed to the mantra 'Pace makes the race.' And to judge the pace accurately it had to be recorded along the lines of lap-timing in track athletics. On the race-track this involved timing every quarter (two furlongs) and occasionally one furlong (towards the finish). The barometer of pace was 'even time' – a quarter in 24 seconds. The resultant splits or fractions, as they became known, promoted an understanding of how a race was run – e.g. a gallop slower than even time prompted a late sprint for the line by animals with plenty left in reserve; a taxing gallop favoured the stamina-laden by eliminating the likelihood of a sprint finish. Astute students of the data were able to identify the preferred running style of a horse – its running profile: a 'grinder' enjoyed a strong gallop; a 'kicker' or a 'closer' preferred deploying a burst of late acceleration off a slower pace. Nowhere in sport might the maxim 'knowledge is power' be demonstrated to better financial effect.

American racehorses are barned and trained at the tracks on which they are about to run, which, thanks to them being homogenous, flat, left-handed dirt ovals, facilitates time comparisons for both workouts and races. To this end, American apprentices – 'bug boys' – grow into fully fledged jockeys, having had the lessons outlined in the previous paragraph engrained into them by riding to the clock during work in the morning and races in the afternoon; if a trainer instructs a work rider to go 'four-eighths in 52', he'd better get his mount to complete those four furlongs in 52 seconds or face a volley of abuse. And every track possessed a 'Clockers Corner', a vantage point where assorted rail-birds – jockeys' agents and speed handicappers, hustlers and 'hardboots' – gathered every morning to get a heads-up on the hand-clocked workouts destined to appear in *Daily Racing Form*.

Such was the racing environment in which Steve Cauthen matured from bug boy to a 17-year-old champion jockey in less than two seasons. That he made the transition so rapidly brought super-stardom. And switching from Eastern Standard Time to British Summer Time didn't cause much disruption to the 'clock in his head'. Of course, the concept of even time needed revision, owing to the physical diversity of the tracks he now faced: a 24-second quarter on an undulating track like Epsom or Goodwood described a different pace to a flat one like Chester or York. Cauthen soon got to grips with the problem. And solved it.

It quickly became apparent to English racegoers that Cauthen rarely, if ever, misjudged a mount's running profile. And, more importantly, he seldom, if ever, misjudged the pace; it was as if Cauthen had the finest chronometer ticking away under his skull cap. No finer juxtaposition of this acuity may be found than in a pair of Group Ones at Royal Ascot in 1990 run over the Old Mile: he won the St James's Palace Stakes on Shavian by making every yard and then added the Coronation Stakes on Chimes of Freedom after lying off the pace and coming late. If any rider deserved to be nicknamed 'Nobody' it was Steve Cauthen. Why? Because 'Nobody's perfect'.

The American possessed other qualities that set him aside from his colleagues in English weighing rooms from 1979 to 1992; for one, hands looking more suited to holding a pick-axe instead of a set of reins down which the rider transmits the most sensitive of messages, belied their heft to gossamer effect. Yet Cauthen's understanding of pace was his most sublime trait. Consequently, Cauthen became a God-send to the various columns based on sectional timing that I contributed to Turf newspapers and periodicals. On English tracks, however, the fractions had to be hand-timed, usually reinforced with the aid of video recordings. Some derided my efforts at bringing the subject to wider attention. But when the message is worth communicating it's worth persevering. Eventually the naysayers began singing from my hymn sheet.

In that early land of the blind, the one-eyed man could be king. Even hand-timed fractions gave the watch-holder some objective idea of race rhythm; notably, whereabouts came the telling injection of pace that settled the destiny of Group races, the battleground for elite performers who

INTRODUCTION

tended to play tactical games of cat and mouse – as opposed to handicaps habitually truly run from gate to line. One of the sport's biggest outfits recognised the value of the data quicker than most, regularly seeking assurance how a particular Group race had been run and whether their horse had shown itself to be a 'grinder' or a 'kicker'. The discussion about future tactics invariably ended with questions such as: 'Do we need a pacemaker to force the pace for a grinder or one to slow it down for a kicker?' or 'When should we inject pace into the race to expose any vulnerabilities in rivals X or Y?'

In 1997, thanks to the good offices of Brough Scott and Andrew Franklin, *Channel 4 Racing* chose to involve me in showcasing sectional timing. Over a number of seasons I'd stand alongside Graham Goode or Simon Holt in the commentator's booth for Group One events and act as their personal teletimer, letting them know the splits and whether that meant the pace was fast or slow – the various repercussions of which we'd discussed beforehand. That, to me, was fulfilling the main aim of sectional timing: objective information in running.

Sectional timing drew greater attention, however, when its financial implications became apparent thanks to the 1997 Eclipse Stakes. I asserted odds-on Bosra Sham, the new star in the firmament following stunning successes in the Guineas, Champion Stakes and, freshest in the memory, the Prince of Wales's Stakes at Royal Ascot, could be overturned in a five-runner renewal. Her fractions suggested she was a grinder. Compromised by a pedestrian gallop, I argued, she could be exposed. And that's what happened: Pilsudski, at the remunerative odds of 11/2, beat her by two lengths – an against-the-odds prediction that led to Brough conducting a live *Channel 4* dissection of the race with me. Five weeks later, the runes were again read accurately in a four-runner Juddmonte International. Once more Bosra Sham was odds-on and running without a pacemaker. Might she force the pace this time? Singspiel's running profile suggested he could cope with that, and prevail if it came to a sprint down the long York straight. Singspiel beat her by four lengths into last place – at equally rewarding odds of 4/1.

A suitably impressed John McCririck, always quick to bestow a moniker, instantly christened me 'Mystic Mike'.

Two from two spoke well of sectional times as an aid to winner finding. But it's no more than an aid. Ground, wind strength and direction, positioning of running rails and weight carried must all be factored into the equation when assessing their true value. And racehorses are athletes not robots; there's a limit to quantifying body and soul – particularly when the athlete in question is deaf and dumb to any entreaties. Above all, the jockey must be able to read the pace and adjust to its ramifications for his mount, quite literally, on the hoof. Once the gates slam open he's on his own. Judgement and coolness are the only currency with any value now. And you could bank on Steve Cauthen. He was as safe as the Old Lady of Threadneedle Street.

That example of Bosra Sham becomes relevant to this work because, although not partnered by Cauthen, she was trained by Henry Cecil on whose horses Cauthen demonstrated his acute awareness of pace during a six-year tenure as stable jockey at Warren Place. It was a rare column of mine that did not extol the accuracy of the clock in Steve's head: 'Classy Cauthen' was the headline to one piece that pinpointed the 'outstanding tactician currently performing in these islands.' Another ventured to say: 'We have not seen his peer at the art of winning from the front – Lester Piggott included.'

And didn't things change when Cauthen vacated the track in 1992. As the 1993 Derby approached I found myself lamenting his absence in the *Sporting Life Weekender* under the headline 'Missing You, Cauthen.' Back in the 1920s, I mused, the cry of 'Come on, Steve!' used to fill the air when the Derby came around. In 1993 the exaltation could've been amended to 'Come back, Steve!' – for Donoghue, read Cauthen. You see, a recurring trait had blighted the season's middle-distance Pattern races: a marked lack of pace that did scant justice to their race description. When Cauthen was around, I reminded readers you could put money on this rarely, if ever, being the case. But in his absence the middle-distance category had been replete with instances of woefully tentative early pace. Was this

INTRODUCTION

merely coincidental? Or were we gathering abundant evidence to support the hypothesis that our jockeys lacked the fine judgement of pace frequently found in their American counterparts? Did they lack sufficient confidence to show initiative in this respect?

There's no question riding a winning race from the front is a far more difficult proposition than riding one from behind. Even if the leader is left to its own devices, the jockey must judge pace to perfection; he has no other horse in sight by which he may gauge pace. All he has is the 'clock in his head'. And he's a sitting duck for opponents stalking him; they can tuck in while he takes the strain, physically and psychologically. They can see him; but he's no wing mirrors to check what they're about. Alternatively, he may be hassled along faster than he wants, owing to the presence of a horse upsides; possibly a rival put in the race deliberately to make him compete to exhaustion. Preventing a rush of blood to the head from inciting a false move during the cauldron of battle consequently demands of any jockey colossal sang-froid. And the blood flowing through Cauthen's veins as the bugle sounded was glacial.

I confessed to having lost count of the numerous occasions I'd been afforded just cause to attribute a victory to the so-called 'clock' in Cauthen's head – a veritable Rolex among a tray of Mickey Mouse timepieces. The majority of Group One races over a mile and a half will see at least one pacemaker in the field that can afford to sacrifice itself, I argued, with few or no questions asked regarding 'running on its merits'. But Cauthen's acute sense of pace made a pace-making stable-mate superfluous: in the 241 renewals of the Derby up to 2020 there have only been eight certain instances of the winner making virtually every yard of the running – two of those successes stand to the peerless American within the space of three years.

Steve Cauthen, unlike Caesar, was no braggart. He was an unassuming champion; modesty became him. Often he confessed to feeling uneasy being labelled some kind of 'god' just because he won horseraces. Nevertheless, to us rail-birds there was something joyous about watching how Cauthen applied the guile and the horse supplied the power to leave us believing in centaurs. He dazzled us with talents based on an acute understanding of the thoroughbred and its foibles that only materialises when horseman and jockey are one and the same – which is not always the case. Few bar the Philistine would deny the sight of a running horse being one of the most beautiful and stirring sights in the natural world; any human impediment to that vision is as ugly as it is unwelcome. Watching Cauthen on a thoroughbred racehorse was to gaze upon a thing of beauty: his streamlined aerodynamic crouch so low that from head-on he could barely be spotted tucked away behind his animal's neck; his flat back tantamount to a second skin atop its hide; his toe-tips caressing the irons with the delicacy of a raindrop on a blade of grass. Thus did we appreciate the transatlantic mantra 'down low and go for dough!' And understand why one Belmont regulare swore, 'You could serve drinks on the Kid's back at the furlong marker and you wouldn't spill a drop before he hits the wire.'

Yes, the image of Steve Cauthen on a thoroughbred racehorse came as close to perfection as rationality allows. He once acknowledged that opinion in his own quiet way: 'The horse is such a beautiful animal, when you're on him, in control of him, moving with him as one, it's a beautiful feeling. And the best is when you're almost getting him to know what you want to do.'

The extraordinary thing was Cauthen made the extraordinary happen so regularly the extraordinary seemed normal. It made watching him constantly instructive and infinitely pleasurable. He may or may not have been a genius – whatever that means – in the saddle. But if he was a genius, he was one of the few of that ilk both intelligent and articulate enough to give us some explanation as to how he worked his wonders. During his 'English Odyssey' it's safe to assert he gave more pre-race prognostication and post-race analysis on live television than all his weighing-room colleagues put together. For that alone the English race-goer must give thanks because many of our great jockeys burdened with 'genius' down the centuries, from George Fordham and Fred Archer to Lester Piggott and Pat Eddery, have struggled to translate their philosophy or methodology into words. But it

INTRODUCTION

is Steve Cauthen's words that provide the warp to the weft provided by sectional timing throughout this book.

We in England may not have claimed Steve Cauthen as one of our own for long, but for as long as it lasted it was a blast of fresh air. And that's why it demanded recording in print.

Venit, vidit, vicit.

PROLOGUE

IN EARLY 1979 three friends were chatting over a meal in a Newbury Italian restaurant called The Sapient Pig. One was an owner – and a leading owner at that with racehorses and cash a-plenty. The second was a trainer who handled three dozen of his horses. And the third was a former jockey. The diners were Robert Sangster, Barry Hills and Jimmy Lindley. Over pasta and red wine, this was the triumvirate who brought about Steve Cauthen's 'English Odyssey'.

Jimmy Lindley takes up the story. 'Barry had rung me and said Robert was coming over and we should meet for lunch. During the course of the meal Robert said he was fed up with changing jockeys in mid-stream because it wasn't good for decent horses not to have a good jockey all the time. George Blackwell, the bloodstock agent, had been staying with us and had been talking of this kid in America. It had gone through one ear and out the other at the time. But in the restaurant the bell went in my head and I suggested Steve. Barry said, "If he's that good he'll stay in America." I said, "Not necessarily, you've a card up your sleeve because he's getting a bit heavy for over there." And, he might be ready for a change because at the time Steve was going through a bad patch, a losing streak he'd never experienced before. He'd go a month without riding a winner. The next day Robert rang me and said, "Go and get on a f***ing plane and get him." They paid for me to go over and put the proposition to Steve in person.'

Sangster had approached Cauthen before. Cauthen had ridden a winner for him in South Africa and the previous summer he'd needed a jockey for

Hawaiian Sound in the Derby. Though flattered, Cauthen felt it wouldn't be fair to everyone concerned with his Kentucky Derby and Preakness Stakes winner Affirmed if he accepted, as there were only a couple of days difference between the Derby and the Belmont Stakes, the third leg of the American Triple Crown. The mount went to Bill Shoemaker. 'The Shoe' almost pulled off a miracle: trying to make every yard of the running only to be grabbed on the line by Shirley Heights. Now Sangster sensed he might get his man.

Lindley's visit afforded him first-hand experience of an American sporting phenomenon. 'I rang the Cauthen farm and arranged to meet Steve in the coffee bar at my Lexington hotel. I had never met him and when the kid walked in wearing a pair of jeans and sneakers, that was it! Wham! I thought it was bloody Frank Sinatra. Everyone was going mad. Women were rushing up and saying, "Can I have your autograph for my daughter?" I put the positives to him; assured him that he'd benefit from our higher weights, an extra 5lb or so that he might use to his advantage. He asked me to come for lunch the next day at the farm to meet his parents, Tex and Myra. It was like real old America, with even a hound dog on the veranda. I came back and was able to tell Barry that I thought we had a chance of getting him.'

> Robert Sangster came over and asked to have dinner with my father and I, and offered me the job. At dinner he said, 'You'll need to ride in England eventually because of your weight – so why not come now.' It was obvious to him that I was still growing. He struck me as very genuine and a nice guy to be around and I could sense he was a winner, and that's the kind of person you want to be around in the racing game.
>
> After I'd given it some thought, I realised what he'd said was true and, talking with my dad, decided it was a great opportunity. Jimmy had explained that he would be trying to help me with handling the different courses and in any way that I needed. I thought I had nothing to lose and everything to gain and that if it didn't work out I could come back.

PROLOGUE

God presents us with things. He runs the show. I don't run the show. For whatever reason, I took it that going to England was obviously something that was maybe meant to happen. I came over thinking I'd try it for a month and then go back if I didn't like it. But it turned out I had the best job in England.

The negotiations were handled by Sangster's Californian 'fixer', Los Angeles-based Ulsterman Billy Macdonald, managing director of International Horse Broker Limited. Macdonald was a charmer of the first order whose claims to fame allegedly included being engaged no fewer than seven times, selling the record number of Rolls Royces in one day and being a buddy of Frank Sinatra. With that pedigree as a 'spieler' *par excellence,* there was only going to be one outcome of his discussions with Cauthen's parents. 'Steve thought this would be a wonderful time to race in Europe,' said Myra Cauthen. 'It would be a learning experience. It would be different if he had some stakes horses going for him here but Steve has nothing to hold him back. Racing right as well as left-handed? He races in both directions out in our pasture so that'll be no problem.'

News of Cauthen's defection caused quite a stir. 'Cauthen's decision surprises his agent' was the headline in the *New York Times* in the wake of Cauthen breaking the news to the Press at Santa Anita on 23 February; Harry 'The Hat' Hacek, it reported, had only heard about his client's new job from the television. The contract was duly signed on 24 February. It involved a retainer rumoured to be of £100,000 plus a share in every colt winning a Group race and 7.5 per cent of their prize-money; and 15 per cent for fillies likewise successful. Cauthen has insisted the retainer was less than half that amount, but, in any case, he knew very well he had to justify himself 'by earning a great deal more'. Whatever the precise amount, Sangster and his seven partners (who included Sheikh Mohammed, Prince Khalid Abdulla and Tony Shead) could afford it.

The 'English Odyssey' destined to bequeath Cauthen's adopted country a legacy beyond rubies was about to begin. It would last 14 seasons. And leave us with infinite memories. Not just memories of great horses given great rides to win great races. Cauthen stamped his presence with something indelible. It's with us every day of the Flat-racing season. By the time he retired in 1992 our up-and-coming riders had watched and taken the hint. Some took to riding in California during the winter to acquire a 'clock-in-the-head' of their own. Champion jockeys such as Frankie Dettori and Kieren Fallon reaped the benefit from working horses on the track to time. Others followed; with the result that our riders are far less wary nowadays of making the pace. Winning from the front is a challenge no longer dodged. And as for style: 'Imitation is the sincerest form of flattery,' according to that noted literary 'stylist' Oscar Wilde. The Cauthenesque 'toe-in-the-iron' has inspired so many copy-cats as to become the norm.

Cauthen's legacy was not built in a day. To appreciate its evolution we must resist the temptation for undue haste. For gaining genuine understanding of any Homeric exploit demands we delve into its origins besides chronicling its narrative. Homer, for example, might divide Cauthen's story into four *cantos*: Rise: Fall: Redemption: Acclamation. The 'English Odyssey' encompasses parts three and four. To put the scale of their impact into perspective, however, we must explore the depths plumbed in the second *canto*, and demonstrate how extreme they were by referencing the astonishing feats that preceded them.

Thus did an eventful journey bring Cauthen to our shores. Its long and winding course came by way of New York and California. But it began in that bluegrass country where the thoroughbred racehorse walks tallest. It began in Kentucky.

ONE

THE RISE AND FALL OF 'STEVIE WONDER'

ONE DAY in the late 1970s, so the story goes, a reporter who arrived in Lexington, Kentucky, searching for the Walton home of Steve Cauthen was advised: 'Just drive about 70 miles up the Interstate and look at the sky – there's a star in the East.'

Cauthen may not have been born in a stable, but his parents most certainly knew their way around one; and the emergence of their jockey prodigy would be looked upon as nothing short of divine intervention. He came out of nowhere. He looked like a cherub in a Titian fresco. He wore a halo of innocence that made you think he'd fallen from a cloud. And he was destined to perform his own kind of miracle from the back of racehorses.

Stephen Mark Cauthen weighed in for the first time on Sunday, 1 May 1960 at 7lb and 'change'. The latter 12oz most likely accounted for the clock and metronome stored for future usage; while any gifts from three kings surely numbered soft hands, exquisite balance and an equine empathy that found its finest expression on the backs of thoroughbred racehorses. His birthplace was Covington, a small place 80 miles north of Louisville, Kentucky. He would be the eldest of three brothers born to Ronald 'Tex' Cauthen and Myra Bischoff. His birth did not create headlines. That month they were dominated by the shooting down by the

Russians of an American U2 'spy-plane' and the resultant fizzling out of a summit meeting between the two countries.

Cauthen's future, however, did seem foretold in the stars. Anyone who has ever sat on a horse of any description knows how daunting it feels to be stuck on the back of another living creature with a will of its own far above terra firma. And the prospect of sitting on half a ton of thoroughbred capable of going from 0 to 42mph in six strides that take all of 2.5 seconds at any signal from its passenger (deliberate or accidental) does not bear thinking about for the majority of the population. The infant Steve Cauthen was not among the lily-livered. The blood coursing through his veins amounted to equine positive. The army trained Tex as a meteorologist but he'd completed a deferred course in Michigan State University's blacksmith programme and was now a $27-a-job farrier; Myra was a licensed trainer. Their first-born was perched on a horse before he was out of diapers and rode his first pony when most infants would be concentrating on keeping a tricycle upright; saw his first Kentucky Derby aged three; and was a kid on the backstretch when Majestic Prince won in 1969 and his mother was given a rose from his winner's blanket. Aged six, he was flicking flies off horses for his father as he shoed them and was receiving $4 a week from his mother (that went into the bank) to muck stalls and put horses out to pasture each morning. Two years later he got a horse of his own, but only on the condition he did everything for it: brushing, rubbing and picking feet; cleaning and filling the water tub and cutting out a flake or two of hay; forking soiled straw; and applying poultices to any wound – each and every task defined by the sweet musk of horseflesh and the pungent whiff of horse urine. And in all weather. No boy ever grew up in rural Kentucky without learning how the cow ate the corn: the youngster learned to appreciate the easy way by learning things the hard way.

When their eldest son was five, the Cauthens had relocated 20 miles south to a 40-acre farm at the southern end of Main Street in Walton (population 1,600; biggest building its High School), close to the Cincinnati area racetracks of River Downs and Latonia (subsequently rebranded as

THE RISE AND FALL OF 'STEVIE WONDER'

Belterra Park and Turfway Park respectively). Here, to the background clatter of passing freight trains, there was room to breed the horses on which the youngster might learn to ride. Father often took his son on his blacksmith rounds to track and trainers. It was during one such visit that a seven-year-old Cauthen performed his first sleight of hand by accepting Lonnie Abshire's tongue-in-cheek invitation to ride the stroppiest animal in his barn, one Slade by name.

Those present experienced what might best be described as an equestrian epiphany. Much the same as no less a personage as Queen Victoria experienced a century earlier when renowned Ohio horse tamer John Solomon Rarey was invited to Windsor Castle to work his magic on the monarch's most ill-tempered animal. Rarey had a quiet way of pacifying even the most obstreperous of horses with kindness instead of brutality: he placed his hands on Her Majesty's horse, coaxed it to the ground and, to everyone's astonishment, lay down beside it and used the hooves that were usually thrashing with hostility for a pillow. Then Rarey heard about Cruiser. Once a decent enough racer to run second in the Criterion Stakes, he was now a six-year-old stallion of such bulging black-eyed fury that he was forced to wear an 8lb iron muzzle to prevent him attacking anyone who entered his stone-walled prison of a box. However, after a three-hour visitation from this American horse 'whisperer', the erstwhile savage was led out minus muzzle and mental scars, as placid as a geriatric sheep. Rarey took Cruiser back to America and they toured the country giving demonstrations of what kindness and insight could do: so compliant did Cruiser become he'd even lie down on Rarey's command.

What ensued in Abshire's barn would've pleased Rarey. It was as if this slight seven-year-old boy had read his book *The Complete Horse Tamer* from cover to cover and absorbed every word. Slade bared his teeth at the boy. The youngster bared his in reply. But his pearly-whites were revealed by a broad smile as he walked the half-ton of snorting equine round Abshire's shed row to the trainer's absolute bewilderment. Stevie could understand how kids might be scared of some things but it never occurred to him that might include horses. It was as simple as any 'nuts and bolts' job: if the rider's nuts, the horse bolts. For brute strength wasn't the only, or the best, way to handle an unruly horse. A cool head and soothing words work better than a short temper and a long stick when you're dealing with an animal 20 times bigger and stronger. You had to be cute. The kid had the gift. Just like Rarey. Tex Cauthen realised he'd a child prodigy on his hands. He and Abshire had just witnessed the birth of a horseman extraordinaire. 'He could ride everything that moved,' said Tex Cauthen. 'And even some things that didn't.'

But like most all-American boys, Stevie loved sports of all kinds. He yearned to be a quarterback for an NFL team as he idolised Johnny Unitas of the Baltimore Colts. But the summer he came back from vacation to discover all his pals had grown six to eight inches and he had not he realised he was not going to be physically cut out for football. Conversely, he might be small enough to become a jockey. Some deep thinkers swear we become who we're going to be upon attaining a dozen years. Cauthen had just made 12.

It made sense. He'd thought about being a lawyer or a doctor: he reckoned it was possible because he was very focused. But he'd been around horses all his life and the dream came alive in his mind. That road became his choice and he'd concentrate on it. However, at this stage it was only *maybe* he could do this. Tex and some of his friends appreciated the kid had something on a horse – a feel and a balance – and they knew his determination would stand him in good stead. Horses became his lifeblood. Most Kentucky kids his age wanted nothing more than to 'hang out': go to the movies; run around in cars. But all that bored him. Cauthen listened to his father, who drilled into him the maxim: 'If you find something you love to do, you'll never have to work another day in your life.' Steve reckoned he had found it.

Tex Cauthen vowed to help his son achieve his aim on the condition he agreed to concede defeat if it ever came to starving himself to satisfy the scales and that he'd never get swollen-headed if it brought success. The pact was made and the gifts from God were polished by countless hours of practice and refinement. The reins, for example, are the telephone

THE RISE AND FALL OF 'STEVIE WONDER'

lines through which the jockey talks to the horse. The large hands of the blacksmith's son may at first glance be suggestive of nothing more than finding restraint facile, but they belied an equal facility for transmitting 'sweet nuthins'. Tex Cauthen enlisted the help of his friend Jackie Flinchem, a former jockey renowned for his exquisite 'hands'; rising at 4am, Steve would spend two hours astride a bale of hay flicking a set of reins attached to the wall until they became extensions to his fingers; and swishing a whip in either hand until there were wisps of golden debris carpeting the floor and he could flick the whip to within a hair of where he aimed it. He lifted weights for strength and did yoga exercises to keep his limbs supple enough for him to stretch in the saddle and hit his mount freely. During the summer he'd then head to the track and the den of cacophony that doubled as the clockers' stand until he could recognise a 12-second furlong when he saw it, and replicate it or variations on it: the 'clock in the head' was being wound. Picking up tips from stall handlers about how to avoid screwing up at the gate, and visiting the camera patrol shed in the afternoons and poring over race film of an evening, developed an appreciation of how races might be won or lost by adopting the right or wrong position and asking your mount for its effort at the right or wrong time. And, above all, the youngster kept asking questions. There were always new ideas to ponder, fresh minds to pick. 'It's the feet, the hands and the head that matter,' stressed Tex Cauthen. 'That's the balance. They all go together.'

So, while his peers were still languishing abed and the rising sun reddened the dirt of Latonia's backstretch, 12-year-old Steve Cauthen began exercising thoroughbred racehorses. Morning track lore was soaked up like a sponge: trot clockwise on the outer; 'breeze' or gallop anticlockwise up the middle; a 'blowout' was shorter and faster than a 'pipeopener'. His first task was to take Abshire's Be a Saint an easy three furlongs in around 40 seconds. Some jockeys will admit to counting the seconds under their breath. To Cauthen, however, the learning process was more matter of fact. Observation. Replication. Application. The 'clock in the head' now appreciated perpetual motion. The clocker's watch stopped at 39.50. 'The

Kid' knew what he was doing. Four decades later he puts into words how this came about:

> I'd watched horses work and soon learned to distinguish an 11-second furlong from a 12-second furlong and I was able to transfer that awareness onto the back of the horse when I began riding work myself. I'd be told to work a horse in 11 and two fifths and I could guarantee doing it. If I didn't, I'd get a rollicking!
>
> There are a lot of things to take into account in gauging time. You need to know what kind of horse you're on, his stride pattern, how much ground he's covering. For example, it would be much harder effort for a $5,000 claimer to run a 12-second furlong than a stakes horse.
>
> It's hard to explain. But I seemed to have an innate ability to judge it. I suppose I was blessed. But I give my father credit for everything I learned. How to get a good seat and hands. Pace. How to switch the stick in one stride. The basics came from him.

Whilst absorbing one set of laws another was being broken: Cauthen was underage. Fortunately the authorities turned a blind eye. Their Nelsonian touch ensured that when Cauthen turned 16 he'd be able to go on and do what he wanted to do more readily. Every ounce of the teenager's energy was poured into realising the dream which his heart insisted he could do. Noting his son's burgeoning enthusiasm, Tex Cauthen took him to doctors to discuss any potential weight problems because he didn't want his son's dreams of becoming a jockey to be dashed cruelly. For a small boy he had huge hands and feet; but there was no way anyone could tell whether, or how, he'd grow. However, one thing was certain: by the time he made 14 Cauthen's 'apprenticeship' around the 'Cincy' tracks was complete. The two years until he became eligible for a jockey's licence couldn't pass quickly enough. The first sit, the first 'breeze' had all come and gone. He'd paid his dues. He was ready. 'The Kid', as the rail-birds dubbed him, was a natural. Three days after his 16th birthday, Tex took his son to see Kentucky racing steward Keene Dangerfield to ask for a licence. The teenager was worried: Dangerfield would look him up and down and see an 11-year-old as skinny as a rail. The Cauthens were told they'd better come back in a few days while he thought about it. For those three days Steve was sweating bullets, his stomach tighter than a drumhead.

And so the first race-ride came to pass. On Saturday, 12 May 1976, one week after Bold Forbes had won the Kentucky Derby in the hands of Angel Cordero, Steve Cauthen walked into the jock's room at Churchill Downs. If any of the jocks assumed this latest whippersnapper would be greener than a seasick frog they were in for the rudest of awakenings. He entered as if it were the family lounge back in Walton. Not with the hip-rolling strut of a dandified bantam like a Tod Sloan or Steve Donoghue. But the confident swagger of a 16-year-old youth going on 36-year-old man. After all, he'd been preparing for this moment for half his life. He'd served his 'apprenticeship' before he even began one. He'd become an overnight success who had been working at being an overnight success for years.

Tex Cauthen had had to work over-time to secure his son a debut ride. The animal was called King of Swat. His odds were 136/1. They were perfectly accurate. He was thought only fit enough to run four of the six furlongs at pace. Cauthen rode King of Swat through an even-time opening half-mile in third or fourth – before they fell away to beat just one of the 11 to the wire, 16 lengths behind the winner. But the teenager had given the horse a 'proper' ride. An hour later Cauthen rode a second no-hoper, Singing Saint, into sixth.

Cauthen was now a bona fide 'bug boy' – so named from the insect-like asterisk beside the name of an apprentice on the race chart. A triple bug denoted the rider got a 10lb allowance; after riding five winners, only a double bug equating to a 7lb allowance presented itself; 35 wins equalled a single bug and 5lb; and after a year the bug was removed altogether.

Getting rides, decent rides, was the greatest challenge for any bug boy; out of an annual crop of 150 apprentices, only 25 will eventually make a living – and maybe five of those will become truly successful. When trainers have invested months of endeavour in a horse with one opportunity in mind, perhaps the only opportunity to win that might come the way of an ordinary, moderate animal, the last thing he wants is for an inexperienced jockey to screw it up in a matter of seconds. Cauthen was in a fortunate position. Five days after his debut, his uncle, Tommy Bischoff, chose to exploit the 10lb weight reduction by giving him the leg-up on Red Pipe in a five-and-a-half furlong sprint at River Downs. Uncle instructed nephew to relax his mount on the sloppy track and bring him through with one run down the stretch. The jockey practised what the trainer preached. He must have been 15 lengths out of it at the three pole. But when they hit the stretch and Cauthen finally went to the whip, the horse really charged home. For the first time he felt the joy of a horse responding to win his race. It felt just as good as he'd always envisaged. Red Pipe passed under the wire one and a half lengths to the good. His young pilot was lathered in the jock's room with shaving cream and boot polish. His initiation was complete. Cauthen's life was about to change from black and white into colour. American racing had caught lightning in a bottle. It just didn't know it yet.

It got its first inkling one week later when Cauthen nursed Mary McCullough, a filly bred and owned by his mother, to his second win. Within days the triple bug beside his name disappeared. Then, at the River Downs summer meeting, the 16-year-old set trackside tongues wagging with a record 96 wins in 56 days of racing at a winning average of 24 per cent. It was the forerunner of many records 'The Kid' would smash in the next two years. The word soon got around. Something special was happening. Those racing gods that had entrusted Cauthen with a spark of genius now blew on it and made it glow. One trainer mused: 'You can give a violin to a thousand kids, give them all the same encouragement and lessons, but only one ends up playing beautiful music. And we're lucky to be around that one of a kind.'

THE RISE AND FALL OF 'STEVIE WONDER'

While a Cauthen 'bug' remained, it amounted to 'stealing money'. Trainers got the real deal in the saddle and vital weight missing from the saddle cloth. Cauthen didn't so much 'steal' the money as empty the cash registers, make off with the safety deposit boxes and raid Fort Knox. Cauthen had become so hot so quickly he needed an agent to sift the offers and sort the live from the dead. In August the Cauthen roadshow hit the mecca of American racing, Saratoga in upstate New York, before coming to rest at Arlington Park in Chicago – where he fell under the scrutinising gaze of two-time champion jockey Ted Atkinson, whom Tex Cauthen asked to find any flaws in his son's riding. 'I looked for several days before I could find one,' said the Hall of Fame inductee. 'Most races are stolen in the first and last quarter. Getting position and pacing your mount is crucial.' Cauthen listened; and agent Paul Blair (taking over his book from Eddie Campbell) put him on 160 horses at Arlington, and Cauthen surpassed the track average by winning on one in four of them. However, if the teenager was to prosper on the grander stages of New York, Florida and California he'd require the services of a top agent. Campbell told the Cauthens to seek out Lenny Goodman.

Agents didn't come any bigger than Lenny, who knew every note on his trumpet and loved playing them at every opportunity. Lenny only kept the finest Cuban cigars between his lips, the snazziest cashmere coats on his back and shiny snaffled loafers on his feet. He'd read the rave reviews and heard the scuttle-butt. He agreed to take a close look at 'The Kid'. He couldn't have expected much: the rookie was on two slowcoaches. 'Even though he finished last both times, I liked what I saw. Bad horses can't keep a rider from showing that he can ride a horse. He came out of the gate clean, got a good position, had good balance, and I liked the way he rode so low. So I did something I rarely do. I took an apprentice. Trainers knew that I hadn't taken on a bug boy in 25 years so they knew I must've come across something special. They knew I wouldn't try to sell them crap.'

Some couldn't believe their eyes when Goodman introduced his new protégé. 'Hey, Lenny!' joshed Lazaro Barrera, 'You gonna go to jail for this!

31

This kid looks like he's 12!' Someone else reckoned the cherubic Cauthen looked as if he should be 'sweeping chimneys in 19th-century London'. But Goodman sensed a new meal ticket. 'The Kid' was as American as deep-dish apple pie at a time when Spanish-speaking riders dominated the New York scene. On 30 November 'The Kid' came to the big time: New York's Aqueduct – the 'Big A'. The bug boy, equipped with gloves, ear muffs and Saran Wrap (cling film) around his feet to combat the cold, would light up the dark winter days and ensure Goodman could dine at Sardi's whenever he wanted. The first winner was a humble filly called Illiterate at odds of 20/1. He was riding against people he'd been reading about all his life. He split horses at the top of the stretch and came on to beat Angel Cordero by a neck. To Cauthen it was like beating Joe Frazier your first time out. Now he knew for certain he could hold his own. 'The Kid' soon got the hang of the 'Big A'. By the Christmas break he'd accumulated 29 wins. And when he coaxed a nonentity by the name of Frampton Delight to win the $50,000 Gallant Fox Handicap, his first stakes race, *Daily Racing Form* declared: 'Never has so much been done by one so young in such a short time.' He finished his rookie year, only commenced in May, with a total of 240 winners – enough to have made him champion jockey in 12 of the previous 50 years. Dick Meade, the youngster's 'Man Friday', enjoyed a closer view than most and was unequivocal: 'He's smart and cool with a mind like a steel trap. He's all steel; eats and sleeps horses.'

Cauthen's New Year's resolution for 1977 was 'You ain't seen nuthin yet!' 'The Kid' began burning up the track – and shredding the record books. In one week of January he had 23 wins, which was a record for any track in the country, not just the 'Big A'. On 22 January alone he rode six winners, a New York feat usually associated with a Shoemaker, Cordero or Turcotte; and he'd replicate the feat twice more. By mid-February Cauthen had won over $1m and passed Shoemaker's apprentice record. After 47 racing days his score reached 124 – a new national record; and his Aqueduct total of 133 for January and February was twice the number won by his nearest challenger. When he rode only one winner on a March Wednesday, *The New York Times* ran a banner headline 'Cauthen in Doldrums?' He responded with a treble. He was the toast of the town. Bettors were backing his mounts 'blind'. One confessed: 'He's driving everybody crazy! You don't know whether to keep looking at the form of the horses or just bet everything Cauthen rides.' Those horse-players who vainly bet against him were heard lamenting, 'We've been Cauthenised again!'

All these numbers were being racked up to an insane beat. When Saturday afternoon's Aqueduct card was completed, Cauthen would be driven to Kennedy Airport to catch the 6pm California-bound jet to ride at Santa Anita on Sunday; his first appearance generated the year's largest attendance and the headline 'Cauthen Captures LA' in the *Los Angeles Herald Examiner*. After competing against the big beasts of the west, Shoemaker, Pincay and Hawley, it would be back on a 'red eye' to resume at Aqueduct on Monday morning. In the first six months of 1977 Cauthen rode 276 winners – and he still wasn't old enough to drink, drive or vote. Even though this frenetic lifestyle would've taxed the endurance of Pheidippides, it didn't stop 'The Kid' from enrolling in a High School correspondence course with the University of Eastern Kentucky that consumed an hour or two each evening, rather than see the good grades attained at Walton-Verona High School go to waste.

Superlatives tend to be thrown around willy-nilly in the modern world – and nowhere more so than in the world of sport. But in this instance there can be no cavilling. Cauthen had become a phenomenon. He'd got the great and the good shaking their heads in admiration. Laz Barrera reckoned Cauthen's gifts were extra-terrestrial. 'Maybe he came to us as a gift from some other planet on a flying sausage,' he suggested with his habitual disregard for the English language. 'Steve Cauthen is no teenager, he's an old man. I think he rode a long time ago and came back with 80 years' experience. Maybe Stevie's the 1,000-year-old man! He came off that spaceship with the coolness of Georgie Woolf, the old Iceman, and the talent of the Master, Eddie Arcaro – and there was some Shoemaker too!' And even if he was a mere squirt, his ability to extract 100 per cent from any animal across which he slung a leg prompted one grizzled New York bettor to bestow what may be the ultimate citation: 'When you're betting against him, The Kid is poison. Pure poison.'

Being elevated to god-like status worried Cauthen. He insisted he'd no magic touch and pointed out how often he'd been thrown off or run off with. He'd calculated, rightly, that the horse was the stronger partner in the relationship. The horse weighed 1,000lb and he weighed 95. So he set about getting it to co-operate. He could never overpower him; he must outsmart him. He succeeded pretty much most of the time. They responded to his way of thinking and ran for him. Communication was the key: enticement not coercion was the message. In the hands of 'The Kid' the reins were a hot line.

> You can 'feel' the horse through the hands. Sometimes I'd yell at a horse if he's young or not paying attention. Sometimes I might talk in a soothing tone to calm one down. But the horse gains confidence in you through your hands. Horses are not dumb animals. They're very intelligent. When they wanna run, they run. You gotta try to get them to pick the bit up and do their own thing. Horses respond to a rider's 'feel' and the rider senses this and makes them believe in themselves.

Cauthen thought he could do 'good' in New York; but not *that* good. Respect emerged from all sides of the sport. 'He's too cool for a bug boy. I don't see any weaknesses in him,' reckoned Angel Cordero. 'Every now and then a natural comes along and you can see this kid was born to it,' added the retired, but revered, Johnny Longden. Starter George Cassidy opined, 'He even looks more experienced than some of the top riders'; NYRA executive Pat Lynch agreed: 'This kid is more of a horse rider than a race-rider. He gets on some of these tough old claimers and they run better than they have in years.' Even Arcaro, often the curmudgeon when asked to rate jockeys other than himself, conceded: 'Sure, the kid can ride. He knows a lot about pace, has a good seat, good balance, he's very quiet in the irons and has good hands. But jockeys fall and lose their nerve.' Cauthen soon passed that test when Bay Streak snapped a foreleg at Belmont and gave him the kind of spill usually associated with a jockey fatality. The teenager was as resilient as rubber: concussion, busted rib, wrist and two fingers, and ten stitches to a cut above his right eye couldn't keep him out for long. A month to the day from Bay Streak's demise, he rammed the aptly named Little Miracle through the narrowest of gaps to win on his comeback ride. Arcaro had his answer. This kid was no ordinary bug boy.

But nothing escaped Willie Shoemaker: 'He thinks well, sits nicely, but there's something else too. Horses simply seem to run better for some riders than others. And you can see this kid has that gift.' Shoemaker's observations implied the difference between horsemanship and jockeyship. The two are frequent bedfellows but they are not one and the same. There's a subtle distinction. Horsemanship refers to a rider's technique and rapport with his mount: the strength to control horseflesh ten times his own weight without forfeiting the silken touch of his hands on the reins that transmit his will to the horse's mouth; maintaining a balanced posture that adds impetus not resistance; when, how, and not, to use the whip and the dexterity to switch seamlessly from hand to hand. Jockeyship relates to tactical intelligence during a race: the rider's ability to adapt to different circumstances and the needs of different horses; the guile and reflexes to judge pace, grab a position, and, particularly, assess the relationship of one to the other, viz position near the front off a slow pace and at the back off a rapid gallop. 'It is the gift of brains which makes the jockey,' insisted champion English trainer Richard Marsh in his autobiography of 1925. 'They have been given the brains which enable them to do the right thing at the right time. They have no time in a race for hesitation. Their brains must act quickly.' Latter-day American handler John Nerud made no bones: 'Of all the jockeys I've seen in 25 years, the only two that consistently exhibit real intelligence are Shoemaker and Steve Cauthen.'

Horsemanship and jockeyship: riders often possess one of those skills more than the other. The beau ideal is the perfect blend of both. Some have that gift. The net result is reliability. It presents itself in the jockey who loses the fewest races he should've won. His horsemanship and jockeyship hold up under pressure. His technique never lets him down and he makes fewer tactical errors. Whether they were born with the gift, or whether it developed through practice during the formative years of their life with thoroughbreds, is frequently a mystery to them. Truly great English jockeys such as George Fordham in the 19th century and Lester Piggott in the 20th century couldn't explain why and how they did things on a racehorse even if they bothered to try. To steal a Churchillian phrase on an unfathomable political issue: 'It's a riddle, wrapped in a mystery, inside an enigma.' More simply: in racing, as in all things, there are stars; then there are real stars; and then there's genius. The possibility presented itself that in Cauthen horse racing had unearthed another gem.

Goodman knew he had precisely that in his care and was busier than ever. There are two sorts of agents: those who make calls and those who take calls. Agents have a phone for each eventuality. Goodman was now picking up way more than he was dialling and frequently was spoiled for choice – although he did see fit to turn down a request for Cauthen to lead the circus into town riding an elephant. All Goodman now needed to do was deliver 'The Kid' that one good horse, the flagship horse, to put him front and centre when the curtain lifted on the big show. In fact, he found two. The first, and unlikelier conveyance of the pair, was called Johnny D.

Johnny D was the antithesis of his new partner: large and ungainly, his late development saw him gelded. However, once switched to grass at three, he reeled off a four-timer culminating in the Lexington Handicap that prompted connections to pit him against older and classier horses in the Man o' War Stakes (Grade One) over one and a half miles at Belmont in early October. He put up a brave show, finishing third to Majestic Light and multiple European Group One winner Exceller. Two weeks later, Johnny D filled the same position to the two four-year-olds (Exceller winning on this occasion) in a second Grade One Canadian International Championship run over 13 furlongs at Woodbine. All three horses were invited to compete in the

THE RISE AND FALL OF 'STEVIE WONDER'

$200,000 Washington DC International at Laurel Park on 5 November. For this third tilt at a Grade One, Johnny D would be assisted by Steve Cauthen. Goodman could've put his jockey on the favourite for a $100,000 race in California but took a gamble because the gelding's chances of turning the tables on Exceller and Majestic Light appeared slim. And the participation of the 1976 St Leger winner Crow and the globetrotting Australasian star Balmerino, recently runner-up in the Arc, made this a white-hot contest.

Johnny D was fifth best of the eight runners on 10s. Cauthen had more faith in the gelding than the odds-makers. He'd worked him six furlongs at Belmont and noted his speed. He hoped to use it to break quickly, get a good position to avoid any trouble on the first turn, and then perhaps control the pace. And if the favourites made any mistakes he'd be right there to take advantage.

'The Kid' duly put international stars Cordero, Hawley, Turcotte, Hutchinson, Saint-Martin and Paquet to sleep; and left them snoring. The turf was very soft. An opening half-mile as pedestrian as 55.60 would normally suggest a teletimer malfunction because Grade One performers should be clocking something closer to 50 seconds. The message was not lost on Cauthen, however. Entering the backstretch, he urged Johnny D into the lead and opened up a yawning six-length lead on the pack. Nothing could recoup the lost ground in the conditions. Cauthen's early position and mid-race surge had nicked the race. 'Cauthen Posts International Upset,' declared the headline in *The New York Times*. *The Washington Post* was more specific: 'The race figured to be a jockeys' race – there was no early speed – and 17-year-old Steve Cauthen turned out to be THE jockey. Young Mr Cauthen showed he's not only one of America's best jockeys but that he also is one of the smartest.'

The inaugural Turf Classic Invitational at Aqueduct a fortnight later offered another $200,000 bonanza. Inevitably, Johnny D had a re-match with Majestic Light and Exceller – now assisted by Lester Piggott instead of Cordero. The bettors gave no credit to Johnny D for his win at Laurel, allowing him to start at 7/2 behind his two old foes. Another helping of humble pie had to be swallowed. 'Johnny D Again Trounces Turf Rivals,' proclaimed *The Washington Post*. In truth, the paper might've reprinted its report of the International. Soft ground again prevailed and the opening fractions posted by Cauthen were tawdry: he was merely 'waiting in front'. Once stoked up, Johnny D drew away inside the final furlong to beat Majestic Light cosily.

Johnny D's pair of Grade Ones contributed relatively little to Cauthen's unprecedented 1977 earnings of $6,151,750 (the aptly-named Little Happiness breaking the $6m barrier at Aqueduct in December) and even less to the total of 487 wins (accumulated at 23 different tracks and including 23 stakes races) that made him the leading rider in America. To those watching from afar, however, that latter figure smacks of incredulity – in the 1970s a European champion jockey might need three seasons to reach that number. 'The Six Million Dollar Man' aka 'Stevie Wonder' had arrived; though he deflected any questions on that score by confessing to be more pleased at 'winning $45 from his fellow jocks at racehorse rummy'. Nevertheless, he proceeded to pick up awards like loose change. Three Eclipse Awards, the most treasured accolades on the American Turf, came his way: Outstanding Apprentice; Outstanding Jockey; and the Award of Merit. 'What he accomplished is without parallel, not only in racing but in sports,' eulogised Joe Hirsch in *Daily Racing Form*. He was voted Sportsman of the Year by *Associated Press* (the only jockey ever so honoured), *Sporting News* and *Sports Illustrated* (sandwiched between no less than Chris Evert and Jack Nicklaus). *Time* magazine had him on its cover, a big cigar clamped between teeth, with the headline: 'A Born Winner'. *Sports Illustrated* responded by putting him on its cover three times, one announcing 'The Cauthen Phenomenon' went on to state: 'Steve Cauthen seems touched by both luck and genius, a storybook figure whose tale is wholesome, warm and uncomplicated. Television would hesitate to invent him, but it certainly cannot resist him. Neither can advertisers who are dangling $1 million in contracts.'

The suitors were impressive. He filmed a commercial for American Express; he endorsed Trident chewing gum; his face greeted children from their box of 'Wheaties' breakfast cereal. He appeared on *Good Morning*

THE RISE AND FALL OF 'STEVIE WONDER'

America and the evening news with the iconic broadcasters Barbara Walters and Walter Cronkite. Johnny Carson told his *Tonight Show* audience he was trying to get Cauthen on the programme with the quip, 'If he keeps going from the finish line to the winner's circle as often as he does, the racetracks will have to hire crossing guards.'

The fresh-faced country boy was being treated like a rock star. Indeed, he even cut an album featuring tracks called 'Riding High', 'One Mile to Go' and 'Win, Place or Show'. Walton erected a sign for all to see as they entered the town announcing this was 'The Home of Steve Cauthen'; in time, they'd even re-name a stretch of highway in his honour; and 'Steve's Pub' (adorned with murals of Walton's favourite son) opened on Main Street to emphasise the point – even though he was not old enough to drink in it. Yet Cauthen didn't play the 'high hat', even though 'people were hugging him from morning to night' according to Goodman. His lack of arrogance and braggadocio was a feat the equal of his riding. Many a young man's head might've been turned. But there's a saying folks use in Cauthen's neck of the woods: 'Don't get above your raisin.' And he didn't. His family saw to that. They might concede he was doing great but they reminded him he was still a 17-year-old kid who wasn't as great as everyone was saying – and Cauthen was smart enough to realise they were right.

Just as well Cauthen was so grounded because the hysteria triggered by his exploits in 1978 was stratospheric by comparison. This was the year of Affirmed's Triple Crown. And what a Triple Crown it was. Affirmed was a chestnut the hue of a wire-woolled penny who raced in the colours of Louis Wolfson's Harbor View Farm. Cauthen and this half-brother to his old partner Little Miracle were united for the first time at Saratoga for the Sanford Stakes on 17 August 1977. They made it four from five with no apparent effort. Affirmed's single setback had come on his third start, inflicted by a colt he'd beaten out of sight previously in the Youthful Stakes. This second youngster was Alydar.

The story of Affirmed and his Triple Crown is not so much the story of his relationship with an 18-year-old Steve Cauthen, the youngest jockey to win a Triple Crown, as much as it is the story of Affirmed's relationship with Alydar, his chestnut alter ego with whom he tussled ferociously through a Triple Crown that proved tighter than bark on a Kentucky coffeetree. By the first Saturday in May 1978, the score between the pair stood at four to two in Affirmed's favour. All was set for three bouts of equine combat seldom, if ever, witnessed anywhere in the Turf world. It was calculated that if their six previous encounters were strung together the pair would've raced four and a quarter miles and finished a neck apart – Affirmed's neck. The four miles or so on which they were about to embark would see them at each other's throats from Churchill Downs to Pimlico and then Belmont Park with Affirmed's margin of superiority being whittled away from one and a half lengths to a neck and then a head. Disraeli once averred that, 'There are lies, damned lies – and statistics.' But if there's one statistic that told no lie about the comparative abilities of Affirmed and Alydar it's surely the aforementioned.

Those seeking a Triple Crown face an ordeal the equal of any that confronted Arthur's knights in pursuit of the Holy Grail. It's a source of debate whether the American or the English Triple Crown demands more of its competitors. The English Triple Crown became an accepted concept with the three successes of West Australian in 1853. It demands versatility and durability over a period of five months; the straight mile of the Guineas in the spring; the twisting and undulating mile and a half of the Derby or the Oaks in early summer; and the physical slog of an extended mile and three-quarters in the St Leger as the leaves begin to fall. The American Triple Crown, comprising the Kentucky Derby, Preakness Stakes and Belmont Stakes, didn't gain currency until an article appeared from Turf writer Charles Hatton in the 1930s – by which time Sir Barton and Gallant Fox had already achieved the treble. Unlike its English counterpart, however, the American Triple Crown places less emphasis on versatility, being restricted to distances between a mile and three-sixteenths and a mile and a half: any horse must be primed for the initial ten furlongs of the Derby; then it must come back two weeks later for the Preakness and shorten-up slightly on a tighter track; and finally, within three weeks, the horse must be relaxed and stretched out for the Belmont. Under such a schedule as this, physical and mental toughness is paramount if three increasingly draining contests inside five weeks are to be secured by an increasingly battle-sore horse.

More saliently: could a tenderfoot like Steve Cauthen handle the pressure of riding a top animal in a Classic in front of 130,000 bouncing race fans and raucous pleasure-seekers? Laz Barrera had no concerns about his horse or his jockey. Returning to his tale of the 'flying sausage' (but finding the word right on this occasion), the malaprop-prone Cuban regaled reporters with a Runyonesque tale that would've enthralled the Lemon Drop Kid and Nicely-Nicely Johnson over dinner in Mindy's: 'One night when the racing world was sleeping a small flying saucer landed out in the desert and Stevie got off. He stands by the spaceship and waits three minutes. Horses come from everywhere toward the spaceship. They come out of California and Chicago and New York. They line up and say, "Stevie, come be my jockey." Stevie doesn't say anything for a few minutes, then waves his hands for silence. "Horses, I will get to you all eventually. Be patient. I am looking for a special horse, one that can win the Kentucky Derby. You there, big chestnut, what is your name?" This horse says, "Affirmed." And Stevie says, "Affirmed, I choose you to be my first Derby winner. We will win before a huge crowd and I will put up a ride that people will talk about for years to come."'

By the time Barrera ran out of breath his audience were in tears of laughter. But the racing public would soon see the truth of his prophecy. Not two years on from first entering the jocks room at Churchill Downs, Cauthen returned on 6 May 1978 to ride Affirmed in the race that means more to Kentuckians like Steve Cauthen than any race in the world. The teenager seemed unfazed: the night before the Derby he spent in a sleeping bag on the floor surrounded by relatives, denied a bed because it wasn't his turn. He slept like a baby. So relaxed was he on Derby Day that he left for the track without his goggles and had to ride the biggest race in his young life in a borrowed pair. But six years' hard graft had brought the Kentucky

Derby within touching distance of 'The Kentucky Kid'. The Derby – 'The most exciting two minutes in sports' – had been his abiding dream. It wasn't the one-two-three that mattered. It's just to be there. It's the Ball. The Big Dance. The Senior Prom. It was hard trying not to let things get out of hand in his mind and keep it all in perspective: make it like just another race. But once on Affirmed's back the relaxation that comes to any sportsman when finally able to start doing his job kicked in. He inhaled the atmosphere unique to Kentucky Derby Day and waited for the strains of 'My Old Kentucky Home'. When he brought Affirmed out onto the track as the band struck up that familiar refrain, Myra Cauthen brushed away the tears and from high in the clubhouse blew her son a mother's good-luck kiss.

The odds of a rookie teenager winning the Kentucky Derby six days after his 18th birthday were remote. Only two jockeys in the previous 25 years had won the Derby at their first attempt; and he'd be the youngest ever to compete. For the fifth time in seven clashes the public favoured Alydar at 6/5. Nevertheless, Cauthen had implicit faith in Affirmed. Barrera reckoned Affirmed was smart enough to gain his jockey's attention if something was charging at him by twitching his ears – the right ear for the outside and the left ear for the inside. Cauthen believed Affirmed saved himself for the racetrack. He never overdid himself in work-outs. He did as much as he needed. He was tractable, and could accommodate whatever Cauthen asked. This gave Cauthen tactical options that Alydar lacked. But he had no way of knowing if Alydar had improved. It looked like maybe he had because lately he was just kicking everybody out of the way.

The track had been rolled hard to generate speed. But Cauthen wasn't suckered into allowing Affirmed to burn himself out up front: he could be spotted stalking the pace. The half-mile fraction flashed on the track monitor: 45.60 – fast, way too fast. Affirmed, five lengths back, posted a more sensible 46.60; Cauthen had married pace to position perfectly. Alydar trailed him by a dozen lengths. When the pace dropped, Cauthen shot Affirmed to the lead. Then the colt began to loaf like he always did. Cauthen waited, wondering where Alydar was, figuring he'd move sooner.

But Alydar was struggling to close with his usual rush. Affirmed was now powering his way to the wire. The race was over. The Calumet colt had too much ground to make up. The Derby is considered the toughest of the Triple Crown races to win because it attracts the largest field: usually the first time all the cracks meet having dodged each other for comfortable prep races. But on reflection Cauthen felt this Derby actually proved the easiest of the three races to win.

The clock stopped at 2:01.20, the fifth fastest in history, with Alydar one and a half lengths in arrears. En route to the winner's circle, Cauthen doffed his cap as awkwardly as a polite teenager accepting his graduation certificate from a visiting VIP. 'The Kentucky Kid' had come home. He'd proved to his own folk he not only knew how to ride but how to cope with the big occasion.

The caravan moved on to Pimlico for the Preakness, but was prefaced by a scare. Three days beforehand, Cauthen was speared into the dirt when pulling up a horse at Aqueduct. He took the rest of the afternoon off with a sore arm. The next day he rode a four-timer. Panic over. Cauthen got to Pimlico at noon on race day, ate a hearty lunch and went out to win an early heat.

The Preakness that unfolded provided a differing spectacle to the Derby. The pace was slow. Cauthen pushed Affirmed into the lead going into the first turn. Alydar was within five lengths of him down the backstretch and into the final turn he began accelerating in a blur of chestnut muscle and sinew. The two horses entered the stretch neck and neck. Some observers swore they saw Affirmed bare his teeth like a tiger moving in for the kill, and cock a right ear at Alydar as if to say, 'I know you're there and I'm ready for you!' Cauthen sensed he had a lot horse left. Both horses flew down the stretch. Both jockeys asked for all they had. Their mounts gave it. And Affirmed had just a mite more to give. It was as comfortable a neck as you could get in a Triple Crown race. The clock took another battering: it was the third quickest Preakness since the present distance was adopted in 1925.

Alydar's trainer, John Veitch, assessed the two Triple Crown losses and decided to implement two changes for the final leg of the trilogy over the longest trip. Alydar had always been a 'closer'. He'd run everything down in the stretch – except Affirmed. Veitch now instructed Jorge Velasquez to ride Alydar on the pace; Affirmed must not be allowed an easy lead over the longer distance and be fresh for a stretch battle. He wanted Alydar to test Affirmed's resolve from a long way out. Second, he removed Alydar's blinkers in the hope it would freshen him up. 'Alydar will be right there at his throat! And if we get beat it won't be because we let Affirmed gallop along on his own. We'll make it a real test for him.' Race fans trekked to Belmont Park on 20 May 1978 to see if Veitch's strategy would triumph. Cauthen's adrenalin had been marking time since the Preakness. The three weeks separating Preakness and Belmont are the longest in the world for any jockey, let alone an 18-year-old kid who now felt the weight of the world on his slender shoulders. He was itching to get on with the job. And although wanting to treat the Belmont the same as any other race the sense of anticipation wouldn't allow it.

He realised how lucky he was to get on a horse as talented as Affirmed this early in his career and he didn't want to let the horse down or the humans who'd placed such faith in him. That aside, his principal worry concerned Affirmed's ability to stay a mile and a half. His pedigree raised some doubts. Cauthen put his trust in Affirmed's tremendous heart and Barrera's intuitive training: Laz, he assured reporters, reckoned Affirmed could go three miles! Cynical members of the media reasoned he was due to foul up. Might this be the day: after all, he'd never ridden in a race as long as one and a half miles. The teenager acknowledged the facts but Belmont was his home track and held no mysteries for him. Moreover, he had rock-solid faith in the tactical advantage Affirmed offered. He was sure Alydar wanted no part of being on the lead.

His plan: send Affirmed to the lead, nurse his speed, and count on his love of a fight to get them home. The 65,417 paying customers would bear privileged witness to the barn-burner to end all barn-burners. Five went to

THE RISE AND FALL OF 'STEVIE WONDER'

post to the accompaniment of a band playing *The Sidewalks of New York*. But only two mattered: at the wire the other three would be 13 lengths and more adrift. Early on it seemed Veitch's plan was unravelling. Cauthen engineered a sloth's pace on the lead: the quarter passed in 25, the half in 50. Alydar moved alongside. The duel had begun, a full mile from the finish. Now Alydar began trying to grind down Affirmed; 'thrash' the finish out of him. The ensuing quarter passed in 24 flat; the next flew by in 23.40. Alydar was 'at Affirmed's throat'. This was the slug-fest Veitch had ordered – and Cauthen had been anticipating. He knew it. The crowd knew it. This would be a knock-down, drag-out battle right to the end. It had to be – and was.

There comes a point in any horse race when a decision taken or not taken by a rider, a move made or not made, decides the outcome of his race. A coup is landed or lost; glory secured or let slip. In the 110th Belmont Stakes that moment came when Affirmed on the rail and Alydar on his outside drove down the stretch close enough for their jockeys to exchange stirrups had they wished. Cauthen's inability to whip Affirmed right-handed at this critical moment was suddenly compromised; and just as suddenly Affirmed was in trouble. Maybe the distance was taking its toll. Nothing was coming easy to him any more. He was having to work at it. Alydar stuck his head in front. Now, one of two things could happen: Alydar would hold his lead to the wire and the Veitch plan would be gloriously vindicated, and a gallant Affirmed would be carried out on his shield; or Affirmed would reach into the depths of his competitive being and find an improbable response. It was Cauthen's lot to search for it. His window of opportunity was no more than an arrowslit. And the noise rolling down from the stands like the sound of surf was enough to dull the brain. The destiny of the Belmont – and the Triple Crown – would be decided in the next few ticks of the teletimer. It was sufficient for Affirmed's jockey to sprinkle magic dust.

Cauthen resorted to something he'd not done before with Affirmed. He'd always wondered how Affirmed would react if he switched the stick from right hand to left. Now was the time to give it a try. All those hours flaying hay bales back home in his father's barn bore the rich fruit they'd promised. Cauthen perceived and determined and responded in the same instant. The three actions were sequential. But so infinitesimal were the time intervals between them that they appeared simultaneous to the naked eye. Cauthen executed the move that stole the inches by which the Triple Crown would be won. Jorge Velasquez believed he'd got Alydar home in front until he saw 'the little head coming again and thought, "Oh, my God! Here we go again!"' Cauthen's move may have surprised Affirmed, but it sure made a difference. Affirmed reached for more. He fought back, and got to Alydar about 20 yards from the wire and then ground out a head advantage. Alydar had nothing left to give. Affirmed willed himself to the wire. What really got him home was his heart.

> It's a thrill to send a horse to the lead and judge the pace perfectly so he keeps going to the wire. It's also exciting to save a horse and make one run through the stretch. But I think the most satisfying feeling I got on a horse was to hook up in a head-to-head duel with another good horse. I love the sense that two horses are really trying, giving it everything they have. Coming down the stretch with a chance to win the Triple Crown and pulling it off in such a great race – I don't think it gets any better than that.
>
> I realised afterwards that one mistake and we were beaten. I got everything right and won by three inches. So perhaps I made the difference. When you do something near perfection, that's a good feeling.

The words of track race-caller Chic Anderson give some sense of what the finish to the 1978 Belmont was like, but words alone cannot convey an atmosphere that accompanied Affirmed and Alydar to the wire: just shut the eyes and conjure up the picture. 'The two are heads apart ... Alydar's got a lead ... Affirmed under a left-hand whip ... Alydar's on the outside driving ... Affirmed's got a nose in front as they come on to the wire!

THE RISE AND FALL OF 'STEVIE WONDER'

When you want to define the thoroughbred racehorse from now on you just have to say those names: Affirmed and Alydar! Alydar and Affirmed!' Anderson's call demanded a suitably Wagnerian soundtrack: a spontaneous outpouring of affection for two gladiators, cheering for the sake of cheering, neither for Affirmed nor Alydar specifically – just an involuntary salute to a momentous event about which they'd be privileged to say in years to come: 'I was there when ...'

Thus, did Affirmed become the 11th winner of the American Triple Crown by a few coats of paint; and to Alydar the dubious honour of becoming the only horse to finish second in all three legs. Just nine jockeys (Eddie Arcaro won two) had landed a Triple Crown in the 99 years it was possible after the inception of the Kentucky Derby in 1875 (the Preakness wasn't run in 1891/92/93; nor the Belmont 1911/12). And none came younger than 18-year-old Steve Cauthen, who stood up in the irons and raised his whip to the skies as he crossed the line that precious head to the good. Then he broke down in tears.

> I experienced a million emotions as we headed toward the winner's circle. Relief. Elation. Pride. Pride in Affirmed. Pride in myself. More than anything, I could not wait to share the moment with my parents and my brothers. My father, not big on compliments, complimented me that day. He said, 'That was pretty exceptional.' My father died in his sleep in 2009. I will never forget those words. I will never forget him. I will never forget the greatest day of my racing life. It was one of the pleasures of my life, both then and now. I've probably come to appreciate it even more now.

It surely was 'exceptional'. Woody Stephens averred: 'Been around racing for 50 years but that was the best horserace there's ever been'; Joe Hirsch wrote of 'the most remarkable chapter in the Triple Crown'; while the *New York Post* offered the best overview: 'A horse may luck into winning the

Derby or the Preakness but luck never wins the Belmont – heart wins the Belmont.' Such opinions were endorsed by the clock. A time of 2:26.80 had been bettered only twice; more significantly, that gruelling last mile was run in 1:36.80 – the quickest ever. The final edition of the *Daily News* to hit the streets of New York that Saturday evening saw the front page stolen by Cauthen: 'The Kid wins the Triple Crown', declared the page-filling type.

Cauthen was not minded to disagree with the notion that the '78 Belmont was the greatest Triple Crown race of all time, even the greatest race of all time; or that his Triple Crown was probably the greatest. He reasons two extra-special horses in a great rivalry, going at it, investing all the heart and ability they possess into the fight, created something magical. It was like the Ali and Frazier trilogy. Both showed up every time. Barrera even suggested, 'Affirmed is greater than Secretariat, or any other Triple Crown winner, because only Affirmed had to face Alydar.' Like Ali needed Frazier and Arkle needed Mill House, Affirmed needed Alydar to stamp the 1978 Triple Crown as a great event and enshrine its greatness.

> The Triple Crown is probably one of the toughest things to do in sports. It wasn't done again for 37 years. There are so many variables. All the little things that can wrong. You need a little divine intervention. It all has to happen at the right time. It takes a very special horse to check all the boxes. It's so difficult to have a horse that's good, overcomes many obstacles, and is that consistent. Affirmed and Alydar were race-tough. They were special horses.

It's been said racing encompasses hours of agony and moments of glory. Such were these three battles of heart and speed that saw chestnut flank and flaring nostril matched by chestnut flank and flaring nostril, familiarity not breeding contempt, Bucephalus and Pegasus oblivious to *Daily Racing Form* or the Tote board, fixed only on stiffening the sinew and summoning up the blood – just to be better than the other. The cost to each horse can be more than just imagined. After the Belmont, Affirmed was so tired his head was practically hanging on the floor and he weighed 72lb less than he did before starting the Triple Crown quest.

Praise for the protagonists was universal. *Daily Racing Form* placed Affirmed at number 15 in its *Great Horses of the 20th Century*; in its book *Top 100 Racehorses of the 20th Century* a panel of distinguished writers from *The Blood-Horse* ranked Affirmed number 12; Alydar was at 27, ahead of four Triple Crown winners – which serves to emphasise how near he came to being a Triple Crown winner and yet how far. Ultimately, their 14-month and ten-race rivalry, half of them ending in photo finishes, saw them gallop ten miles with barely a millimetre between them. That's how entwined were Affirmed and Alydar. As for Cauthen, he'd not ride in another American Classic for 14 years.

Once Cauthen had assisted Affirmed to that Triple Crown, it seemed there was no water he could not turn into wine. Whether he liked it or not – and he didn't – he was an unanointed miracle worker to horse-players; Saint Stephen, delivering them from evil and sending them to the pay-out windows. Nothing was impossible when 'Stevie Wonder' was aboard. His powers were supernatural. Hymns of praise were sung in his honour from every corner of the racing parish. JT Lundy, the President of Calumet Farm that bred Alydar, had this to say about the rider who'd humbled its latest prized asset: 'That boy could ride a swamp hog naked through the Louisiana bayous and still win 25 lengths.'

Then came the Fall.

* * * * *

When a sportsman seems incapable of doing wrong, fate has a nasty habit of sneaking up behind him with a length of lead piping. Yet there's something mean-spirited about dwelling on someone's misfortune – even when dealing with anything as intrinsically unimportant as a jockey's run of bad luck. We can take our time – especially in print – glorying in the triumphs. There's something joyous in a success story: reading it cheers the soul; it's life-affirming. But expending equal time belabouring a jockey's errors and dissecting a horserace lost betrays a sour streak any fair-minded human being can do without. Bad memories are like the minestrone soup served in a lousy trattoria: best not stirred.

One is mindful of such caveats when describing the trials and tribulations of a teenage jockey burdened with the tag of 'Boy Wonder'. Even when we know there's a happy ending to the Cauthen story, there's nothing to be gained by 'stirring the soup' any more than necessary to demonstrate how unsettling were the events of January 1979 to Steve Cauthen and how uncomfortable they made him feel – both at the time and on recollection. It's worth reiterating, and stressing: at the time he was just an 18-year-old youth who by rights should still have been attending high school. If coming to terms with instant and premature adulation had been tough to handle without increasing a couple of hat sizes, coping with vicious and cold vivisection by the Press ensured a double helping of soul-searching.

> I look back on it and think everything can seem to be going so right one minute and so wrong the next. It's an up-and-down game. I knew that from the start. But when things are not going right, it's not necessarily your own fault. People can expect too much of anyone. I knew that an awful lot was expected of me because of those two great years. Maybe because they expected so much of me, they tended to get down on me real quick. People were already calling me washed up. I don't hold any grudges, but at the time it was tough emotionally.

When you're travelling as high, wide and handsome as Cauthen was at the end of 1978, there was only one direction the meteor could go: down to earth with a thud that could be heard from the Atlantic to the Pacific. Those the gods raise up, they will in time surely bring to their knees. Homer knew it as *hubris*. Icarus had flown too close to the sun; both the gods of racing and their representatives on earth, the Press, were ruthless when Cauthen's wings melted. A jockey in dire straits can invariably depend on one trusted trainer or owner to put him up on a 'sure thing' just to shoo the monkey off his back. But in California during those early weeks of 1979 succour was fast asleep and benevolent arms were folded. It was even spread about that some disgruntled jocks were trying to freeze the youngster out. Cauthen was no longer 'hot'. In the graphic words of Woody Stephens, 'suddenly it's toilet time.'

Cauthen's winter of discontent had been brewing; the slump had been building. Following the Belmont on 10 June, Cauthen won barely a handful of races prior to winning the Jim Dandy Stakes on Affirmed at Saratoga on 8 August. This downturn in fortune may be linked with a pair of dramatic interventions. On 6 July Lenny Goodman's high-life caught up with him: he had a heart attack. He'd not return to working full time until September; 'Red' Fenton filled the breach temporarily. Then, on 9 August, Cauthen had a smashing fall when the filly Cute As A Button broke a leg at Saratoga. A dislocated shoulder and 'messed-up' knee cut him inactive for a month. Cauthen resumed in early September to win the United Nations Handicap (Grade One) at Atlantic City on Noble Dancer II. But two months of his season had been effectively chalked off. The chain of trackside connections Goodman had built with trainers was interrupted, damagingly. Instead of half a dozen mounts being on offer for every race, the requests for Cauthen's services began to dwindle. On 10 November the *New York Times* was asking whether he'd been 'spoiled by success, money, injury, girls or "old age".' The paper reasoned: 'He's ridden only 191 winners at an average of 16 per cent compared to 21 per cent and 24 per cent in 1976 and 1977. Instead of living with Laz Barrera's son Larry or trainer Chuck Taliaferro and his wife as previously, he now lives in a penthouse near Belmont Park and drives a ''77 Cougar to the track'.

Goodman leapt to his jockey's defence: 'Nonsense! If anyone's in a slump it's me not "The Kid". It's not the jock's fault. It's mine. He's been floundering because I'm not there. He had 45 seconds at Belmont which tells you how narrow is the difference between hot and cold. Has he discovered girls? He discovered them a long time ago! They're everywhere. Mostly he likes to play cards and eat. But every morning he's at the track early for the work-outs. He's all business.'

Nevertheless, the 'numbers' were making uncomfortable reading for one unused to anything other than the exceptional. Cauthen finished the 58-day Belmont meeting 26 winners behind Velasquez and languished 16th in the national table. Cauthen moved to Santa Anita on 26 December and welcomed the New Year by riding a double on its first day. Things might be looking up: a new year, a fresh slate. His poorer neighbours in Appalachia were apt to describe the variable diet of their hand-to-mouth existence as 'chicken and feathers'. Cauthen had feasted on chicken for over two years. Now he was about to choke on feathers. Loser after loser piled up. By 27 January the losing streak had reached 97 and, as *The Washington Post* observed, 'The laurels have turned into hemlock for the snake-bitten ex-wonder of Santa Anita.' People were writing in, offering prayers to help break the slump; one correspondent offered to lift the curse by hypnotising the hapless jockey into winning. Cauthen decided to go trout fishing instead.

For the new superstar of the sport to be plagued by a slump of such proportions became a story too good for the Press to play down. In days of yore, men had to contend with the rack; in modern times they had to endure the Press. Once reporters had sung his praises like a choir of angels. Now a mug-shot of an abject Cauthen in a newspaper was captioned: 'Portrait of a Struggling Superstar.' In the eyes of those erstwhile journalistic acolytes 'Stevie Wonder' had become 'Stevie Blunder'. In the heat of a race he'd zig when he should zag and zag when he should zig. The resultant pain was worse than any spill. Homer would've had his tormented hero fall on his sword.

> It was beyond my worst nightmare. I can't explain it. Nothing was going right. Every jockey goes through slumps but I didn't understand why this one kept going. I went to people I respected and trust to ask what I was doing wrong and the answer was usually, 'Stevie, you're riding as good as ever.'

THE RISE AND FALL OF 'STEVIE WONDER'

> All I needed was a horse who could run fast enough! I was just getting a lot of crappy mounts. Nobody wins with slow horses! I didn't find that people were throwing great mounts at me and I was frustrated. I thought that they were people I'd won a lot of races for and they should want to help me. I had no doubt whatsoever I was still the same person. But you're only as good as your last winner. I felt the Press treated me terribly, for no reason. The newspapers in LA made a big deal out of every race I lost and how many mounts since I'd last won a race. They were treating me like a criminal.

Some acknowledged Cauthen's stoicism. 'Who could handle being covered by the Press for a month of losing?' asked Elliot Burch, trainer of Paul Mellon-owned cracks like Arts and Letters, Key to the Mint and Fort Marcy. 'Nobody – until Cauthen!' Jorge Velasquez's laconic summation came from the heart of a jockey: 'You can't get off and push!'

Cauthen began to learn how Robinson Crusoe must've felt as the pressure intensified. Some began questioning his nerve in the aftermath of the Saratoga spill. The one accusation that clung to him like flour on a fillet concerned his weight. The teenager was experiencing the growth spurt his large hands and feet (he wore size six boots whereas at his age Arcaro wore four and a half and Shoemaker one and a half) had always predicted. He'd grown two inches to 5ft 1in and his riding weight ballooned from 95lb to 112lb. The pact made with his father was going to be tested sooner than he'd wanted: the words 'don't starve yourself to make the weight' echoed inside his brain like the hunger pangs in his stomach. Forced to ditch his beloved shrimp and lobster, his daily intake now comprised a dozen unsalted peanuts mixed with bran for breakfast and a lunch of boiled egg and crackers followed by a second helping of breakfast in the evening. No wonder Cauthen began to question himself.

> You second guess yourself in those times and lose confidence, like a hitter who can't put the bat on the ball. You put stress on

yourself, partly because people start glorifying you and you start to think 'Yeah, I guess if I don't ride five winners today I'm no good any more.' I saw both ends of the spectrum. I was glorified and then five minutes later I was called a has-been. It hurt. It made me grow up a lot quicker.

Circumstances worsened. Lenny Goodman returned to New York. His successor, Chic McClellan, lasted two days before what was fast assuming the guise of a poisoned chalice was handed to Harry 'The Hat' Hacek. And then the worst cut of all: Cauthen lost the ride on Affirmed. A slipping saddle had ruled them out of contention in October's Jockey Club Gold Cup that went to the previous season's Triple Crown hero Seattle Slew. That was no fault of Cauthen's. However, after moving west in the New Year, consecutive losses in the Malibu Stakes and San Fernando Handicap got to Laz Barrera. Affirmed had now lost five in a row after winning ten in a row. On 29 January, with his losing streak at 105, Cauthen was taken off Affirmed for the Charles H Strub Stakes on 4 February and Pincay reinstated. 'I'm worried about Stevie. He isn't my son. But he is,' explained Barrera. 'Racecourses are tough, cruel places. Maybe Stevie needs to go some place else for a while to get out of this slump. I thought the best thing was not to have him lose on Affirmed again. Maybe something good will fall from the heavens.' It really did seem as if supplies of the milk of human kindness were short by several pints.

Then the dark clouds parted and something good did fall from the heavens. On the Thursday before the Strub, 1 February, Pincay was down to ride a four-year-old Wolfson-Barrera gelding called Father Duffy. The jock cried off racing that day with illness. Barrera had no hesitation putting Cauthen up, even though Father Duffy bore all the hallmarks of becoming 'Loser 111'. He hadn't a win to his name in ten attempts. Cauthen got him racing, stalked the leaders to the top of the stretch and then kicked him clear. Out of the pack came a 'closer'. Vaslov stole an advantage. Cauthen pulled out all the stops and Father Duffy fought back to break his maiden by a

THE RISE AND FALL OF 'STEVIE WONDER'

neck. Cauthen's left arm went up, his whip pointing heavenwards. Surely, if ever there was evidence of divine intervention, this was it. The throats of 13,645 race-goers emitted a sound like the 65,000-odd at Belmont when Affirmed hit the wire to secure the Triple Crown. The roar triggered, in the words of William Leggett in *Sports Illustrated*, 'a series of reactions as bright and tender as one could ever hope to see on a race-track. Thank Heaven for Father Duffy.'

Cauthen dismounted to chants of 'Stevie! Stevie!' He was suddenly a fresh-faced country boy again. But no longer one of the troubled kind. He buried his head in Barrera's paternal chest. An emotional Barrera spoke for many: 'The whole slump has been so crazy that something crazy like this might cause it to end. Maybe now the monkey can get off Stevie's back and everyone along with it.' Even when the inquiry light began flashing there was an unspoken feeling that it was of no account. The gods of racing had spoken. They'd had their sport with Cauthen. Now they gave him release. There was no change in the finishing order. The losing streak was over. Cauthen booted home another winner the following day.

> I'd only brandished my whip once before, when Affirmed won the Belmont and the Triple Crown. I normally didn't do things like that. But it was that kinda feeling.
>
> Two days before I was ready to go back East. New York was really my back yard where I'd won plenty of races. My car was packed and I was going to stop off back home for a couple of days and think things out. At the track the morning after making the decision, several trainers came up to me and said, 'Don't go. Things will change.' I decided to stay and see the slump end.
>
> I knew before I started times like this would probably happen. I guess I was lucky I didn't start out with a losing streak. I had the attention when things were going good and the attention when things went bad. The bad days were over.

But there would be no reunion with Affirmed. The story of Affirmed ended without Steve Cauthen. Under Laffit Pincay, the chestnut won seven races on the trot and earned his third consecutive Eclipse Award. He retired the winner of 22 from 29 starts (a dozen with Cauthen; 14 of them Grade One) with record earnings of $2,393,818. And, by way of numerically expressing his *leit-motif*, he never lost one of his nine photo finishes. Despite the sad dissolution of their partnership, it's only right and proper that the groundbreaking names of 'The Six Million Dollar Man' and 'The Two Million Dollar Horse' should be entwined forever.

> We had a connection, no doubt. Affirmed knew exactly what I asked him to do. He was an exceptional horse, in mind, spirit and heart. Riding him was like floating. I knew he was the real deal when we won the Hopeful – I'd never accelerated that much on any horse before. There was nothing he liked more than a fight. He was like that guy in a bar who loves to fight! And he beat a great horse in Alydar, who would've won the Triple Crown in any other year. He was good at two, three and four and from five furlongs to a mile and a half. He's the best I ever rode.

It was said that if Affirmed were human he'd be Steve Cauthen; and there'd be few doubting Steve Cauthen's identity were he equine. Like all first loves, Affirmed would not, and could not, ever be displaced in Cauthen's affections. The teenager had said 'Goodbye' to Affirmed. Now he bade 'Farewell' to the United States. The past was of no importance: its legacy would be qualified by what ensued. The present was of no importance: its wretchedness might be nullified by what ensued. It was the future with which Cauthen now had to deal. He'd ridden the whirlwind and seen it out. The winds had changed. They were now firmly in the west. And Cauthen was blown to England. The refrain heralding Tod Sloan's departure a century earlier once more became apt: 'Yankee Doodle went to London just to ride the ponies.'

THE RISE AND FALL OF 'STEVIE WONDER'

Homer lay down his reed and pushed the papyrus aside. He'd garlanded his leading player with superlatives; then brought him to his knees. What now for his fallen hero? Either the jaws of despond or the arms of redemption lay in wait for 18-year-old Steve Cauthen on the far side of the Atlantic.

TWO

ADAPTATION & REDEMPTION

IF 1978 bore the hallmarks of *annus mirabilis,* those early weeks of 1979 suggested Cauthen was in the throes of *annus horribilis*. The heights of one and the depths of the other conspired to make what followed something to render Lazarus green-eyed with envy. Someone once said the art of success was to be where the lightning was about to strike. On Friday, 30 March 1979, one such bolt struck the English Turf when the aircraft carrying Steve Cauthen, possessed of his first passport and a work permit, touched down unannounced in Surrey.

> I flew into Ireland and then they snuck me over to Blackbushe Airport near Camberley, so nobody would know I was coming in. I met Barry and his car, and I say, 'Hi, Barry, nice to meet you. Shall I put my case in your trunk?' And he says, 'Over here it's called a f***ing boot!'

Forty-two-year-old Barrington William Hills had long since won a gold medal in calling a spade a shovel; and he was renowned amongst the training fraternity for possessing a mind as sharp as his suits. The early bird would need to stay up all night to beat Hills to the morning worm. He'd used his brain to climb the ladder from five shillings a week apprentice to travelling head lad and finally trainer thanks to some fearless, yet judicious, punting. He was the son of a head lad who'd won decent races on Lord Derby's Peter

ADAPTATION & REDEMPTION

Pan as an apprentice in 1955. Hills never lost his 7lb claim: National Service beckoned in the King's Troop of the Royal Horse Artillery where he landed the plum job of the RSM's horse holder.

Owing to his father's parlous health, Hills was discharged on compassionate grounds after just eight months of 'musical rides and 21-gun salutes' and rejoined George Colling as travelling head lad until the trainer's death, whereupon he served in the same capacity to the new occupant of Hurworth House, John Oxley.

Barry Hills knew his way around a stable yard. He'd also given plentiful evidence of knowing his way around the betting ring. In 1967 he got odds of 50/1 about Stewards' Cup winner Sky Diver; and scooped a whole lot more when Ovaltine won the Ebor at 100/8 and Lacquer the Cambridgeshire at 20s. The big wager, however, was yet to be me made. Hills staked all he could muster on Oxley's Frankincense to win the 1968 Lincolnshire Handicap. His work on the Newmarket gallops told Hills he was as close to a certainty as exists in a competitive 31-runner handicap, even with top weight of 9st 5lb. Hills backed him at 66/1 and all the way down to the starting price of 5/1 favourite. Frankincense won by half a length, and subsequently demonstrated his class – and the perspicacity of Hills's punting – by finishing fourth in the Eclipse behind Royal Palace. Hills pocketed £60,000 – over £1million in today's money. 'Job done,' said Hills. 'After that it was simply a matter of looking for a stable to buy.' The hunt was brief. Hills paid Keith Piggott, Lester's father, £16,000 for Lambourn's 28-box South Bank Stables and moved in with 14 horses for the 1969 Flat season.

His first winner was the aptly named £200 purchase La Dolce Vita since Hills had a hankering for 'The Sweet Life'. He'd come up the hard way but he worked the 'system' to a tee. Being conversant with the echo of mash buckets and the whine of horsebox engines was all well and good, but an aspiring trainer had to think higher. Hills had made a point of drinking in the swankiest racecourse bars and dressed accordingly: 'You might meet someone in the smart bar that you wouldn't in the others,' he explained. Yes, Barry Hills never missed a trick in what Stephen Potter called the game of 'one-upmanship'. Establishing himself amongst the leaders of his new profession thus proved no surprise and pretty rapid. Rheingold propelled Hills into the sport's stratosphere when, in only the trainer's fifth season, the colt won the 1973 Prix de l'Arc de Triomphe. Classic success followed as a matter of course. Dibidale would have won the 1974 Oaks but for a slipping saddle that left Willie Carson riding bareback in the final stages. But she put the record straight by winning the Irish equivalent. At the conclusion of the 1978 season, Hills stood third in the trainers' table, having won 86 races worth £260,949. He'd go on to win 13 Classics: five English; five Irish; two Italian; and one French – though including the Welsh, Scottish, Austrian and Slovakian Derbies might be stretching matters. And, of equal if not greater merit, he'd finish outside the trainers' top ten just once in 30 years.

Hills definitely emerged from the box marked 'No Fools Suffered Here'. He could come to the boil pretty quickly: in the pantheon of 'Mr Men' books Barry Hills had first claim on 'Mr Combustible'. But no grudge was borne; and, like many a crusty individual, beneath that gruff exterior hid an infinitely softer core. He was the perfect father figure and tutor for Steve Cauthen. His twin sons, Michael and Richard, both became quality jockeys under his tutelage (and the odd lesson from Cauthen riding their ponies); as did Darryl Holland later on. After initially having his new jockey to stay as one of the family, he arranged for Cauthen to live in a rented bungalow in Lambourn. Jimmy Lindley, once as stylish an English jockey as any this side of the Atlantic, came on board as the manager, advisor and track guru who'd prepare Cauthen for every course; he'd handle Cauthen's bookings for the first six months until John Hanmer, respected *Raceform* analyst and BBC commentator, eventually became the new Lenny Goodman. It seemed no effort would be spared in the cause of enabling 'The Kid' to strut his stuff. And perhaps even shake up the established order. Tim Richards announced the forthcoming arrival of 'The Young Pretender' in the *Daily Mirror* by quoting Robert Sangster: 'At this stage I can tell you Steve will be under a year's contract with an option on a second season. He will be first jockey to Barry Hills, who trains 35 horses for me, and will ride my others in England

and France. Lester has a two-year contract with Vincent O'Brien and myself to ride the horses trained at Ballydoyle. When you're dealing with the best horses and the best trainers you must have the best jockeys. There's only one Lester. Steve is coming to strengthen the team.' Barry Hills agreed: 'Steve is a professional and seems to have the same uncanny balance as Piggott and Saint-Martin. He can do 7st 12lb. His most important ride this season will be Hawaiian Sound, whose major target is the Prix de l'Arc de Triomphe.'

The man underwriting Cauthen's salary was one of the major players on the English Turf: the millionaire managing director of Vernon's Football Pools founded by his father. 'I wish this day could last forever,' Robert Sangster had said at the celebration party following his first big success in the Liverpool Autumn Cup of 1960. And it pretty much did. Known as the 'Fat Owl' to his many mates, Sangster had invested millions on bloodstock – at his zenith he'd 400-odd horses racing worldwide in his colours – and won millions. He lived a life, according to one friend, 'of delightful scams and tasteful skulduggery'. That life was lived high on the hog: whenever Sangster flew Concorde to New York he'd be greeted on arrival by his butler with scrambled eggs at the ready. 'His pleasures,' wrote another wit, 'were boxing, champagne, golf, racing and beautiful women, in no particular order, and, more often than not, more than one at the same time.' Given that Sangster once sparred with light heavyweight world champion Freddie Mills, the aforementioned scribes were thankful for their subject's humorous disposition.

In the mid-1970s Sangster had joined forces with dynamic young stud manager John Magnier of Coolmore Farm and the iconic Irish trainer Vincent O'Brien (soon to be Magnier's father-in-law). 'My job is to be the middle man, to put the right animals and people together,' said Sangster. 'We weren't looking for glory – we were looking for stallions and we got them.' Sending mares to the top sires was an expensive business. 'The Brethren', as the triumvirate was known, decided to make their own stallions. They knew perhaps only one purchase in ten or 20 would pay off: 'Our secret is to spread the investment,' Sangster explained. 'We eliminate the gamble.'

The aim was to buy the choicest yearlings at America's Keeneland Sales (investing a cool $9m annually) with a view to cornering the market in descendants of the influential stallion Northern Dancer; and then eventually replicate him through a conveyor belt of stallions created by success in the most prestigious events in the global calendar. The strategy worked like a charm. In 1975 'Sangster's Gangsters', as they were also dubbed, paid $200,000 for a flashy chestnut yearling by Northern Dancer they named The Minstrel: two years later the colt won the Derby, Irish Derby and the King George VI and Queen Elizabeth Stakes. The Brethren had got their first home-grown stallion. The elite winners rolled off the production line, whose running costs exceeded £40,000 a week, with awesome regularity: that same season of 1977 Lady Capulet won the Irish One Thousand Guineas; Godswalk was a top sprinter who won the King's Stand Stakes at Royal Ascot, and Try My Best and Sookera were leading juveniles following successes in the Dewhurst and Cheveley Park Stakes respectively. The following year Jaazeiro won the Irish Two Thousand Guineas, St James's Palace Stakes and Sussex Stakes, whilst Alleged, a $175,000 yearling, won his second successive Prix de l'Arc de Triomphe to become a stallion worth $16m. To no one's surprise, Sangster topped the owners' list for the second year running. All the aforementioned were prepared by O'Brien at Ballydoyle in County Tipperary. And they were invariably partnered by Lester Piggott. If things went well for Cauthen he looked to be Old Stoneface's heir apparent.

Yet that was the question: would things run smoothly? Cauthen was not the first American jockey to test his mettle in England. As long ago as 1857, American owner Richard Ten Broeck had brought over the finest jockey of antebellum America, the magnificently bearded Gil Patrick (winner of the inaugural Belmont), who couldn't cut the mustard and was swiftly repatriated. Modern 'greats' Willie Shoemaker and Johnny Longden made fleeting visits: the former to come second on Hawaiian Sound in the previous year's Derby; the latter to finish tenth in the 1954 Derby on Major Lionel Holliday's Blue Sail – Longden did win a race the day before; and two years later flew in to add the Edinburgh Gold Cup. These sightings amounted to rare treats for those who appreciated global contrasts in riding styles. Of late, English racegoers had become accustomed to the quiet whip-twirling Australian style of Scobie Breasley, Ron Hutchinson, Bill Williamson and George Moore. Now they'd be able to run their eyes over the sweetest style contemporary American racing could offer.

Those glimpses of Shoemaker and Longden amounted to blink-and-you-miss-them experiences. The legacy Cauthen's 'English Odyssey' would be measured against was that bequeathed by the full-blown invasion of England (and Europe) by American jockeys around the turn of the 20th century. And that legacy was decidedly double-edged.

Virtually to a man these jockeys were mercenaries fleeing the 'Message of Salvation' sweeping through America that rejected the Devil's tools such as gambling; and after New York had passed anti-betting legislation in 1894 they arrived in company with assorted gamblers used to fixing races and fleecing mug punters. Massive betting coups were engineered by the judicious application of dope and a willing co-operation from the saddle that saw £2m taken from the Ring (a staggering *£8m* in modern money) by the time these bandits high-tailed it out of the country. Anything American was viewed as cancerous. The 'American Disease' had struck: 'The sport was,' asserted leading Turf writer Alfred Watson, 'more healthy before the American jockeys came.'

Nonetheless, many of those jockeys proved champions: Lester Reiff (England) and brother Johnny (France); Danny Maher (England); Frank O'Neill (France); Winnie O'Connor (America and Germany); Guy Garner (America); Jay Ransch (America); George Archibald (Germany); Jimmy 'Black Maestro' Winkfield (Russia); Cash Sloan (Russia); and Fred Taral (Austria-Hungary) – and that's ignoring the conceited and crooked little genius that was James Forman 'Tod' Sloan. These sons of Uncle Sam franked their ascendency by winning six out of seven Derbies during the opening decade of the new millennium and were prone to stealing half the lucrative prizes at Royal Ascot and 'Glorious' Goodwood.

STEVE CAUTHEN - ENGLISH ODYSSEY

Steve Cauthen was at a crossroads. In which direction would his own English adventure take him? Whose lead would he follow? Would he, for example, be sent packing with tail between his legs like Gil Patrick or Willie Simms?

Simms had proved himself by winning the two most recent renewals of the Belmont and was fresh from winning the American jockeys title with 228 winners – a total only surpassed in England by Fred Archer – when he arrived in Newmarket in the spring of 1895. He was a negro and had been taught to ride like his peers by being thrown up onto a horse's back equipped with just a rug instead of a saddle; in consequence he was compelled to 'cling like a monkey' to the animal's mane to keep his balance. Thus was born the 'monkey-on-the-stick' epithet. Simms instantly silenced the ridicule heaped on him while taking Eau Gallie to post on his debut by winning. Chewing his mud were the five leading jockeys in the table. In four months, however, Simms only managed a further 18 rides and three more wins and he returned stateside to resume Classic-winning ways with two victories in the Kentucky Derby.

Or would Cauthen revolutionise English race-riding only to crash and burn spectacularly like Tod Sloan?

Doing justice to Sloan's meteoric flight through the firmament of the English Turf is akin to replicating a flash of lightning with the end of a wet matchstick. Yet time can't dim his brilliance. Outweighing his innate corruptibility was the legacy he bequeathed English race-riding. His short trunk and stumpy legs – drawing the name 'Toad' from his father, shortened to 'Tod' – helped forge his style. He'd watched his idol Harry Griffin adopt the negro 'crouch' with effect and determined to use it himself. Hands clasped close to the rings of the bridle, cap hardly discernible above the horse's ears, this streamlined seat reduced wind resistance and redistributed weight to allow his mount freer hind leverage; trainers reckoned the 'crouch' was worth up to 7lb over five furlongs. His first visit, in 1897 to aid gambles in the Cesarewitch and Cambridgeshire, came unstuck, but when he returned the following September his impact was instant and sensational.

ADAPTATION & REDEMPTION

He won on no fewer than 12 of his 16 rides at Newmarket and within six weeks he put 43 winners on the board for an astounding winning percentage of 43.8. Sloan's staggering success soon had English racing folk laughing on the other side of their faces. And all of a sudden English jockeys began to shorten their stirrups and reins.

That wasn't all. Sloan implemented avant-garde race tactics. To ascertain how much speed he had at his disposal, he let his mount sprint for a furlong on the way to the start. Then, instead of the slow, muddling English fashion of waiting, he thought nothing of shooting out of the recently introduced gate to capitalise on his knowledge of pace. Thanks to Sloan's influence, the average time for the Derby between 1899 and 1908 improved on the preceding ten years by 4.3 seconds and the Gold Cup by a whopping 14.1.

Unfortunately Tod's integrity was as loose as his tongue – which eventually cost him his licence and a £6,000 annual retainer from Edward VII. In less than four seasons Sloan accumulated 253 wins (at 31.6 per cent); and he'd become the first American jockey to win a Classic, the 1899 One Thousand Guineas on Sibola. Washed-up at the age of 26, his life went downhill faster than an avalanche. At his peak allegedly worth $½m (almost £5m), fat cigars, flash clothes and expensive champagne were to Sloan like plankton to a blue whale – and promised only one outcome. He went bust. His remaining years were those of a nomad in search of a buck, even as far as advertising himself for dimes on a street corner as 'the strangest dwarf in the world.' He died in the charity ward of a Los Angeles hospital from cirrhosis of the liver aged 59.

Or perhaps Cauthen would be a baby-faced sensation to be banished just as quickly like Johnny Reiff?

'Little Johnny' arrived in the summer of 1899, the 14-year-old kid brother of Lester (who achieved a couple of notable American firsts: champion jockey in 1900 and a Derby a year later on Volodyovski). Blessed with baby-blue eyes set in a cherubic face, Johnny stood barely 4ft and weighed 4½st. Within a week he gave the English Press its first opportunity to sing his praises, winning the New Biennial at Ascot on Bettyfield; and so miniscule the trainer had to carry his saddle back into the weighing room. Elegant ladies oohed and aahed. The hysteria peaked at Newmarket after he rode Bishopswood to win the Alexandra Plate. The horse had not run all season and on going to post everyone knew why: he was a brute made to appear even beastlier by the mite trying to control him. Reiff fought him for furlong after furlong, until, by dint of steering him against the rail, he settled the colt – and got up to win. Then, as the 'baby jockey' slipped exhausted from the saddle, a handsomely dressed woman caught him in her arms and kissed him rapturously.

Johnny's 'boyishness' served as a convenient smokescreen for those manipulating him. The statistic that itched was the number of occasions the Reiff brothers occupied first and second – and the number of times the American gamblers backed the right one. The Jockey Club went gunning for the Reiffs. High noon came in a minor race at Manchester in September 1901: Johnny beat his brother by a head. Lester's 'suspicious riding' was reported to the stewards of the Jockey Club – who withdrew his licence. The message was not lost on Johnny, who thereafter based himself in France (where he was champion in 1902) or Germany, establishing himself as a gun for hire in any showdown. In the 1907 Derby he landed a huge gamble on Richard Croker's Irish-trained Orby. Five years later Walter Raphael booked him for the grey filly Tagalie in the Derby. Reiff rode a copybook race from the front, putting all the other jockeys to bed, to win by four lengths.

Or, maybe, just maybe, Cauthen's conduct in and out of the saddle might win the respect and admiration of the racing parish like Danny Maher.

Maher had proved the acceptable face of American jockeyship. Arriving in 1900 aged 18, he set out to charm the racing community, not insult it. Despite mixing with his fair share of seamy characters, he zealously guarded his good name. When his riding of a loser at Leicester was referred to the Jockey Club, for instance, he refused to ride at the track ever again. Debonair and rakishly handsome, he married the actress Doreen Frazier and for a spell lived at Cropwell Hall, near Nottingham, and regularly supported the local hunt. Well could *The Sporting Life's* Meyrick Good write of him: 'Danny was the "aristocrat" of all the jockeys I have known.'

ADAPTATION & REDEMPTION

Key to this exalted status was the patronage of several Turf worthies, none greater than the 5th Earl of Rosebery, who invited him to cruise on his yacht and stay at his Scottish country seat, was witness at his marriage and stood guarantor when he successfully sought British citizenship. He also paid Maher an annual retainer of £4,000: in return Maher rode him Classic winners. Maher rewarded likewise Australian millionaire AW Cox (who retained him at £2,000), Lord Derby, Sir James Miller and Major Eustace Loder. Boasting such lofty patronage, Maher could hardly fail to become champion jockey, and did so in 1908. Maher's undoing was his weight and a delicate constitution: he was frequently rendered virtually speechless after a strenuous ride through shortage of breath – not helped by heavy smoking. He secured his second championship in 1913 but inside three years he was dead from tuberculosis aged 35. 'Sloan was the revolutionary,' observed journalist Sidney Galtrey, 'Maher was the true artist.'

So, which road would 'The Kentucky Kid' take in 1979? There were lessons to learn from each of his American predecessors. Yet there was never any doubting Steve Cauthen's 'English Odyssey' would stick to the straight and narrow, enabling him to combine the finer points of Sloan's innovation and Maher's charm offensive: he would be both 'revolutionary' and 'artist'. For in his father he possessed a *consigliere* worthy of Don Corleone's respect; in Barry Hills he possessed an astute mentor in the nooks and crannies of English racing; and in Jimmy Lindley he possessed a guide to every bend and dip on English racetracks.

The job as retained rider to Sangster at Hills's South Bank Stables had one potential snag: Hills trained more than 100 other horses that were not Sangster's. In all probability Cauthen would also ride those of other owners whenever possible. Hills's stable jockey Ernie Johnson, a Derby winner on Blakeney for Arthur Budgett a decade earlier and the rider of Hills's first English Classic aboard Enstone Spark in the latest One Thousand Guineas, was not likely to be enamoured with the new arrangement. The American eagle was about to land in England and Johnson would be obliged to like it or lump it. He decided to 'lump it' and would soon quit South Bank Stables.

Such concerns were not within Cauthen's power to influence. He was keen to see what the venture might bring.

> One nice thing about being a jockey is that you aren't tied to one place. I wasn't so narrow-minded as to think that there is racing only in America. The world doesn't revolve around America. At the time a lot of people assumed I was running away from a bad losing streak, but even before that I had been thinking of moving to England. I'd always wanted to see Europe and the European tracks and I realised this was the time to do it. I was getting the feeling that American racing was a day-in-day-out affair. I'd been riding non-stop for 365 days a year for two and a half years. I was burnt out and stale. If it didn't work out I was young enough to go back to the States. I thought 'what the heck'.

Lending Cauthen a solid refuge of affection and trust during the bedding-in period was the presence of his father. 'My boy has grown up with horses,' Tex Cauthen reminded the first journalist to question his son's ability to cope with the move, 'so that he understands you have to be suspicious of both success and failure. People talk about the pressure on him, but they forget, he is doing what he loves. You say he looks calm. He don't! That's not surface, that goes right through! T'aint a gamble because he can't lose. If it doesn't work out he could go back to New York and start climbing on winners. But if he makes it here, he'll start becoming a world-class rider. He may have missed some parties and some necking in the back of the car, but he knows he's got a rich life in front of him.'

That 'rich life' recommenced in England on Monday, 2 April, when Cauthen dropped onto an English thoroughbred for the first time and made his acquaintance with the Lambourn gallops. That was the easy part – even if it did mean 'riding two miles to the gallops and four miles home in the rain and wind and cold.' Two days later he faced the ordeal of fielding questions at a Press conference in west London's Heston Centre. It proved nothing of the kind.

As a public figure used to attracting as much attention from the mainstream Press as the Turf Press, 'The Kid' had become accustomed to the usual mix of sensible and stupid questions – and treated them with equal courtesy. To someone who'd sparred verbally with Barbara Walters and Walter Cronkite on live coast-to-coast American television, the task of dealing with English hacks amounted to a walk in the park. It's no exaggeration to say Cauthen had the denizens of Fleet Street eating out of his hands as he sipped from a glass of wine while father Tex filmed the exchanges on his cine camera. Used to slim pickings from the laconic Piggott and Eddery, who exhibited the taciturnity of men searching for a gas leak with a naked flame, the eloquent, cordial and, most significantly for reporters seeking 'good copy', the eminently quotable responses from Cauthen were akin to finding the oyster that held the pearl. Looking whip-smart in blue-striped suit, and brandishing his Jockeys' Association membership badge, this is the gist of what the newcomer had to tell them: The Challenge: he was looking forward to the fresh new experience; this wasn't just a one-year thing; if it all went well he could be back in 1980; and might stay for the rest of his riding life; there was no chance of him feeling homesick because he'd been travelling since he was 12. There were things to learn, new problems, but he thought he could do almost anything on a horse.

His Reception: no adverse reaction was expected from British riders. He'd met 'Mr Piggott – nice and kinda quiet.' And Willie Carson had offered some advice: 'Just follow me anywhere you like – as long as you keep on following!'

On Adapting: it would be a bit difficult judging pace at first, but in America he could judge a furlong to one-fifth of a second and had won many races from both laying off the pace and making the pace. The great variety of tracks will be a new and exciting challenge because he'd never ridden a course with an uphill finish. His weight was no problem; he could eat virtually what he wanted.

His Losing Streak: he was disappointed, of course. But all the top riders were out in sunny California: so he was getting long-shot horses and not much luck. He'd checked his riding on videotape and listened to advice from other jockeys. But he was the same jockey who rode Affirmed to the Triple Crown; everyone confirmed as much.

On Pressure: he wasn't concerned what people expected of him; he could do more than his best – but 'you can't win without the horse'. Whenever he came to a bridge, he generally gave it a bit of thought to find the best way of crossing it. That's what he was doing right now.

Watching 'The Kid' deal with reporters like a master was the 'Master' himself, Eddie Arcaro, with TV crew in tow to capture the moment for American audiences. The rider of Triple Crown winners Whirlaway and Citation nodded his approval: 'Cauthen's always been the same and nothing ever seems to worry him. I can't think of an American jockey who would be a better advertisement for us over here.' The following day's newspapers agreed with the beloved 'Banana Nose' of American racing. All featured pictures of the beaming teenager atop favourable reactions to his arrival and demeanour.

'Young Steve takes it all in his stride,' said the front-page headline of the sport's principal trade paper *The Sporting Life*. 'If Steve Cauthen displays the same composure on his British racing debut at Salisbury on Saturday as he showed at his introduction to the Press in west London yesterday, he is assured of a successful season. He handled a plethora of questions with an authority and assurance that belied his years.'

James Lawton in the *Daily Express* went with: 'Ice Kid: Cauthen shows just how tough he's going to be. He has been wrapped so carefully, he might be a piece of porcelain, but the moment Steve "The Kid" Cauthen says "hello" to England after five days behind the doors of a big house on the Berkshire Downs, you know this is no porcelain. This is the kid with the melting point of tungsten; this is 5ft 2in of rare metal.'

The *Daily Mirror* settled for 'Super Steve's a winning Yankee', as its headline. Tim Richards reported, 'It's a winning double – the smile and style of teenage wonder jockey Steve Cauthen. The cool, composed 18-year-old from Kentucky is more articulate than most sportsmen; the boyish looks and frail figure belie the adult approach to his already legendary career; the vice-like handshake when we parted confirmed the first impression – Cauthen is a cool, confident kid.'

In *The Daily Telegraph* John Oaksey wrote, 'If he rides even half as well as he talks it is going to be a real delight to watch him in action: the impression one got was of a modest, highly intelligent young man who is quite used to facing challenges and has come to England looking for a new one. Cauthen looks what he clearly is – a strong, highly co-ordinated athlete; his hands are noticeably a size bigger than the rest of him and not least among his weapons may be a pair of cheerful eyes above a broad urchin grin. Only time will tell, but my bet is we are going to like him fine.'

Anyone who fancied 'The Kid' for the jockeys' championship could get odds of 20/1 from Corals; reigning champion Pat Eddery was 6/4 on; ex-champ Willie Carson 5/4. Cauthen's price couldn't be disputed. The key questions had still to be answered. Did Hills have the artillery for Cauthen? And could the American adapt his style to the totally contrasting character of English tracks and English races?

English racing professionals and public did not have to wait long for clues. A glimpse of the Cauthen magic touch quickly made itself evident: the wait was not weeks; nor days; just a couple of minutes after Cauthen was legged up for his first ride at Salisbury on Saturday, 7 April. Hills had 'laid out' one for him. The first ride would be a winner. This, so the cliché goes, is the kind of fairy-tale Hollywood shies away from for being too fanciful. But in Cauthen's case this was no cliché: the fairy-tale was an established fact by now. This was merely the latest, vaguely unbelievable, page.

The 'cert' was a three-year-old called Marquee Universal owned, not by Sangster, but by Keith Hsu. Its one run as a juvenile was successful. The Grand Food Stakes wouldn't take much winning for a horse later to prove himself a useful handicapper by winning both the Esher and Thirsk Hunt Cups. 'Steve and Marquee for a fairytale start,' declared the *Daily Mirror*. Plenty came to see whether that headline would prove accurate. Racegoers, 8,000 of them, were still clicking through the antiquated turnstiles as Cauthen fought his way through a battery of cameras to the parade ring in the company of his new colleagues, who included top-table riders in Messrs Mercer, Hide and Eddery. Cut off from him in the scrum, one of them was heard to plead, 'Let a few poor English jocks through ... unless he's gonna race on his own.'

Cauthen's problems, if he even considered them as such, was coming to terms with riding his debut race over what amounted to a straight mile (albeit with a slight right-handed elbow) culminating in gradually ascending final furlongs. There are no straight mile courses in America; and certainly no undulations. Furthermore, whilst there was no evidence of the Almighty hurling a thunder bolt at Salisbury to announce Cauthen's English debut, it was accompanied by rain of biblical proportion that in places was transforming wet grass into treacherous mud. So desperate did the surface become as the afternoon progressed that the car conveying the stewards down the course for an inspection before the fourth race slithered to a halt and got stuck in the mire. That was not all: the new number board failed to function properly; race commentaries were lost owing to a power failure; a shaggy pony somehow managed to escape its field and lollop down the track, passing the winning post to an ovation; and anyone expecting to buy a drink or visit the lavatory would've been better advised to stay at home. The odds were stacked heavily toward a Cauthen calamity rather than a Cauthen coronation.

One minor snag immediately presented itself: Cauthen had come without any waterproof breeches – 'mud pants' to the American; weighing room stalwart Brian Taylor loaned him a pair. As for the track presenting further unforeseen snags, he'd walked the course with Lindley two days before to absorb all he needed to know. 'We walked every one of the southern courses before Steve rode them,' Lindley recalls. 'It's like walking a golf course before you play it to learn the undulations. His very first race at Salisbury was tricky because the ground was heavy from rain. But I couldn't have done better myself. Steve has always ridden like a European jockey and takes in everything he is told. I could see his eyes practically counting the blades of grass. I told him to come across to the stands side and he did just that. When Salisbury was like that, at the finish you don't stay near the rail because the ground is too heavy there. You have to swing away from it and that's what Steve did. He rode that first race down our footsteps and he won. He went right on course with our bloody footsteps! That's racing intelligence; very rare. That impressed people, especially the other jockeys. He's smooth, a great hands-and-heels rider. But we knew that before he came. The bonus was his mental approach.' Lindley chuckles at a final memory of an unusual but special day and adds a postscript: 'I watched the race with Tex from the stand. We got up there and Tex looked baffled. He said to me, "Where's the racecourse?" And I replied, "Over there, to your right!" The Salisbury stand is built at an odd angle and faces the wrong way, away from the straight! Poor old Tex wondered what on earth was happening!'

Marquee Universal won as Hills promised he would, tracking Twickenham until Cauthen – and the crowd that was reviving the old Donoghue chant of 'Come on, Steve!' – gave him the signal to put the race to bed. One slap from Cauthen's whip was enough to remind the 9/4 favourite of his task so that hands-and-heels only were needed thereafter to record a stylish victory by one and a half lengths. On dismounting, Cauthen thanked his horse with 'Okay, Pal.'

> It surprised me – I didn't expect to feel that good. It's always nice to be warmly greeted and the crowd gave me a great reception. I enjoyed it all. I preferred the atmosphere, including the interior of the weighing room, which might not have been quite up to the clinical standards of similar outfits in the States, to the daily grind at home.
>
> It was good to get that first winner out of the way. Winning it meant a great deal. I felt a big relief. The pressure was off

me. We were always travelling well and I knew we had it won a furlong out. All the English jockeys were fine and congratulated me on my win.

The racing public had been gifted a new style to savour on a daily basis. The one riding posture hitherto known to every English racegoer was the Piggott 'Perch', that human paper-clip bent over the horse's withers forcing Lester's posterior high in the air. But through the thick curtain of Salisbury rain, racegoers might've been forgiven for thinking Marquee Universal was riderless, so low was Cauthen crouching behind his mount's neck. 'When Steve started,' said Tex Cauthen, 'he had a tendency to get his rump up a bit when he got near the money at the wire. Now he rides awfully flat – butt down, back straight – and has all the power there to move with the horse.' Other transatlantic traits helping him 'move with the horse' were also instantly recognisable. The toe in the iron so tenuous as to be anonymous. The 'acey-deucy' leathers: left stirrup deeper down the horse, enabling the jockey to lean into the left-handed turns on America's cambered ovals – but also to enable the seasoned pro to lock his left leg round the right leg of any greenhorn stupid enough to try and get up his inner. And the whip held in the forehand position like a periscope beside the horse's head.

Cauthen's two other mounts contested the pair of Guineas trials over seven furlongs. Sangster's Ring Lady ran second in the fillies' race and Tony Shead's Tap On Wood fourth in the colts' trial behind Lake City. Subsequent events proved Cauthen was equally adept at saving a horse to win another day as he was at accomplishing a steering job.

> The ground was getting worse as the day wore on. When Tap On Wood's chance had gone I didn't want to punish him and give him a hard race. That could have ruined him for the year. I didn't want to do that.
>
> Everything was so well planned. I got so much help from Barry Hills and Jimmy Lindley. It wasn't as if I was going into

things on my own. They were teaching me all the time. Jimmy was the best thing Barry did to help me out. He opened doors for me. People wanted to see me in Germany and Austria, for example, and Jimmy had the contacts to make it happen. He rode for Jeremy Tree for years and introduced me to Jeremy. I remember working Known Fact for him before he won the Guineas – Khalid Abdulla's first Classic winner and the only horse other than Tap On Wood to beat Kris. Jimmy was phenomenally helpful because it was hard for me to figure things out otherwise. Simple things, for example, like going to the outside on soft ground – in America we always go the shortest way. Jimmy told me you may travel further but you'll benefit in the end, where it matters. I listened and it made sense: 'When in Rome, do like the Romans.'

Cauthen's afternoon concluded with two Press conferences, one impromptu out in the rain after his victory and a second under canvas after racing for the benefit of every media outlet on site. He departed with a crate of champagne from a grateful course directorate for the sell-out. By now he was showing every symptom of having caught his first English cold. But he still managed a few giggles from the back seat of the Hills's Jaguar at the sight of Tex having to lend a helping push out of the marsh that was once the car park and being splattered with flying mud when the driver revved the engine.

The Cauthens were squired to nearby country pile Wilton House for tea by Sangster camp follower Charles Benson. Currently employed as 'The Scout' of the *Daily Express*, the Old Etonian was just the man to introduce the Cauthens to the English aristocracy since he seemingly had the key to the front doors of country seats throughout the land. Renowned as a *bon viveur* and incorrigible gambler (Sangster had twice cleared his gambling debts), the tale of him flogging his son's Falklands War medal for a tenner which he put on a horse that came fourth may have been apocryphal but

Benson still roared with laughter at its re-telling because he accepted it could easily have been true. He was a member of John Aspinall's Clermont Club crowd (that included the likes of Lord Lucan) and a devotee of the global high life, nicknamed '1A' in deference to his preferred seat in first class. The scribe's subsequent exclusive began, 'Rain-swept! But the Cauthen style was immaculate despite the almost Marx Brothers aspects of the whole day's activities.' Benson went on to describe Cauthen, glass of champagne in one hand, egg sandwich in the other, musing on the events of the day. 'I'm a simple guy and I love simple things. While I appreciate the magnificence of these surroundings, I really like best of all this big log fire, this friendly dog right here and the countryside around.' Benson ended the piece, 'There can be no doubt whatever that his style is just as effective here as it is in America, and detractors must surely be silenced. Cauthen has added a new dimension to our racing, and it is to the credit of our own jockeys that they have recognised this and have so far been unstintingly fair and friendly to him.'

Other Press coverage trod similar paths. 'Steve starts like a dream!' stated Alan Smith in *The Life*, complete with no fewer than six photographs. 'Salisbury racecourse has never seen anything like it in its history stretching from the 16th century. The Kentucky Kid could not be faulted; his British prospects cannot be judged on one performance but he could not have had a more encouraging start. I have a growing belief that Lester Piggott will retire the season after next and I believe Cauthen is being groomed to take over on Vincent O'Brien's horses.' In *The Daily Telegraph*, Christopher Wright saluted, 'The Steve "Kid" Cauthen show. The picturesque little Wiltshire course may never be the same again. The star of the show negotiated all the traumatic mishaps with the aplomb of a veteran. Perhaps after being subjected to the glare of American publicity, he is immune to all the razzamatazz.' The *Daily Mail* had some fun at the sight of 'his dad pushing away at their bogged-down car like the Bionic Man,' before adding, 'This American wonder kid wore the slight immovable smile of a master who had lost not a second in proving that his prodigious talent would travel.' It ended with the prediction that, 'The Kid's ready to upstage Red Rum and company.'

ADAPTATION & REDEMPTION

Swapping his *Daily Telegraph* persona for his weekly guise as 'Audax' at *Horse and Hound,* John Oaksey summed up Cauthen's debut very nicely: 'By modern European standards he rides a pretty reasonable length – made to look shorter than it is by the fact that only the tip of his toe is lodged in the stirrup. This almost universal American habit always looks horribly precarious to me, but in Cauthen's case it is part of a beautifully poised and streamlined seat. One day and three rides is pathetically inadequate evidence on which to judge, but nothing we saw at Salisbury has altered my conviction that watching Steve Cauthen ride this season is going to be not only a regular source of interest and discussion but also, for anyone who likes to see a job well done, a constant and abiding pleasure.'

Within a week of his first winner, Cauthen got, said the *Mirror*, 'his first taste of English justice.' After making every yard of the running to win Kempton's Easter Stakes on Joleg for Hills he found himself in the stewards' room after Bruce Raymond lodged an objection for 'crossing'. The margin of victory over Man of Vision was only a head; the objection was upheld. On the same horse he even managed to outwit Lester in a three-horse race on his first visit to Epsom when Lester continuously moved this way and that to block his path. However, the early weeks only got better and better. 'Cauthen in Big Demand,' proclaimed a *Mirror* headline. Thanks to Jimmy Lindley's extensive contacts throughout Europe, he'd ridden in Italy, France and Germany (scoring a treble on his 19th birthday) within his first month; and won six Group races – five of them for Hills.

To no one's surprise the newcomer was showing every sign of being a quick learner (he was obliged to ask one trainer who wanted him to ride his horse like a 'non-trier' exactly what that meant). It helped that Hills ran his yard in such a meticulous and organised fashion. One owner insisted if Hills hadn't been a trainer he'd have made 'a damned good prime minister'. Morning work on the Lambourn downland gallops couldn't be any further from stateside track work-outs: it's the same activity but on different planets. Cauthen hadn't seen, let alone experienced, anything like it before – as he told Robin Oakley for the writer's 2010 biography of Barry Hills.

The first morning I rode out there was a bit of mist. It was eerie - 60 horses in one string, walking across the ridge on a misty morning with a bit of sun; so beautiful. It was so efficient. Groups of horses arrive at the gallops at five-minute intervals. The work riders are ferried to the bottom of the gallops by car after each lot. That way I was getting a feel of perhaps half a dozen horses in quick succession. He was a traditionalist but a great thinker. He was always looking for ways of doing things better – new open-air barns, walking machines.

I understood how he wanted his horses ridden and he understood that I understood. We hardly had to talk. We had a great connection. Barry gave me a lot of confidence and told me all the peculiarities of the horses and courses. It was fantastic riding for him because he'd give me a plan of the way he thought a race should be ridden but always said that it was basically down to me and I must do what I thought was right. I think that's the best advice you can give a jockey.

The one facet of his new life the teenager considered a drawback was the travelling:

It was soon brought home to me by going racing somewhere different most days – in America we're at a track for weeks on end, and you have to be close to the tracks in order to ride work.

Penny usually drove the Mercedes. I would sit in the front and Barry would be in the back doing the entries, smoking a cigar. I'd been dying to drive and one day Penny felt a little tired and asked me to drive to Nottingham. I had very little experience of smaller English roads. I kept pulling out to get by trucks and swerving back in again. I didn't quite understand how to kick the Merc in the belly. After a few of these manoeuvres, Penny started looking nervously for the reaction in the back but there wasn't a word from Barry, who went on with his work. The comment was saved for when we got to the track.

B Hills climbed out and said to me, 'I hope you give my horses a better f***ing ride than you've just given me!'

The Johnny D or Affirmed that Cauthen needed to establish himself in his fresh surroundings entered right on cue. It was Tap On Wood.

When it came to selecting yearlings, Hills's policy was to examine the horseflesh first and, if he liked what he saw, the pedigree second: 'What it boils down to is that I value the horse according to the pedigree, after I have seen it.' Hills was suitably impressed by the conformation and swagger of a chestnut yearling by leading miler Sallust to buy him for 12,500 guineas on behalf of Tony Shead. Named after one of Shead's favourite Cole Porter songs, Tap On Wood had not been wrapped in cotton wool as a juvenile, entering the stalls on no fewer than 13 occasions and winning seven times. No great surprise there. His handler was no stranger to stretching South Bank's two-year-olds if they were sufficiently hardy: his filly Nagwa set a record by winning 13 of her 20 starts in 1975. The Hills credo was simple: 'I never ask my horses much at home. The secret is to get them to peak fitness without really testing them.' From the outset, achieving this with Tap On Wood wasn't entirely straightforward. 'He was a rather funky individual,' Hills recalled, 'worried about the whole job and broke out in terrible sweats.' The colt, often partnered by Penny Hills on the gallops, was notoriously lazy and even after he'd won the Guineas he allowed a poor maiden to beat him five lengths one morning. The canny individual developed a habit of pulling himself up as soon as he caught sight of his trainer at the top of the gallop; until one foggy morning fooled him and he worked brilliantly as a result. Clearly, Tap On Wood would only consent to earn his oats on the racetrack.

Hills decided Tap On Wood needed 'toughening up' by plenty of racing. Accordingly, the colt was out early, making his debut at Newbury on 14 April and finishing a promising second – that saw him sent off favourite on his next start. He came fourth; but third time of asking he opened his account at Pontefract, cruising home by eight lengths. Further success came quickly at Lingfield and Windsor before a troubled passage saw him come unstuck at Bath. Any money forfeited was soon recouped when, stepped up to seven furlongs, he justified favouritism at Doncaster. Two more facile wins at Pontefract and Newbury convinced Hills he was worth sending to Ireland for the Group Two National Stakes over seven furlongs at the Curragh on 2 September. Hills was not one to miss an opportunity; he'd entered no fewer than 28 horses because a recent injection of prize-money had raised the stakes to almost £20,000, greater than any juvenile Group Two in England bar the Gimcrack Stakes. Sent off at the generous odds of 10/1, Tap On Wood pipped Dickens Hill by a head in a messy finish that triggered an unsuccessful objection by the second. Hindsight made this success more significant than it looked at the time because Dickens Hill went on to win the Irish Two Thousand Guineas and Eclipse Stakes and finish runner-up in both the Derby and the Irish Derby to an above-average winner in Troy.

Suitably emboldened, Hills aimed higher still. Tap On Wood's 12th race of the season was to be the Group One Grand Criterium over a mile at Longchamp. Once again he accounted for Dickens Hill but his limitations were brutally exposed; he proved no match for the French crack Irish River, who already had a pair of Group Ones to his name and would develop into an unbeaten miler as a three-year-old. For his final outing Tap On Wood was dropped back in grade and trip to contest the Horris Hill Stakes at his local Newbury on 26 October. Although looking well beforehand, it's possible his arduous campaign had caught up with him. He was never in the hunt and passed the post some 14 lengths behind the winner, the odds-on favourite Kris. Tap On Wood might be forgiven were he pining for a break. He'd been hard at it for seven months.

Tap On Wood was allotted 8st 6lb in the Free Handicap; no fewer than 31 juveniles rated his superior. He was 6lb below Kris (unbeaten in his four races) and 15lb behind the top-rated Tromos, winner of the Dewhurst Stakes and winter favourite for the Two Thousand Guineas. Hills knew Tap On Wood would need a couple of runs to bring him on if he was to contest the Guineas. Consequently, a fortnight after Salisbury, he was sent north for the one-mile Thirsk Classic Trial with Ernie Johnson in the saddle. He readily put paid to the filly Abbeydale. Shead loved a bet when the odds were in his favour: he'd already backed his horse at 100/1 for the Guineas and when Abbeydale came second in the One Thousand (Cauthen finishing fourth aboard the Geoff Wragg-trained Topsy, on whom he'd landed his first Pattern race, Newbury's Group Three Fred Darling Stakes), he invested quite a few quid more at 66/1 – shortening the price still further. Cauthen was reinstated for the Classic: a birthday present of sorts, coming four days after he'd turned 19. Johnson took understandable umbrage and stalked off in a huff.

By post time on Two Thousand Guineas day, Tap On Wood had been backed down to 20s thanks, in no small measure, to Robert Sangster getting in on the act. The starting price might've got more cramped had there not been so much confidence in Kris, a warm favourite following his win in the Greenham Stakes. Henry Cecil, who'd landed the One Thousand Guineas with One In A Million and was hoping to become the first trainer since his father-in-law Noel Murless in 1967 to win both Guineas in the same season, fielded a second live contender in Lyphard's Wish, winner of the Craven Stakes (from Tromos – a Guineas absentee) over course and distance.

Cauthen's introduction to Newmarket Heath could scarcely have gone better. Hawaiian Sound had taken the Earl of Sefton Stakes earlier in the meeting (despite a saddle slipping after two furlongs leaving him half-way up the horse's neck) and he climbed aboard Tap On Wood buoyed by having notched a double the previous afternoon. Nor would it have escaped his notice that this day back home the Kentucky Derby was being run; it was a year since Affirmed had elevated him to superstardom. There was a thought from which he might draw inspiration. Nevertheless, it's worth emphasising how daunting a proposition it was for an American jockey used to racing round a left-handed oval to adapt to the wide-open spaces of the dead straight Rowley Mile on Newmarket's wind-swept heath. In 1979, furthermore, there were no running rails to shepherd the runners through the first five furlongs and prevent them from running out. Once again Jimmy Lindley's input was critical: 'Whether you're racing on a straight or round turns it's still all about timing. This is where Steve had the advantage on our riders. We never rode to the clock. We referred to half speed or quarter speed, but Steve had a clock in his head – which is all he needed. I passed on to him the advice I'd once been given by the great Charlie Smirke before I won the Guineas on Kashmir II in 1966. He was a "short runner" and Charlie told me the way to win on him was to go on at the Bushes and get momentum down the hill into the Dip. That way we might hold on. And we did by a short head!'

The stalls were placed on the far side of the track with Tap On Wood drawn in two (with Kris in three) and thus toward, the centre of the track. Standaan set off like the natural sprinter who'd win the Stewards' Cup three months later. This was precisely the pace to suit a lazy animal like Tap On Wood: he had to work. But recognising the implications of racing too close to the fast gallop, Cauthen was content to drop him to the rear of the 20 runners where he raced almost alone and detached. And he waited. He'd ridden the Rowley Mile a few times by now, most pertinently in the One Thousand Guineas on Topsy. Its two distinguishing features for race-callers and jockeys alike are the Bushes, located about two-and-a half-furlongs out, and the Dip, between the two and the one-furlong poles. The norm sees a challenging position sought at the first and the challenge delivered at the second. These twin signposts emphasised by Lindley allied to Cauthen's innate sense of where he should be in a race based on its pace gave him all the ordnance he needed. He just had to stay calm and await the moment to unlimber.

> I never psyched myself up. I psyched myself down. I think clearer when I'm not psyched up.
>
> I liked being the go-to guy, the guy in pressure positions, calling the plays, making decisions in the big moments. It's exciting, it's thrilling, and there is a lot at stake because a lot of people are counting on you. You're the pressure guy, the

quarterback – the guy who gets all the glory if it works out and blamed if it doesn't.

I always had an idea of what my horse could do but I'd check the form to see what to expect from the other horses. All horses tend to have patterns. You can only learn this by watching them a lot. Some horses always bear out when they're getting tired, so you try to move up inside them. Others bear in and close off the rail, so you avoid getting trapped inside them. Which ones will run on the front end and which ones will come from behind.

Everybody realises a jockey should know his own mount. But to really do your job, you should also know all the other horses in a race.

There's a lot more to riding than having balance and a good seat. You have to judge the pace; judge what the strong horses are doing; judge openings and when to make your move. You have to know where you're at and where the strong horses are.

By the time the running rail materialised three furlongs from home, Cauthen had tacked across to sit on the tail of Joe Mercer and Kris, who was starting to make inroads on the leaders. Passing the Bushes, he got first run on the favourite and capitalised on the ground falling away in the Dip to generate momentum for a race-winning move. Kris gave chase but Tap On Wood responded gamely to every one of the dozen cracks from Cauthen's whip and meeting the rising ground to the winning post it was Young Generation on his outside who looked the likelier threat. Tap On Wood hung on resolutely to beat Kris and Young Generation by half a length and a short head.

Shead was justifiably ecstatic: 'I owe it all to Steve. He doesn't get flustered and he doesn't fluster a horse. He was magnificent. He had it all to do but he waited for it to come right.' Back in Cauthen's home state the hardened members of the Press gathered at Churchill Downs to report on the Derby burst into spontaneous cheering at the news.

It was great for me, probably the moment when the English public decided to accept me into their hearts. The cheers weren't just for winning. I know they were a sort of welcome as if to say 'Glad to have you.'

Barry gave me instructions to get him settled, use a long rein on him, so that when we came to the Bushes he would be in a position to make one run. It went that way. I always had my eye on Kris and when he made his move I had my sights set on running him down. I had him covered and got first run on him down into the Dip. Then it was just a case of continuing to the wire. Kris proved a great horse; he only lost once more in all his 16 starts. But this was Tap On Wood's day to shine. Barry knew he had a horse. He was quietly confident he was going to be in the frame. I'm sure he had a few bucks on him!

Tap On Wood's success enabled Cauthen to replicate the Classic-winning deeds earlier in the century of fellow Americans Tod Sloan, Lester and Johnny Reiff, Danny Maher, 'Skeets' Martin, Matt McGee and Frank O'Neill – the last to score with Straitlace in the Oaks of 1924. '"Kid" Cauthen wrecks Cecil's Classic dream,' reported *The Sunday Express*. 'It was pure magic, Steve, "The Kid", Cauthen sending Newmarket race crowds into orbits of delight.' In the *Daily Mail*, Jim Stanford chose to highlight the post-race party in Lambourn: 'The Kid thanks the lads. He took the party in his stride before slipping away to telephone the good news to his mother and father back in Kentucky.'

The Sporting Life, on the other hand, shone the spotlight on another aspect of Cauthen's Guineas victory: 'Kid wins – Johnson quits.' Alan Smith's interview with South Bank's erstwhile rider was soaked in Johnson's sense of betrayal: he'd partnered almost 200 winners for Hills, including the very first, La Dolce Vita, and the trainer's first Classic winner, Enstone Spark. Now he'd been denied the opportunity to ride a horse on which he'd won six races the year before, and at Thirsk only a fortnight ago. The piece also seized the chance to expose the circumstances that expedited the granting of Cauthen's work permit. Smith related how Barry Hills had approached an MP for assistance. And how the Department of Employment had told him that Cauthen was treated as an 'equal' rather than someone who'd be 'taking someone's job' – which now appeared debatable. Geoffrey Summers, on behalf of the Jockeys' Association, assured Smith that 'we have never adopted a policy of seeking to prevent overseas jockeys from riding here.' What had always seemed a matter of time had come to a head quicker than anticipated. Johnson had been 'jocked off' from Rheingold by Lester Piggott after the 1972 Derby and missed the colt's subsequent Arc victory. Being jocked-off by 'Old Stoneface', however, was an occupational hazard for any jockey – Johnson joined a lengthy list of victims. Johnson didn't like it but he could live with it. Being replaced by Cauthen was a pill too harsh for his digestion. But he'd swallow his pride for a second time and was back riding for Hills in the Oaks.

Tap On Wood's participation in the Derby had to be in doubt on stamina grounds. And although a jockey seldom deserts a Classic-winning partner, even if he did run Cauthen's presence on his back couldn't be assured. At one point it seemed South Bank housed three other Derby candidates in Cracaval, Two of Diamonds and Galaxy Libra. The last-named soon fluffed his lines but Tony Shead's Cracaval and Two of Diamonds both won their Derby rehearsals at Chester (the Vase and the Dee Stakes) to earn places in the Epsom line-up, finishing eighth and 14th respectively. Thereafter, like many of South Bank's inmates, they were affected by a virus. In the autumn, however, Cauthen partnered Cracaval to a short-head victory over the Coronation Cup and King George VI and Queen Elizabeth Stakes winner Ile de Bourbon in a ding-dong battle for Kempton Park's newly instituted September Stakes. As a result of this performance, Cracaval started co-favourite for the St Leger seven days later. But there would be no second Classic in his first English season for Cauthen. Probably owing to those Kempton exertions and his lengthy illness, Cracaval could only manage 12th place. Two of Diamonds returned to the track in the Group One Joe McGrath Memorial Stakes at the Curragh; a decent second earned him a spot in the Prix de l'Arc de Triomphe; he and Cauthen finished a long way behind Three Troikas.

But Tap On Wood did take his chance in the Derby. His trainer hoped the colt's innate laziness might enable him to cope with the extra half a mile. Cauthen, understandably, stayed loyal to his Classic winner. They finished 12th of 23. In mitigation, Tap On Wood may, like numerous stable-mates, have been already ailing from the virus that was to keep him out of action until the Kiveton Park Steel Stakes at Doncaster in September. Conceding weight all round on Town Moor, he won convincingly to set up a mouth-watering re-match with Kris in Ascot's Queen Elizabeth II Stakes at the end of the month. But he coughed on the way home following his last piece of work and was retired to stand at the Kildangan Stud in County Kildare. Kris won the Queen Elizabeth II Stakes and was duly lauded as the champion miler of his generation. Kris certainly improved after his Guineas defeat to Tap On Wood. Yet that critical afternoon on the Rowley Mile Tap On Wood beat him fair and square.

For Cauthen's debut season to have progressed in the rich vein it had begun proved too much of a pipe dream. Group winners dried up: after that initial burst in the spring, he had to wait until September to add a seventh, and last, Group race in England; one Group Three apiece in Germany and Ireland completed his haul. Quantity proved as disappointing as quality. A total of just 52 winners (plus 15 on the continent) caused the same circling of Press vultures overhead as contributed to him leaving America at the start of the year. This disappointing score owed less to Cauthen's talents than Hills's horses. They'd not provided the expected spate of winners owing to the yard being hit hard by the bane of every stable: the 'virus', that all-embracing term describing a variety of equine afflictions. The common denominator was seemingly healthy horses running below par when put to the racecourse test. Yards frequently shut down rather than run the risk of exacerbating the problem by placing undue strain on a horse before it had genuinely recovered. The outcome saw the number of winners sent out by Hills drop by 30 from 1978's score.

ADAPTATION & REDEMPTION

Winners continued to arrive in a trickle rather than a flood in 1980: an improvement of just nine to 61 – though still enough to enable Cauthen to break into the top ten – and just four lowly Group races at home plus one in Germany and one in Ireland. The last, however, was the highlight of this – on face value – mediocre campaign since it resulted from a late pick-up ride at Leopardstown that saw him united with the best juvenile he was to ride in Europe: Storm Bird, trained in Ireland for Sangster by his principal ally, Vincent O'Brien. They won the Larkspur Stakes in a canter by four lengths. Next time up, the unbeaten Storm Bird stretched his streak to five by adding the Dewhurst Stakes to top the Free Handicap and earn a *Timeform* rating of 134. Storm Bird's three-year-old career amounted to a series of set-backs amid rumours of home brilliance that spawned just one disastrous outing before he was packed off to stud – where he sired a striking grey daughter destined to come Cauthen's way in the form of Indian Skimmer.

Consequently, as the 1980 season petered out, the question broached whenever Pressmen gathered over a drink was whether Cauthen might be forced to pack his bags and head back stateside. In fact, as Jimmy Lindley recalls, he had one other option: 'He was toying with the idea of moving to Ireland as one of the top yards, possibly Dermot Weld if memory serves, had offered him a job. He asked my advice and I told him to stick in England. There's not so much racing in Ireland to keep you busy.'

Cauthen was not for quitting. However, his fortunes in 1981 did little to scotch the tittle-tattle even though South Bank's total returning to the 80s helped him to 87 and seventh in the list – albeit the best part of a hundred behind Lester Piggott's championship-winning total. But quality was even more conspicuous by its absence: just a trio of Group Threes, one of them in Ireland. The character of 'The Six Million Dollar Man' was being tested. Cauthen remained stoic.

> There was something about the place that made me want to stay. I suppose the pace of life suited me. England is small, it's beautiful and the whole little place is just horse crazy. Sure there

are class barriers but it didn't bother me. I know my class and I was happy to stay in it.

Then a surge: a maiden century in 1982 of 107 for third place in the table behind Lester Piggott – still over 80 adrift. Press coverage began tilting in Cauthen's favour. A piece from *The Times* is typical: 'The young American rider has now been completely accepted as part of our racing scene – a far cry from the inquisitive hordes that descended on Salisbury in April 1979 to watch his British baptism. Cauthen has improved his race-riding tremendously in his three full seasons here, but too often he was caught out by the different tactics used by top jockeys in this country. Not for us is the flat-out, open-throttle style of racing. Our riders must adopt a more leisurely, subtle set of tactics to offset the wide variety of racecourses. Here the timing of the final challenge is crucial.' The doyen of English racing correspondents went further: 'Cauthen is a maker of horses,' wrote Richard Baerlein, 'not just a rider of winners.' Yet possibly the ultimate accolade came from an Ascot gateman: 'A fine ambassador for his country! Makes up a bit for that bloody feller McEnroe!'

Cauthen was no fool. He knew he'd have to make minor adjustments to his style, though the toe-in-the-iron and back so flat and steady it might invite a table setting for two with a floral centrepiece for good measure remained instantly recognisable from the stands. His whip had gradually moved its forehand position like a periscope into the backhand, but was secondary armament to his elbows edging out and upwards (the opposite sequence to English jockeys) in pumping rhythm with his horse's stride to seize a gap or launch a race-winning challenge.

> I was nearly a complete jockey at 18 but the small gap between what I was then and what I became later on in Europe took years to fill. Coming over at that age proved more beneficial than waiting a few years. Myself and Cash Asmussen were both above average riders when we came, but so were Jorge Velasquez and Darrel McHargue when they had a go at riding in Europe. But they were

more set in their ways. It's like trying to teach an old dog new tricks, whereas we were very much more open-minded and able to adapt much more readily. I was intrigued by what European racing had to offer and, as it turned out, it suited me very well.

Cauthen offered a quirky stance on his early problems.

If you've buttered your toast on the left all your life it's tough to switch! But I started out riding the hillsides of Kentucky - you can ride a horse wherever he'll go. So there was no reason why I shouldn't adapt.

In America all the tracks are uniform, left-handed, flat and dirt with a turf track on the inside. All very similar, whereas in England no track is the same, with cambers and uphill finishes. Instead of building courses, in England they made courses out of what's there. If there's a hill, you run up the hill. Or you might have a mile-and-a quarter straight; one would be left-handed, another right or even a figure eight like Windsor.

It's multiple choice. Knowledge of a track is worth 10lb in Britain and Europe. It was a learning process. And I had to learn quick.

There were lots of things I had to learn about each unique course. Dirt is more regular and you don't get such drastic changes in the ground: when the ground is soft you need to be on the outside. But the most fundamental adjustment was learning to balance horses over undulating courses. At Salisbury I remember sliding all over the place to start with. In America, as the tracks are flat, the jockey has to sit up the horse's neck and balance himself so as not to slow its movement down. I had to learn to shift my weight whenever the horse was going uphill or downhill. And I grew four inches taller after I came over! That meant I had to ride a bit longer and had to use a longer rein to keep horses better balanced. But each horse is different. Some are narrow and some are wide. I adjusted my riding length accordingly so that I was comfortable. But I continued to ride with just my toes in the stirrups like most Americans, instead of feet like the English riders, because that was the way I felt most comfortable also.

Cauthen's tactical appreciation also demanded revision.

The rhythm of races differed. In America the horses jump off and go almost flat out from the start. They finish slower, whereas in England they often run the last quarter faster than any other.

A lot of people thought American jockeys only knew how to win from the front. When I came over the only English jockey prepared to win from the front was Lester Piggott; that gave me an advantage in lots of instances. I had ridden a lot of winners from the front and I was happy doing that on the right horse. If I jumped four lengths clear everyone assumed I was going too fast but they weren't comprehending. They thought my horse would fold when they got to me. But I often had plenty left. I won a ton of races that way. But I had to learn to put one to sleep at the back before coming from behind.

I made a lot of adjustments. But a horse is still a horse!

Cauthen's English mentor in the arts of English jockeyship could not have been more pleased with his pupil's successful transition. 'He adapted like nobody I've ever seen,' says Jimmy Lindley. 'When he first came he had a problem keeping horses straight, but every time he went out to ride he improved by pounds. He had a really sharp brain. You only had to tell him something once. I remember walking the round course at Ascot with him; showing him where he had to be running down into Swinley Bottom. Get a good start and then ease off to get the correct position. He saw that straight away. And he'd remember it word for word days later. I knew he'd make it okay over here as soon as I rode work upsides him at Barry's. He could settle horses so well; switch them off. He'd lovely "hands". But they can only do what the brain tells them. It's like picking up a priceless piece of glass but treating it like a clay pot and breaking it because the brain didn't pass on the right information. He changed the style of our boys – they're all based on him now. And he'd be right up there with Ryan Moore and Frankie Dettori.'

Back across the Atlantic, Willie Shoemaker put it succinctly: 'When he left the States he was a boy, gifted but immature. Now he is a man and the complete jockey.' For his own part Cauthen began to appreciate the strengths of his rivals in the English weighing room:

> Each one of the European riders had a definite style. Lester Piggott had a great sense of pace, a great mind, great patience. He'd wait until the last 70 yards to make a move. He didn't worry about what people would say if he got beaten, but he didn't get beaten too often! Willie Carson would seem hopelessly beaten but he comes on. It looks like he's always pushing, but he's really never asked his horse, and then he'll ask it. Pat Eddery was very, very stylish with a good whip rhythm. Joe Mercer was very strong; he never got his horse in trouble.

Carson responded by dubbing Cauthen 'Wonderkid'. He added, 'But afterwards I just called him "Wonder". And he answers to it! He really is a wonder! All our tracks are different and all have got to be ridden. For a kid to adapt so quickly, it's amazing. He's got quite a good brain!' Even the wizened English centaur known as Lester Piggott was prepared to concede: 'The boy is a natural. He has done more in an incredibly short space of time than anyone has ever done before. He is one of the most remarkable jockeys of all time.'

To the majority of jockeys the smattering of Group Two and Three events (and even a Derby of the Scottish variety) that Cauthen managed to accumulate in his first three English seasons would be welcomed with eager arms. But Cauthen needed to mount his show in the West End not the end of the pier. Participation in Group One events was not enough. He wanted to be in a position to win English Classics and others of the calendar's historic races not merely make up the numbers. The next 'good horse', the Group One horse provided by Hills to follow in Tap On Wood's hoof-prints, took a painful while to materialise: a further four seasons to be exact. Although striking up a fruitful partnership with Ian Balding's Diamond Shoal that led to a hat-trick of Group Ones on the continent in the summer of 1983, Cauthen had to remind English racegoers of his talent by scaling such heights on the English stage. And as the autumn leaves fell in 1983, so did a trio of domestic Group Ones fall into Cauthen's lap. Two of them were for Hills courtesy of the fillies Desirable and Cormorant Wood.

If there was one racecourse in England that resembled the dark side of the moon to Cauthen it had to be that occupying the bare and often windswept landscape of Newmarket Heath, defined by its seemingly infinite straight lines and hidden dips rather than those tight bends and short straights he was used to back home. But it's a mark of Cauthen's rapid assimilation into the fabric of the English Turf that he was now both comfortable and highly effective at Newmarket. And he proved it with stunning displays of artistry at the four-day September meeting.

'Cauthen sets Hills alight,' stated *The Times* in uncharacteristically tabloid argot after the first of them. The South Bank representative who triggered the headline was the grey filly Desirable following her victory in the Group One Cheveley Park Stakes. Desirable wasn't the sturdiest of fillies to look at, but she represented on her dam's side one of the most famous families in the Stud Book, that tracing to legendary race-mare Pretty Polly. The Cheveley Park was her fifth start of the year and she turned the tables on the only two fillies who'd lowered her colours, namely Prickle and Gala Event, in the Lowther and Moyglare Stud Stakes respectively. Prickle attempted to make every yard of the six furlongs but never shook off Desirable, whom Cauthen brought with a rare rattle out of the Dip to catch the leader and then withstand the fast-finishing Pebbles by a neck.

Ninety minutes later Cauthen provided a second masterclass in the art of snatching irons from the fire in a frantic battle of short-heads with Messrs Carson and Eddery in a two-mile handicap aboard the Hills filly Hi Love: 'If Cauthen showed style and judgement on Desirable, he added the qualities of tenacity and strength with his performance on Hi Love. It was testimony not only to his now established place at the very top of the riding tree, but also his magical touch.' As Hills had a bet of £5,000 to £350 about Hi Love, it's just as well Cauthen did.

Desirable's generous odds of 12/1 (the longest-priced winner of the race in 18 years) were put in the shade 24 hours later when Cauthen completed the Cheveley Park–Middle Park Group One double on the Charlie Nelson-trained Creag-An-Sgor, who was allowed to start at 50/1. 'Cauthen rides by the copybook,' declared *The Times* after Cauthen had turned over hot-pot Vacarme and a fistful of other Group winners with a colt who'd only a maiden victory to show from his four starts. That this performance was a pronounced improvement goes without saying, but Cauthen deserved all the credit after deploying totally contrasting tactics to those used on Desirable. Urging Creag-An-Sgor to the front early on, he stoked the pace gradually yet had plenty left to repel Superlative and Vacarme up the hill to the line.

The Cauthen-Hills bandwagon hadn't finished rolling. Cormorant Wood maintained the winning run with a convincing success in the Sun Chariot Stakes. Bobby McAlpine's big rangy filly by Home Guard out of Quarry Wood didn't appear until the back end of her juvenile season when she won a seven-furlong maiden at Leicester on the second of her two starts. There was no knowing what Cormorant Wood's optimum distance might be since her sire's best form was over six furlongs (though he got ten) and Quarry Wood's forte was stamina. Hills began her three-year-old campaign over 12 furlongs with the Oaks in mind. She finished a decent second in the Lingfield Oaks Trial to the future Irish Oaks winner Give Thanks, followed by sixth place in the Oaks when aided by Piggott. Cauthen had opted to ride stable-mate Ski Sailing and was proved right as she finished one place ahead of Cormorant Wood; the latter had one more shot at the distance in Newmarket's Princess of Wales's Stakes but when her run again fizzled out in the final quarter it was clear she didn't really get the longer trip. But dropped back in distance Cormorant Wood became a revelation.

She began by upsetting the odds-on favourite Air Distingue in the Virginia Stakes at Newcastle – though she was a mite fortunate to keep the race. Cauthen returned to scale so dehydrated he weighed-in 5lb light: the permitted shortfall is 2lb. Fortunately, since 'Mr Combustible' wouldn't have taken kindly to losing a race in such circumstances, Willie Carson spotted the whereabouts of the needle and applied a surreptitious finger to the scales. Next stop was Newmarket and a step up in class for the Sun Chariot. The outcome was the same. Cauthen took up the running with two furlongs to go and nudged his filly to a routine success by a length from Sedra. 'The ever-improving filly Cormorant Wood kept up the Hills-and-Cauthen run of luck with a convincing success from the heavily backed favourite,' reported *The Life*. A possible tilt at Canada's Rothman's International back at a longer trip was abandoned subsequently in favour of the Champion Stakes (Group One) a fortnight later over the same course and distance as the Sun Chariot.

Cormorant Wood was challenging for one of the Turf's iconic races. First run in 1877, it had been won by such great horses as Ormonde, Pretty Polly, Bayardo and Petite Etoile. Of late, the race had begun to be farmed by females. In the last ten years it had fallen to six females capped by Time Charter 12 months earlier. Fillies and mares frequently seemed to thrive in the autumn; they'd also won six of the last ten renewals of the Prix de l'Arc de Triomphe. One school of thought in the veterinary profession suggested the benefits of coming into season less frequently during the shorter days of autumn may have something to do with fillies showing their best form at this time of year. Whatever its origin, Cormorant Wood's form was starting to peak.

Beforehand Bobby McAlpine expressed the view he'd be delighted if she finished in the first six. It was all he could do to make himself heard. Newmarket Heath can be a bleak spot at the best of times. In the autumn it's frequently battered by winds that must blow all the way from Siberia, raw and bitter enough to make King Lear wrap his cloak around him with more urgency than a man checking his wallet when he thinks he's been mugged. A relentless ten-furlong grind across the Heath with nowhere to shelter from a cutting wind tests a rider as no other. Back home in Kentucky, Cauthen would've headed for the basement when a tornado was nigh. Nothing had prepared him for negotiating a Newmarket typhoon. He'd have to fly by the seat of his breeches. Such was the setting for the 1983 Champion Stakes. The race turned out to be a corker. Even decades after the event some respected judges still consider the ride Cauthen gave Cormorant Wood to be the finest of his 'English Odyssey'. But Cauthen left Robin Oakley in no doubt that the real plaudits for the filly's victory should go to Hills.

> It was one of Barry's best training jobs. He worked a miracle with a horse who two weeks before wouldn't have won a seller. It was a dry year and it was hard getting her going. He'd worked her on the all-weather.
>
> He said to me: 'Ride her like a non-trier. Drop out the back. Wait and wait. Keep her out of the wind as long as you can.' It was a terribly windy day. I was biding my time watching who was going to go and things broke my way. I tracked a few of the right horses and I nailed Tolomeo at the end. Newmarket was a great place for finishes up that hill!

It's no exaggeration to state Cauthen is being unduly modest about his role in Cormorant Wood's mesmerising zig-zagging progress through the teeth of a gale: he'd picked a route with the skills of a London taxi driver during the rush hour. With a furlong to run there were 18 horses being tossed around like autumn leaves, their riders busting a gut to win the richest-ever race run at racing's HQ. But the 19th was Cormorant Wood, whose partner was actually taking a 'pull' while pondering where next to aim her bay nose. Cauthen measured his options and made his decision; his back flattened and his filly stretched; and they side-stepped horse after horse as if they were dodging bullets. 'Cool Cauthen squeezes home, thanks to courageous riding,' announced *The Sporting Life*. 'As near a masterpiece as you will get in race-riding,' wrote Brough Scott in *The Sunday Times* to describe an exhibition of calculated coolness that reminded older folk of threading needles in an air raid.

Cauthen's filly had in fact touched Tolomeo when bursting between him and Flame of Tara to snatch the prize by a head and a short head. According to McAlpine, Tolomeo's jockey, Gianfranco Dettori, was 'squared' afterwards by Cauthen and it was the Italian who took the blame for any scrimmaging during the subsequent stewards' enquiry that relegated Tolomeo to fourth. Three domestic Group Ones, two of them for Barry Hills, was a superb way to bring down the curtain on a 1983 season that saw Cauthen finish fifth in the jockeys' table with 102 winners. And Cormorant Wood did cross the Atlantic after all in 1983: she contested the Washington International but was no match for Arc winner All Along, finishing sixth of eight. The notion of her tackling 12 furlongs was finally abandoned.

Before Cormorant Wood presented Hills and Cauthen with further Group One success, they enjoyed one that came like a bolt from the blue. Gildoran was South Bank through and through: he was the first foal of Durtal, who'd carried the Sangster jacket to success in the Cheveley Park Stakes, by Hills's Arc winner Rheingold. On his final outing the previous season he'd shown much improved form when put over a distance of ground to finish second to Karadar in the Doncaster Cup. Moreover, he loved firm ground and the summer of 1984 proved hot and dry. By the time Royal Ascot came around in flaming June, Gildoran had won the two-mile Sagaro Stakes and carried almost 10st into sixth place in the Chester Cup.

Whizzing round the seven-furlong Roodeye brought back memories of Aqueduct for Cauthen, but two and a half miles round Ascot posed a different problem. If there was one issue more alien to Cauthen's race-riding experience than the disparate topography of Britain's tracks, it was the presence of prestigious races at distances beyond his experience. The Jockey

ADAPTATION & REDEMPTION

Club Gold Cup had been the solitary American Grade One at two miles before America's lust for speed horses saw it reduced to a mile and a half in 1976. Thereafter, it became increasingly fashionable across the Atlantic to talk of 12-furlong races as 'long distance' events. Ascot's Gold Cup had two and a half miles for Cauthen to work out. And he might expect the lactic acid to be burning his calves and thighs inside the last mile.

Gildoran had few supporters for the Group One prize on the day: he started fourth favourite of nine at 10/1. In truth, anyone recalling the recent feats of arms by Le Moss, Ardross and Sagaro appreciated Gildoran was part of an undistinguished field. Besides Karadar, he faced a trio of soft-ground performers from France and Condell from Ireland; some more American spice was added to the contest by the presence of Willie Shoemaker aboard Balitou. While Pretty Picture and Karadar orchestrated a severe gallop, Gildoran lobbed along contentedly in their slipstream until Cauthen pushed him into the lead approaching the final turn. Once straightened up for home, Ore and Condell mounted challenges on his outside and with the three in line abreast it appeared Gildoran might be the one tiring. But Cauthen asked the colt for more and was answered in the positive. Gildoran rallied and showed enormous pluck to see them off. Given the early gallop and the concrete-like conditions underfoot, it came as no shock to see the track record shattered by almost three seconds.

'Cauthen's jockeyship had made the American headline news lately,' said *The Times* beneath the headline, 'Cauthen strikes gold on Gildoran'. It continued: 'The "Kentucky Kid" showed inspired strength in a finish combined with his normal fine judgement of pace as he forced Gildoran's head past Ore inside the final furlong.' The paper pointed out that Hills's yard had been below form for much of the year and quoted the trainer as saying, 'I was beginning to think I couldn't win an argument!' Sangster, on the other hand, had been enjoying a purple patch: Gildoran's success meant he'd won the last four races at the meeting.

Gildoran's next target became a formality: the Goodwood Cup, which over an extra furlong was an even sterner test of stamina. On paper it was a re-run of the Gold Cup with Gildoran's only opponents being Ore, Condell and Karadar and the latter was made favourite to turn the tables in receipt of 4lb. However, since the race wound its way up-hill and down-dale across the Sussex Downs, there were several opportunities for Cauthen to give Gildoran a breather should he choose to make the running and ensure a genuine test of stamina. Hills had been riding work on Gildoran and knew he was as fresh as paint because he'd regularly had his arms pulled out. Making every yard of the 21 furlongs was a cinch, with Cauthen setting the fractions, and he duly turned the Cup into a procession: 'Steve Cauthen rode a superbly judged race as he waited in front,' was the unanimous verdict of the papers after Ore was thrashed by eight lengths with Karadar a further dozen behind.

The Stayers' Triple Crown awaited Gildoran if he could add the Doncaster Cup. Only Le Moss in 1979 and 1980 had achieved the feat in the 30 years since Alycidon. The opposition was again weak; this time he was heavily supported in the market at 2/1 on. But Town Moor in September had some juice in the ground. Gildoran trailed in plumb last. In the Jockey Club Cup at Newmarket he again beat nobody. Gildoran's day in the sun had, quite literally, come and gone for 1984. But the sun that shone once more at Royal Ascot in 1985 enabled him to land a second Gold Cup, only the ninth horse so to do in the 20th century – albeit this time minus Cauthen.

> It was a sweet moment at Ascot, winning that Gold Cup on Gildoran for Barry and Robert. We all knew by then that I'd be leaving them at the end of the season. But they'd brought me over to England, and it was great for me to reward them with such an important success before departing. Barry always said that racing is hours of agony and moments of glory. He's right. And this moment was one of the latter to remember.

Cormorant Wood took some time to regain her brilliant best in 1984. Even so, one shouldn't crab her debut performance in the Lockinge Stakes. Put back to a mile in Newbury's Group Three event (elevated to Group One by

1995), she wasn't fancied to win: only the brace of complete outsiders went off at a longer price than her. But she went clear with two furlongs to run and responded gamely to incessant pressure from Cauthen as Wassl came at her. The pair fought like tiger and tigress: testified by their last furlong of 12.62 seconds being almost two seconds faster that the Newbury norm. Cauthen kept his filly's head in front until the last stride, where the Irish Guineas winner collared her to force a dead heat. Possibly this effort had knocked the stuffing out of her. Made favourite for the Queen Anne at Royal Ascot, she could only finish third to a horse she'd trounced at Newbury; and though subsequently finishing ahead of Wassl and Tolomeo in the Eclipse, she'd the best part of four lengths to find on Sadler's Wells. However, when Hills returned to Lambourn following a buying expedition at the Keeneland Sales, he found the filly bursting with health: and, tellingly, noted her weight of 488kg was the same as before she'd won the Sun Chariot and the Champion Stakes. The filly would go to York for the Benson and Hedges Gold Cup (Group One) on 21 August with no lack of confidence behind her.

Sadler's Wells and two more of Cormorant Wood's Eclipse rivals joined her in the field for the Benson and Hedges: there was, after all, a $1m bonus if the winner proceeded to add the Phoenix Park Champion Stakes and the Champion Stakes at Newmarket. If history was any guide, however, winning the first leg would not be straightforward. The Benson and Hedges had earned a reputation for being a graveyard for favourites. When the tobacco firm took the decision to sponsor a championship race at York's highest-profile meeting over an extended ten furlongs, it could hardly have envisaged the amount of publicity the event would generate. The race succeeded in attracting the cream of Europe's middle-distance stars, but in the first six renewals five odds-on shots were scuppered, causing the Benson and Hedges to become something of a bogey race for favourites. The contest instantly earned this dubious reputation when Derby winner Roberto sank the hitherto undefeated Brigadier Gerard in the inaugural race of 1972, thanks to a consummate exhibition of even-time pace from Lenny Goodman breadwinner Braulio Baeza; Roberto's time smashed the track record by almost three seconds. If the eclipse of the 3/1 on Brigadier was a sensation the subsequent defeats of Rheingold (1973), Grundy (1975), Trepan (1976) and Artaius (1977) at odds-on were equally unwelcome medicine for favourite backers.

There could be no single reason for this catalogue of upsets. Nevertheless, some themes do recur: small fields; the impact of a pacemaker; and, perhaps most controversially, jockeyship. Whatever ensued once the gates clanged open for the 1984 Benson and Hedges, supporters of Cormorant Wood remembered how her jockey had solved a seemingly impenetrable puzzle on Champion Stakes day and felt sure there was more than a decent chance he'd come up with right answers on the Knavesmire. Bookmakers took a different view. Their reading of the formbook reached the conclusion that Cormorant Wood's chances were 15/1; only the two deputed pacemakers in the field of nine were deemed less likely winners. One statistic was safe: there was no odds-on hot pot in the field for Cormorant Wood or anyone else to foil. The favourite was the Sangster-O'Brien representative Sadler's Wells; Tolomeo had his supporters, while 'clever' money rested with Chief Singer, whose season that started with second in the Guineas had gone from strength to strength, with wins in the St James's Palace and the Sussex Stakes over a mile and an astounding victory in the July Cup – over half the distance of today's event.

It proved to be a red-letter day for Cauthen and Cormorant Wood. The filly was majestic. Settled last as Ivano cut out the pace, Cauthen subsequently saw his path blocked when no fewer than seven opponents crossed in front of him toward the fence as the field turned into the straight. Fortunately, York's straight is a long four furlongs. He had time to adjust and was able to follow Sadler's Wells and Raft through as they fought for the lead three furlongs out. But they led only on sufferance. Once Cauthen released the brakes at the one pole, Cormorant Wood quickly burst clear to reach the winning post with two and a half lengths to spare over Tolomeo. This brought up Cauthen's 100th winner of the season. 'Steve celebrates his century in style,' crowed *The Life*. 'Cormorant hits peak – now she goes for gold.'

ADAPTATION & REDEMPTION

That was a good way to hit the target. I knew we were going to win the moment I picked the filly up and it was nice to land a top race for an old friend.

Cauthen's appetite for a crack at the $1m bonus was whetted, but next morning Cormorant Wood pulled out lame, having sustained a tendon injury at some point in the race. She was retired. At the end of the season she was the top-rated older female (2lb above Time Charter) and second only to Teenoso. Hills rated her superior to both Dibidale and Hawaiian Sound and her place in his affection is demonstrated by Cormorant Wood's portrait being among the sextet hung in his drawing room. The best of her progeny was Rock Hopper, trained by Michael Stoute to win a brace of Hardwicke Stakes, a Yorkshire Cup, the Princess of Wales's Stakes and the Jockey Club Stakes.

The Sangster connection resulted in another Group One victory for Cauthen in 1984, courtesy of Committed. Trained in Ireland by Dermot Weld, the four-year-old filly had been butting heads with every crack sprinter all season. Some she lost; some she won. The Cork and Orrery at Royal Ascot over six furlongs and the William Hill Sprint Championship at York over five furlongs by four lengths in a rapid time of 57.24 seconds were her stand-out efforts. She was customarily ridden by Australian jockey Brent Thomson. Cauthen, however, was aboard in the Prix de l'Abbaye de Longchamp (Group One) on Arc day in October. The French seemed incapable of producing a sprinter to win their only Group One over the minimum distance: the juvenile Sigy (1978) was the last. This latest renewal went the same way as most others. Cauthen pushed Committed to the front at halfway and didn't see another horse thereafter. The duo won by an impressive two and a half lengths from the previous season's champion sprinter Habibti.

By now Cauthen's rising profile was gaining him a number of choice 'spare' rides from outside stables. The first star from elsewhere was Sharpo, a lethally fast sprinter usually partnered by Pat Eddery. The Jeremy

Tree flyer had won the last two runnings of York's William Hill Sprint Championship when Cauthen got the late call to ride the five-year-old in 1982 after Eddery had hurt his hand in an earlier race at the meeting. The race was better known, previously and subsequently, as the Nunthorpe and its status within the Pattern oscillated between Group One and Two, just like Britain's other principal race over the minimum trip, the King's Stand Stakes at Royal Ascot. In 1982 the York race was the lower grade and the latter was the higher; the following season saw the 'Nunthorpe' elevated. Somewhat bizarrely, the King's Stand was downgraded in 1988 in exchange for Haydock Park's six-furlong Vernon's Sprint Cup being promoted to the top tier. This demotion persisted until 2008, by which time the Cork and Orrery had been raised to Group One as the Diamond Jubilee Stakes in 2002. The only other sprint in the British calendar in 1982 at the elite level was the July Cup over six furlongs at Newmarket. On the evidence of the Pattern, sprinters, like the stayers, were of minor significance in comparison to milers and middle-distance performers.

Sharpo would aim to replicate the York hat-trick of the gelding Tag End (1928/29/30) so long as the ground had plenty of 'give' in it. He'd jarred himself badly in one King's Stand and had already taken a similar risk on his seasonal debut in the Palace House Stakes, where he finished third. One of Sharpo's trademark late bursts of acceleration had then secured the July Cup. York's ground saw the divots flying: Sharpo would be in his element. Cauthen rode the chestnut in the same fashion as Eddery. He kept him hidden behind a wall of trailblazers until the two-furlong marker, and then gave him a couple of taps. Sharpo reacted like a sling-shot, putting the race to bed so emphatically with a 12-second furlong (in the wake of three in an impressive 34 seconds) that Cauthen was able to down tools and pose motionless with the flattest of backs for the photographers covering the finish. Sharpo's winning margin of two lengths was academic, but his time of 58.68 seconds on the prevailing ground, and unextended to boot, was the hallmark of a great sprinter. Breaking the one minute for five furlongs is a rarity in Britain outside of the two tracks benefitting from downhill five furlongs, Epsom and Goodwood. 'Sharpo fulfilled the hopes of his many admirers,' stated *The Daily Telegraph*, 'and confirmed himself the outstanding European sprinter.' Sharpo went on to add the Prix de l'Abbaye de Longchamp two months later to frank the paper's opinion before being retired. Naturally, Eddery was back on him. But Cauthen had the pleasure and privilege of knowing he'd sat on one of the finest sprinters of the modern era – and, by his own pronouncement at the time, the fastest horse he'd ridden thus far in either England or the United States. Sharpo's *Timeform* rating of 132 put him in an elite group of post-war sprinters fit to be mentioned in the same sentence as Abernant (TR142).

Cauthen developed a more permanent, and lucrative, association with two colts trained by Ian Balding at Kingsclere for the American Paul Mellon: Diamond Shoal and Gold and Ivory. The Mellon-Balding combination delivered a regular flow of classy individuals: from Champion Stakes winner Silly Season in the 1960s to Irish One Thousand Guineas winner Forest Flower in the 1980s – but chiefly with the superlative Mill Reef. Unlike many of his colleagues, Balding was not averse to 'pot-hunting' on the European mainland, with horses that were probably a little below the corresponding level at home. In 1980 and 1981 Balding won more money abroad than any other British trainer. Germany and Italy were ripe hunting grounds, especially for middle-distance horses like Diamond Shoal.

At first Diamond Shoal didn't suggest the promise of his elder sibling Glint of Gold, who'd finished second in both Derby and St Leger and won six Group Ones in France, Italy and Germany. Although much smaller than his brother, Diamond Shoal was a typical son of Mill Reef, being attractive and a grand mover. However, he swam in calmer waters as a three-year-old. Instead of the 1982 Derby, he contested the Rosebery Memorial Handicap – and won it. He concluded his second season in Group One class: third in the Leger; third in the Grosser Preis von Baden; and fourth in the Washington DC International. In so doing, he'd demonstrated his love of travel and indifference to the state of the ground. He failed to win again until united with Cauthen as a four-year-old in 1983. Together they won the John Porter

Stakes at Newbury first time out. To date he'd been ridden as a hold-up horse. But Cauthen began riding the colt far more prominently, resulting in a trio of Group Ones, the Gran Premio di Milano, the Grand Prix de Saint-Cloud and the Grosser Preis von Baden. Unfortunately, a ban for reckless riding prevented Cauthen riding Diamond Shoal in the King George, in which, partnered by Piggott, the colt lost narrowly to Time Charter. The partnership with Cauthen met defeat just the once, in the Arc. With the aid of Cauthen the backward ugly duckling had developed into a glorious swan to stand comparison with his sibling: in fact, Diamond Shoal's *Timeform* rating of 130 was 3lb superior.

As Diamond Shoal exited the stage, Gold and Ivory stepped from the wings. This strong and good-bodied son of Key to the Mint, America's champion colt of 1972, trod a similar path in Europe to his stable-mates: as a three-year-old in 1984, he and Cauthen won the Preis von Europa at Cologne and the Gran Premio del Jockey Club in Milan; the following year they added the Grosser Preis von Baden. In three seasons Cauthen had won six continental Group Ones on the Balding pair and, bagging the best part of £320,000 in the process, reinforced the maxim 'Have horse, will travel'.

> Diamond Shoal was definitely the better of the two. I was grateful to him because, in the summer of 1983, he kept me in the Group One picture: I'd not won a Group One since the Guineas. He'd been a serious Classic contender the previous back end and it seemed every time we went abroad we won. At the time not many trainers fancied travelling abroad on a Sunday like later on, Ian placed his horses extremely well, and they were pretty soft Group Ones to win.

John Hanmer landed an even better booking in 1984. Henry Candy needed a jockey for Time Charter in the Coronation Cup. In February, Candy's stable jockey, Billy Newnes, had received a three-year ban for passing information to big-time gambler Harry Bardsley. The decision was a pivotal one for Cauthen.

ADAPTATION & REDEMPTION

Cormorant Wood was a good filly. But Time Charter was in a higher league. The five-year-old mare had concluded her Oaks-winning season of 1982 by pulverising her field in the Champion Stakes by seven lengths, leaving among the vanquished the Eclipse and King George winner Kalaglow and Guineas winner Zino. The following season she added the King George.

Cauthen and Candy were already allies. Two years earlier Cauthen had very nearly stolen Candy a first Classic success with Wind and Wuthering in the Two Thousand Guineas. Having set a stiff gallop up the centre of the track, the partnership was overhauled only by Zino, who needed to complete the fastest Guineas for 34 years to prevail by a neck. Hanmer corralled Candy at the races and made him aware of Cauthen's availability for Time Charter. There were likely to be only a handful of runners and Candy would be spoiled for choice, with Lester Piggott among those without a mount in the race. He went with Cauthen. Hanmer would confess to not always being so fortunate. The previous summer he'd booked Cauthen for the ride on Horage in the St James's Palace Stakes at Royal Ascot. The colt won well. Trainer Mattie McCormack had also wanted Cauthen aboard his filly Night of Wind in the Queen Mary Stakes the following afternoon. She was still a maiden after three runs. McCormack told Hanmer he could get off Night of Wind in the event of a better ride turning up. Hanmer put his rider on Tony Ingham's My Louie, who at least had some winning form. Night of Wind blew her 14 rivals away at odds of 50/1 to prompt an agent's nightmare.

Time Charter's immediate target was a prestigious prize. First run in 1902, when it replaced the old Epsom Gold Cup won by such cracks as St Simon and Bend Or, under its present title the Coronation Cup had been won by equally luminous fillies in Pretty Polly (1905/1906), Petite Etoile (1960 and 1961), Park Top (1969) and Lupe (1971). However, the emergence and subsequent rise of the King George VI and Queen Elizabeth Stakes from 1951 wrested the Cup's title of Britain's premier mile-and-a-half event for older horses, a trend reflected in the handful of competitors each season. The prize had once attracted plenty of French raiders, who captured 11 renewals between 1946 and 1964. Then the flow began to dry up as French prize-money began to increase dramatically: no Gallic challenger would face Time Charter in 1984.

And the Coronation Cup was fortunate to have Time Charter. She was now a five-year-old. On average no more than 700 of the 9,000-odd horses in training in Britain are older females, and scarcely a dozen will be deemed talented enough to compete in Group One company. 'Can Time Charter beat the colts on level terms?' was the question put to Henry Candy at the start of the season. 'If she can, bash on,' was his answer. 'If not, send her to stud or to a good French trainer.' Candy's point was well made: there were more opportunities for females across the Channel. Of late, France had been producing the finest race-mares thanks in the main to a pair of mercurial trainers. Maurice Zilber and Angel Penna had in their care at the same time two outstanding runners and perennial rivals – Dahlia and Allez France. Egyptian Zilber sent out the globetrotting Dahlia to collect ten Group Ones spread among five different countries: 'She is brilliant, very intelligent, but she is a lady of caprice,' he said of his charge before adding in one word the secret for coaxing older mares into giving of their best: 'She needs to be understood.' Penna's rapport with fillies arguably touched the supernatural. The Argentinian won six English and French Classics with fillies during his six-season sojourn in France courtesy of Flying Water, Pawneese, Madelia and Mata Hari. And he handled the later career of Allez France, who beat Dahlia in every one of their eight clashes. The 'Queen of Longchamp' won Penna his second Arc in 1974 (following another filly San San two years earlier) besides a bevy of Group Ones. It's worth dwelling on Penna's credo for it's as pertinent to the jockey on the filly as it was to her trainer. 'You must treat her as you would a beautiful woman; you must bring her gifts and pamper her a little. Above all, you must never tell her when she is ready. Like all beautiful ladies she will tell you in her own time. The only certain way to make them lay down their lives for you is to love them. A great one will not let you down. She will give you the last drop of blood.'

Perhaps only someone of an exotic background can express his training philosophy in such flamboyant language. It certainly wouldn't be Henry

ADAPTATION & REDEMPTION

Candy's *lingua franca*. But, to his good fortune, Time Charter was no 'lady of caprice.' He admitted, 'Time Charter is a very masculine filly, a real enthusiast, and I didn't need to treat her any differently from the rest. You wouldn't have known she was a filly at all.' Nevertheless, it was Cauthen's task to 'love' Time Charter. And if he did, she'd give 'the last drop of blood'.

Just five opponents stood in their way, of whom Sailor's Dance was acting as pacemaker for the previous year's Oaks and St Leger winner Sun Princess. It was the first outing of the year for both females, and the market favoured the younger Sun Princess following news that Time Charter had injured a heel a fortnight back and missed valuable work as a result; some of Candy's horses had also been coughing. However, Cauthen had been over to Kingstone Warren to partner the mare in a gallop over ten and a half furlongs the previous week and announced himself perfectly satisfied with her condition. The Prix d'Harcourt winner Lovely Dancer, trained in Britain but invariably French-raced, and Ireland's Flame of Tara, a Group One winner at a mile, lent the contest international appeal; Derby third Shearwalk completed the quintet.

'Time Charter could be better than ever,' declared *The Sporting Life* after the mare had treated her opponents like so much 'tackle' on her home gallops. 'You could run out of superlatives describing the brilliance of her victory and the stylish way Steve Cauthen rode her.' The Hern pair tried to draw the sting from Time Charter but once Sun Princess went on in the straight Cauthen played with the leader like a particularly sadistic cat does with a fledgling. She was a 'great one' all right. Cauthen let out an inch of rein inside the last furlong and the mare proceeded to win in a hack canter by four lengths. Time Charter thus joined an illustrious trio who'd completed the Oaks-Coronation Cup double: Pretty Polly, Petite Etoile and Lupe. *The Times* commented, 'She overwhelmed Sun Princess with an exhilarating burst of speed.' Cauthen had enjoyed one of the rides of his life – and knew it:

> She was just fantastic. I didn't like to plan a race because it almost never turns out as you expect. You play it once, the gates open. But before I rode Time Charter I took advice from Billy

Newnes and Joe Mercer, who'd both ridden her. Joe advised me not to move on her till the final furlong. And I didn't. But she was unbelievable! She was one in a million.

The pitfalls awaiting any jockey entering a race with a plan set in stone, however, were never lost on a jockey of Cauthen's stature.

> I knew where I'd like to be at all times in a race but you can't always be there. There are so many things that are almost beyond your control that can totally screw your chance up. There might be an opening that if you're alert enough and paying attention, can make you a hero in an instant. You have to play to your own strengths, not the perceived weaknesses of your opponents, because they don't always turn out to be accurate. You must focus on what you know instead of guessing what might be true about others.
>
> It was my job to get the best possible run out of a horse. That is what I was paid for. So I tended to wait to see how the race developed, judge the pace and only then decide on my tactics. You must react to what you see happening and try to catch the other jocks off balance. Even in a five-furlong dash, I might change my strategy a couple of times.

By quirk of fate, Cauthen rode Time Charter's principal victim in her next race, the King George, replacing the injured Willie Carson on Sun Princess. He'd forfeited the ride on Time Charter in the Eclipse owing to his obligation to Cormorant Wood. His replacement, Joe Mercer, kept the ride on Time Charter – though she'd be reunited with the American in the Arc, finishing a disappointing 11th to Sagace, behind both Sun Princess and Lovely Dancer.

Time Charter was not the only Classic winner to be partnered by Cauthen during the South Bank years. In 1983 he'd ridden, and won, on the

Derby winner Teenoso. The Geoff Wragg-trained colt was a half brother to Topsy, on whom he'd had his first Classic ride in the One Thousand Guineas of 1979, and he partnered him to an emphatic victory in the Lingfield Derby Trial. Unfortunately, his retainer meant he'd no choice but switch to The Noble Player at Epsom. Lester Piggott seized the ride and won the Derby while Cauthen could only ponder what might have been some 20 lengths adrift in 11th. A year later Teenoso won the Grand Prix de Saint-Cloud and a King George.

Teenoso had to be filed in the 'nearly' category alongside a number of other top-class horses that Cauthen rode at some time – with or without success. The afternoon prior to Cormorant Wood announcing herself as a leading lady by winning the Champion Stakes of 1983, Cauthen had chased El Gran Senor home in the Dewhurst aboard Rainbow Quest. The following season the Jeremy Tree-trained colt was one of several up to Classic-winning standard who won none thanks to being part of an outstanding generation. Lear Fan short-headed Rainbow Quest and Cauthen in the Craven Stakes prior to a Two Thousand Guineas that featured a galaxy of stars: the finishing order read El Gran Senor (Irish Derby), Chief Singer (July Cup; Sussex Stakes), Lear Fan (Prix Jacques le Marois), and Rainbow Quest (Coronation Cup; Prix de l'Arc de Triomphe). Perhaps Rainbow Quest was fickle: all five of his wins came under Pat Eddery.

Partnering elite thoroughbreds in Group One races was the icing on Cauthen's cake. The cake was the jockeys' championship. He'd made no bones about this when he came to England: he craved a jockeys' championship to rest beside that won in America. It would be a singular feat. No American had ever come close. No American had even claimed the English title since Danny Maher's second championship in 1913; indeed, no foreigner had been champion jockey since Scobie Breasley in 1963. Cauthen consolidated his 1982 total with a second century of winners in 1983 to finish in fifth spot behind Willie Carson on 159. Could he find another 50 winners to bridge that gap in 1984?

Lady Luck dealt him three cards Nathan Detroit would've sacrificed an arm for. Cauthen's three principal rivals were all to be inconvenienced. Pat Eddery was now Vincent O'Brien's retained jockey, which ensured he'd be riding in Ireland more than ever. Lester Piggott had three spells with injury, and no longer had all the Henry Cecil horses at his disposal after falling out with one of the yard's main owners, Daniel Wildenstein: 'I can't tolerate his whims. There is not a man in the world who can treat me like that and get away with it,' said the French art dealer after Piggott had ditched his filly All Along for the Arc in favour of Awaasif. All Along proceed to win the Arc in the hands of Walter Swinburn – for once Lester, the biter, had been well and truly bitten. And Cauthen's third stroke of good fortune arrived in July when Willie Carson sustained a terrible fall in Italy which kept him on the sidelines for six weeks. 'It looks like this could be the year,' Cauthen told one journalist. It would indeed be the year.

Cauthen never needed the 50-odd winners to bridge the gap between himself and Carson. He only needed to improve his score by 28 to win his first championship. Topping and tailing the season with winners at Doncaster on the first and last days, a total of 130 (Hills providing 36 of them) gave him the title by a margin of 23 over Eddery. This was the lowest total to win the title in peacetime since Freddy Fox pipped Gordon Richards by one to win the 1930 title on the last day with a total of 129. But there was considerable pride in becoming just the third American after Maher (1908/1913) and Lester Reiff (1900) to lift the title. Quality kept pace with quantity: he'd collected six Group Ones, divided equally between home and abroad, another personal best. Most significantly, he was now completely at home on English tracks. Like an aspiring London cab driver, he had to acquire 'The Knowledge' that was essential if he were to adapt successfully to the particular demands placed upon him by the diversity of English tracks.

It took two to three years before I felt comfortable on such a variety of tracks and was riding against the other jockeys on a level playing field, knowing where to be in a race, knowing the different gradients and turns.

You had to learn the right place to be on a given track, the key landmarks to use, like the Bushes and the Dip on the Rowley Mile, or you would lose when you shouldn't lose. The huge fields at Newmarket, with 40 runners splitting into three groups, was also a whole new deal for me. And five furlongs at Chester could be pretty tricky because everyone wants the fence. But Epsom was probably the trickiest of them all. I rode all the smaller tracks, but where I wanted to be was Newmarket, Newbury, Sandown, Goodwood, York and Ascot, with all the excitement of taking on the best.

The kudos associated with the position of champion jockey made Cauthen as hot a property as he'd been in 1977 and 1978. When the offer from Henry Cecil to become his retained rider at Warren Place materialised in the middle of 1984, the reply warranted scant contemplation. Cauthen discussed the switch with Jimmy Lindley. 'I assured him that everyone loved him at Barry's. But he had to look after his own future.' The deal had been struck before Cormorant Wood's victory in the Benson and Hedges, and even though it would spark a smidgeon of justifiable annoyance on the part of Barry Hills, there was little hesitation in deciding where to pitch tent in 1985. Cecil offered quality and quantity in abundance.

Hills and Cecil had precious little in common other than their abilities as trainers. One was a self-made man. The other wasn't so much born with a silver spoon in his mouth as the whole canteen of cutlery. Cecils fought at Bosworth Field and defied the Spanish Armada. Cecil's step-father, Captain Cecil Boyd-Rochfort, was one champion Classic-winning Royal trainer, and his father-in-law, Noel Murless, was another similarly bedecked with honours: between them they'd accumulated a dozen trainers' championships and 32 English Classics – and were both knighted. Henry Cecil had been a dandified wastrel of a youth who failed to get into Eton but did manage

Cirencester Agricultural College, where he seized, in his own words, 'a wonderful opportunity for one last fling before facing up to the serious responsibilities of life.' Cecil's studies featured drinking, assorted pranks and pursuing young ladies with cigarette in hand while kitted out in garish purple and yellow patchwork trousers and tasselled loafers. In other words: a first-rate Henry of the 'Hooray' variety. 'Had I not been a trainer,' he once conceded without a pinch of irony, 'I'd probably have been a porter in a railway station.' It was to the good fortune of railway travellers the length and breadth of England that the 21-year-old Cecil consigned his dissolute youth to the past and knuckled down to a four-year apprenticeship in the fundamentals of training racehorses as assistant to his 'Uncle Cecil'.

At the age of 41 Cecil still loved shopping for a flashy tie or Gucci loafers (he estimated his closet held 100 pairs of shoes). But the suits filling his wardrobe were more sober now, the 150 shirts finely cut, and he drew more fulfilment from tending his rose garden and campaigning his toy soldiers than he'd once gained by dismantling an ancient Morris and transporting it piece by piece to the bedroom of Cirencester's Principal, where it was re-assembled for his nocturnal inspection. Taken together, Cecil's defining characteristics – the statement clothes; the chain-smoking; the hand on hip and tilt of the head; and those verbal ticks – such as a tendency to end every answer to a reporter's intrusive question with a question of his own – seemed to express the kind of tortured soul who in Elizabethan times might've composed love sonnets. This work is no place for cod-psychology, but one can't help wondering the extent to which being frequently deprived of his dazzling, jet-setting, socialite mother's comforting presence during childhood may have marked Cecil for a life prone to a melancholy from the same kennel as Churchill's 'black dog'.

Cecil's idiosyncrasies may have become the stuff of legend but he could now train racehorses as adeptly as his roses. 'Although he was pretty wild when he was young, he always had a great deal of charm, and I honestly believe that this quality has an effect on his horses,' said Cecil's long-time patron Lord Howard de Walden. 'To put it another way, he has, in gardening terms, green fingers, and it can hardly be a coincidence that his other great interest is his garden.' There was no disputing Cecil had clear pictures in his mind of every horse under his care. 'You can detect traits in horses,' he explained. 'Having formed an image in your mind's eye of what a horse might become, you have to give him time to grow into it. Patience is the crowning virtue. To rush young horses can only lead to disaster. To use a horticultural simile, forced horses are like forced flowers: just as the stems of forced flowers are weak, so are the legs of horses treated in a similar manner. Many horses then break down mentally as well as physically, thereby earning the reputations of being dishonest and unreliable because they've been asked to do too much too soon.' If those words are not enough to illustrate Cecil's empathy with the thoroughbred, the following must surely put the question beyond doubt: 'I like to think I understand individual horses, even though I'm not with each one all day long. The horse is a noble animal, abused for generations. Some people are nauseating, but there are very few nauseating horses. Humans are a jealous species, unkind and greedy. But horses are not greedy or malicious. People talk about racehorses being highly strung – they'll kick and bite you. But they won't unless you abuse them. Horses have been good to me and I appreciate them.'

And the public appreciated Cecil to the point of adoration – which ultimately became love. If there's anything the English love more than an eccentric it's a fallen idol who drags himself back from the brink of the abyss and rediscovers his mojo. All it needed to convert Cecil into a national treasure was a much-publicised descent into a personal and professional hell, a miraculous resurrection whilst fighting cancer, and the emergence of a 21st century Pegasus by the name of Frankel. When he died in 2013 Sir Henry Cecil had long won the hearts of princes and paupers alike and entered racing's Valhalla.

Cauthen was in a prime spot to study Cecil's training philosophy at close quarters. It was simplicity itself: 'You want a healthy horse, not a lean and hungry one. And a confident horse. Pit a reluctant one against a poorer one on the gallops so it can sense the pleasure of winning.' Warren

Place animals were always ultra fit, frequently ridden up with the pace, and primed to win. The withering observation of Noel Murless, on first watching his son-in-law's string work on Warren Hill, had struck a nerve: 'Your horses are galloping like a lot of old gentlemen,' he'd admonished. 'You must make them work.' Any hurt Cecil felt at this slight he hid beneath that veneer of eccentricity applied like greasepaint. But the message was taken to heart. 'On galloping mornings, Wednesdays and Saturdays, we ascertain a horse's current form or explore its potential by setting it a harder task or sending it a longer distance than hitherto, as well as putting the finishing touches to getting them fit a few days before running.' Cecil's string soon became renowned for cantering faster and working faster. Seldom, if ever, did they lack strength, sharpness and courage when they stepped out onto the track: spotting a Cecil representative equipped with the rogue's badge of blinkers, for example, was like finding a unicorn in Hyde Park. 'I'm not really a serious trainer,' said Henry in his best self-deprecating manner. 'I think most people wonder how I ever trained a winner.' What all these quips disguised, however, was unbridled ambition: 'I don't want to be an also-ran,' he confessed early in his stellar career. 'One must have a ruthless streak and the competitive spirit.' Eight years after he received his trainer's licence, Henry Cecil won the first of his ten trainers' titles.

Robert Sangster may not have been numbered among the owners at Warren Place, but the likes of Lord Howard de Walden, the Niarchos family, Daniel Wildenstein and Jim Joel were patrons. The yard was packed to the rafters with blue-bloods – 150 of them – with Classic potential written all over their flanks. Cecil had already won five English Classics (the overture to a grand total of 25) and was about to become leading trainer for the fifth time. The winners he churned out propelled Joe Mercer to the jockeys' championship in 1979 with a score of 164 and Lester Piggott in 1981 and 1982 with 179 and 188. Those numbers could do nothing but appeal to Cauthen. They added up to coffee and plenty of cream.

The impending marriage had been foretold in the runes. Cauthen had ridden nine winners for Cecil, most recently on Wildenstein's Claude Monet in York's Mecca-Dante; the partnership started third favourite for the Derby but only beat four of the 17 runners. 'I had him in mind for a long time as Piggott's successor,' Cecil confessed shortly after signing Cauthen up. 'And when Lester and I were forced to go our separate ways over the Wildenstein business, Steve was the obvious replacement. He's adjusted well to English racing and must be the best of the younger jockeys. He's a natural. He's got a good brain and he's a nice person to work with. And he always thinks about what he says.'

Cauthen bid adieu but not goodbye to Barry Hills and South Bank Stables. He left under somewhat of a cloud but his debt of gratitude to Hills ensured his departure was emotionally charged. His erstwhile boss could barely contain his outrage: 'Of course I'm unhappy. It's a question of loyalty. I launched him and stood by him. I won't groom another jockey for another top stable.' But 'Mr Combustible' could forgive even if he did not forget. His relationship with Cauthen, professionally and personally, was too strong to be fractured. Cauthen understood his English mentor's feelings as he related to Robin Oakley:

> I think the world of Barry and it wasn't easy for me to leave. It went better than I had anticipated with Barry because he is that kind of guy. Barry let me know it sucked and I was sad. But we carried on working together, that's what makes him such a special guy. I was in awe of him – as I'd be with Henry.
>
> It was one of the toughest decisions in my life. I'm a loyal person. They'd done so much for me. Barry treated me like a son. I'd race ponies with his sons: played golf and table tennis with them. I lived with Barry and Penny for a while. I felt he was always looking out for me; always making sure I knew what I was dealing with. I probably wouldn't have stayed had I not been with Barry and Penny. I love them both.
>
> Barry's attitude got me revved up and wanting to be champion. I credit him with helping to re-motivate me. But I

knew I'd only got so long to ride and Henry Cecil had a yard full of potential Classic winners. If I wanted to be the best, and I did, I had to do the job properly. If I wanted to be champion jockey again, and I did, I had to ride enough horses.

And I'd given Barry six of the best years of my life since I came to Britain.

Robert Sangster's role is no less appreciated.

I have a lot to be thankful to Robert for. He brought me to England and we had a lot of fun and success together. He was a great guy to work with and to work for. He cared a lot about the people who were involved in his inner circle and had a lot of friends. He was a great man who loved the game. One of my greatest moments was in the Gold Cup on Gildoran. That was a highlight but Robert enjoyed a good punt and we had big wins in the Extel Handicap with Indian Trail early on and again with Risen Moon in the 1990 Cambridgeshire. Barry had a nice touch: he'd backed Risen Moon at 16/1 and then had some more at 8/1. I knew he'd got something coming because when I got off the horse he told me, 'Don't forget to weigh-in!'

I'm sure Robert must've had a punt too!

Cauthen's adaptation to his new Turf environment was complete. More importantly, his resurrection was complete. He'd rolled away the stone from his racing tomb. Redemption was secured. Once again he was a champion jockey. Life was sweet. And it was about to get a whole lot sweeter. As sweet as pecan pie.

THREE

THE WARREN PLACE HAREM

CAUTHEN'S APPOINTMENT as stable jockey to Henry Cecil at Warren Place not only reflected his status as champion jockey, but also his mastery of English tracks. In any race featuring Cauthen, the flat-backed, acey-deucy, American style was still instantly evident even though he'd tinkered with his seat to make the transition from riding on homogenous flat left-handed ovals to the infinite variety of undulations, bends and cambers that proliferated in England. More importantly, he'd also adjusted the American clock under his helmet to fit the new time zone. He knew where and when it had become customary to speed up or slow down on each track, be it at the Bushes on the Rowley Mile or down Tattenham Hill at Epsom. And appreciated how any variation from those norms might be exploited to capitalise upon his mount's particular 'running profile' or expose unwary rival jockeys.

The ensuing six seasons as Henry Cecil's retained rider introduced Cauthen to a profusion of thoroughbreds who sang in tune with the melodies he composed from the saddle. Some of the most hummable were reserved for a harem of beautiful females. Before Cauthen arrived at Warren Place stables in the spring of 1985, one had already filled his eye. No ride was more keenly anticipated than that on Oh So Sharp. Cauthen was smitten. It was love at first sight. Together they'd make the most marvellous music in 1985 by winning a Triple Crown.

This big, rangy chestnut possessed of a raking stride was unbeaten in her three juvenile races at Nottingham, Sandown and Ascot. She was given 9st in the Free Handicap, 5lb below Triptych, winner of the Prix Marcel Boussac (Group One), among the fillies and 7lb below the top colt Kala Dancer. In the Solario Stakes she dispatched the two colts Young Runaway and St Hilarion with an impressive burst of acceleration up the Sandown hill; later in September she reproduced that quality to defeat the smart Deauville winner Helen Street in the Hoover Fillies Mile. In its 11-year existence the Ascot contest had served as a reliable guide to the following season's Classics: Quick as Lightning won in 1979 before taking the One Thousand Guineas; while placed horses Gaily (Irish One Thousand Guineas), Dunfermline (Oaks and St Leger) and Circus Plume (Oaks) also achieved Classic glory. Helen Street would continue this fine record by winning the 1985 Irish Oaks. Yet her achievement would pale beside the achievements of Oh So Sharp who was destined to become the first winner of a Triple Crown since Nijinsky in 1970 and the first female since Meld in 1955.

Oh So Sharp was a product of the Dalham Hall Stud, which her owner Sheikh Mohammed Al-Maktoum had purchased in 1982 from the Phillips family. The Sheikh was the third son of the ruler of Dubai and, serving as its minister of defence, was cast in the mould of the family action man, being an intrepid camel-racer, avid falconer, deadly shot and the pilot of his own jet. In 1970 Dubai was a minute city state in the Persian Gulf few people other than geographers and diplomats had heard about. Certainly no one in racing took much notice of it. But in 1971 Dubai joined six of its neighbouring states to form the United Arab Emirates. This progressive nation, however, was constructed on firm foundations: to be precise, liquid foundations, because it was oil-rich to the factor of ten. The four sons (Hamdan, Maktoum and Ahmed being the others) of its ageing ruler were all devotees of the Turf and they had the financial clout that made 'Sangster's Gangsters' seem paupers. Sheikh Mohammed's first English winner was the filly Hatta, trained by John Dunlop to win four races including Goodwood's Molecomb Stakes in 1977. Pretty soon Maktoum horses dominated the strings of England's leading trainers and the brothers dominated the list of leading owners by prize-money: by 1985 they had 350 horses spread between 30 trainers; and the previous summer they spent $51m at the Keeneland Sales alone. The Maktoums had won five Classics in England and Ireland by 1985; but thus far none had arrived in the scarlet and white colours of Sheikh Mohammed. That was about to change with a vengeance once he placed his first horses with Henry Cecil in 1984.

On breeding Oh So Sharp could not be sure of staying the Oaks distance let alone the extended one and three-quarter miles of the St Leger in order to capture a Triple Crown. Her dam, Oh So Fair, was among the 15 mares Sheikh Mohammed acquired in the purchase of Dalham Hall when she was carrying a foal from the first crop of Tap On Wood's former rival, and Warren Place luminary, Kris. Consequently, any source of stamina in the filly to be known as Oh So Sharp had to come from the bottom line of her pedigree. Oh So Fair had winning form over one and a quarter miles and of her seven-winning progeny My Fair Niece was placed in the Ribblesdale and Galtres Stakes, both over one mile and a half, and Palm Island won at up to two miles. However, the promise of something extra-special derived from Roussalka, a snappy prima donna with whom Henry Cecil won consecutive renewals of the Nassau Stakes over one mile and a quarter at Goodwood when not otherwise engaged kicking out at any irritant or tearing apart her trainer's latest cashmere sweater. If flashes of temperament were any guide, Roussalka's half-sister nurtured the electricity to become a star because Oh So Sharp proved perfectly capable of rearing on hind legs if spooked on the gallops or in the saddling box – actually banging her head on the ceiling before the Solario and then kicking out so fiercely she dislodged both hind shoes.

The romance between Cauthen and Oh So Sharp started brightly with victory in the Nell Gwyn Stakes over seven furlongs of the Guineas course a fortnight before the Classic because four of the previous nine winners had used this race as a stepping stone to Guineas success, including Pebbles a year earlier. Nevertheless, the 1985 Guineas would take some winning. Another six of the top 16 females in the European Free Handicap besides Oh So Sharp were in the line-up: Triptych and Aviance represented the best of Ireland; Antarctica, plus Vilikaia who'd just beaten her in the Prix Imprudence at Maisons-Laffitte, posed the French threat; Al Bahathri (owned by Hamdan Al-Maktoum), Dafayna and Bella Colora (second in the Nell Gwyn) the domestic challenge.

With conditions good to firm underfoot and a brisk tail wind blowing, the competitiveness of the race would be endorsed by a time of 1:36.85 seconds, the fastest recorded in either Guineas since the introduction of electronic timing in the 1950s and the fastest One Thousand Guineas of all time. 'Sharp's oh so late show' was how *The Sporting Life* chose to sum up a hot-blooded finale sufficient to make a bishop kick a hole in a stained-glass window.

As the runners ran down into the Dip, backers of the 2/1 favourite had every right to look apprehensive. The leaders, Bella Colora and Al Bahathri, gave no indication of stopping and Oh So Sharp, in sixth place on the wide outside, had three or more lengths to retrieve. Her initial reaction to a crack from Cauthen's whip reclaimed half the deficit but she now had Triptych for company and outside her the white-faced Vilikaia was also launching a threatening challenge as the rising ground was met inside the final 100 yards. The odds on Oh So Sharp getting up to win still seemed miniscule, but Cauthen conjured an unstoppable surge from Oh So Sharp that saw her inexorably close the gap. Vilikaia's effort died and though the two fillies nearest the rail gave every ounce and were certainly not surrendering, Cauthen had roused Oh So Sharp in the nick of time. In the last four strides she finally got to Bella Colora and Al Bahathri and the trio flashed past the post in unison. Some minutes elapsed before the Judge gave the verdict to Oh So Sharp by a short head from Al Bahathri with Bella Colora a similar distance behind. It was the smallest margin dividing winner and third in the Classic's 171-year history: 'Oh So Sharp's last-stride Classic,' declared *The Times* headline, 'with Cauthen riding like a man inspired.'

Oh So Sharp didn't like firm ground and hated it on Guineas day. She was never going all that well. Lester went off at a tremendous gallop and for the first three furlongs I was just trying to get her into her stride. I knew that Lester on Bella Colora and Tony Murray on Al Bahathri were trying to burst me. It was their only chance of beating me but when I saw them cutting each other's throats I always thought I'd catch them. But in the end it seemed to take a hell of a long time to do it. We barely got there.

She changed her legs a couple of times going down the hill but then she kept running up the hill. I thought I might just have got there, I reckoned I'd just caught Tony and, though I couldn't see Lester, Tony thought he'd beaten Bella Colora, so I was hopeful.

Sheikh Mohammed had secured his first Classic – and the first homebred by his family. Oh So Sharp's stock rose when Al Bahathri went on to win the Irish One Thousand Guineas and Triptych beat the colts in the Irish Two Thousand Guineas. The manner in which she flew up the Newmarket hill dispelled most people's reservations concerning her ability to last the Oaks distance. Indeed, such was her progress on the gallops that Cecil left her amongst the Derby acceptors until the last possible moment in case any mishap befell Slip Anchor. After her stable companion's seven-length romp in the Derby, Oh So Sharp was a 6/4 favourite to complete the Epsom Classic double for trainer and jockey. Her success would be no less stunning.

In very soft ground Cauthen rounded Tattenham Corner four horses wide, knowing the place to be in such conditions was the better ground on the stands side where the steeper camber aids drainage. He immediately latched on to Triptych as the Irish-trained filly, contesting her fourth Classic in five weeks, took command. Thereafter all doubts about the result vanished. Oh So Sharp made light of the ground and made Triptych (on ground she preferred to Guineas day) seem leaden-footed by sprinting away from her to cross the line a regal six lengths to the good. She was the first filly to achieve the Guineas-Oaks double since Warren Place's Mysterious in 1973. 'You can make investments all over the world,' said a proud Sheikh Mohammed, 'but where else would you find a filly like that.'

> I knew from riding out Slip Anchor that the colt was absolutely right for the Derby. But as I was not riding Oh So Sharp in her work all the time I had to accept what other people told me about her. After the Guineas I thought she'd stay further, certainly a mile and a quarter and possibly a mile and a half. Henry said she would certainly stay the trip and told me to ride her like a stayer. So I tracked Triptych into the straight and then kicked on. I had to shake her a bit but as soon as I did she came back on the bit. She was amazing and proved Henry's point emphatically.

Extra syrup was drizzled on Cauthen's waffle in becoming the sixth jockey since the war to win both Epsom Classics in the same year following Rae Johnstone (1950), Lester Piggott (1957), Geoff Lewis (1971) and Willie Carson (1980) – and the first American since Danny Maher in 1906. Cecil, too, entered the history books beside Charles Semblat (1950), Noel Murless (1957) and Dick Hern (1980) for doing likewise in the last 40 years. The terribly slow time induced by the ground failed to disguise the excellence of Oh So Sharp's performance, which drew comparison with Slip Anchor's in the Derby – fuelling some debate as to who was the better. 'Oh So Sharp slips into Anchor league,' suggested *The Sporting Life* headline. Neither Cauthen nor Cecil would be drawn into the argument. They would be kept apart, said Cecil. Defeat in Oh So Sharp's programme of Goodwood's Nassau Stakes, the Benson and Hedges at York and the Champion Stakes could not be countenanced. The King George and the St Leger were earmarked for Slip Anchor – that is until an injury to his near-fore revised Oh So Sharp's schedule. First, she substituted for him at Ascot.

To some eyes the King George VI and Queen Elizabeth Diamond Stakes had been in danger of losing its sparkle as the mid-summer, middle-distance championship of Europe. Were this an equine Olympics, one would expect every potential medallist to be in the gate. However, with so many key defectors latterly the race was beginning to resemble recent Olympics tarnished by the non-participation of American, Russian and African athletes. The French, in particular, were quite emphatic about why they were declining their Ascot invitation. Their priority was the Prix de l'Arc de Triomphe; everything was geared towards peaking in October not July. 'Top races in July are fatal for three-year-old colts,' argued trainer Francois Boutin. 'It would be my idea to rest them until September when they could be prepared for the Arc in the Prix Niel.' As for the fillies, André Fabre averred, 'The race comes too early in the season for a three-year-old filly to compete against older horses. We gear their campaign towards the Arc.'

To the connections of elite mile-and-a-half animals it boiled down to the King George or the Arc. The unpleasant possibility arose that the King George was losing ground to the Arc and the concentrated programme of lucrative autumn prizes capped by the ever-tempting lure of Yankee dollars on offer at the Breeder's Cup. However, even without representation from the current French Classic generation, the opposition awaiting Oh So Sharp was straight out of the top drawer. There were four other Classic winners: the four-year-old Princess Pati (Irish Oaks); the three-year-olds Law Society (Irish Derby) and Sirius Symboli (Japanese Derby); and there was French form in the shape of the redoubtable six-year-old Australian Strawberry Road, winner of the AJC Derby and his country's foremost weight-for-age race over middle-distances, the Cox Plate, before adding the Grand Prix de Saint-Cloud (Group One) three weeks before. In addition, there was a fifth proven Group One performer in Rainbow Quest (Coronation Cup). Also among the dozen who went to post was Petoski, trained by Dick Hern and ridden by Willie Carson. The colt had rebounded from a disappointing effort in Slip Anchor's Derby to claim the Princess of Wales's Stakes at Newmarket; but odds of 12/1 suggested his hopes were forlorn. Although five fillies had won the King George, only Pawneese had followed up an Oaks victory in the same year. Oh So Sharp was made 5/4 on favourite to become the second.

The going at Ascot turned out firm. This presented some concern to Cauthen. His filly had shown herself to be particularly effective on Epsom's soft surface even though her raking stride seemed tailor-made for a faster surface. Would she go on it? Rainbow Quest's pacemaker, August, went off at a gallop guaranteed to give the answer. He rattled through the opening half-mile into Swinley Bottom in 45.63 seconds and rounded out the mile in 1:36.08. These were times on a par with the 1975 gallop started by one pacemaker and continued by a second acting on behalf of Bustino to run the finish out of Grundy. The ploy failed – but prefaced a race record time. Cauthen turned a blind eye. He wasn't about to be duped into any speed duel. He kept his filly covered up in fifth.

August's early self-sacrifice inevitably claimed casualties. And as Oh So Sharp began her challenge entering the short Ascot straight, Cauthen was carried wide by the weakening Infantry. Notwithstanding this interference, she quickened to force her head in front at the two-furlong pole. But charging up the centre of the track was Petoski, who'd escaped from behind a wall of horses and was making ground hand over fist down the centre of the track under a typical head-down Carson drive. The clock showed how taxing the struggle became. Despite that electric early pace, the exhausting tempo barely dropped: the last two furlongs of 12.92 and 12.67 state as much – final quarters below 26 seconds are seldom clocked in Ascot's middle-distance races under even the slickest conditions. Oh So Sharp had a target on her back and, having crossed to the far rail and with Rainbow Quest between herself and Petoski, she couldn't see the arrow coming her way that would steal her unbeaten record. Carson took aim. Petoski hit gold. He won by a neck.

> The race was run on unsuitable rock-hard ground and she was carried wide by a horse in the straight, which meant I had to go sooner than I wanted. She travelled okay, but it's when they're let down and asked to stretch that the hard ground gets to them. At the end she was just going up and down. Had Petoski been

closer to us, my filly might have had time to hit back. As it was,
she never even saw him.

Henry Cecil was as deflated as the filly he greeted in the spot reserved for the second-placed horse: 'She was miserable. If they lose and they're intelligent, then they sulk.'

Despite these exertions Oh So Sharp was still considered ready to fulfil her intended York engagement in the Benson and Hedges. In a small field, which included Triptych plus the St Leger winner Commanche Run and Champion Stakes winner Palace Music from the previous season, she once more started an odds-on favourite. But in a race notorious for its inexplicable results, she was to join Brigadier Gerard and company in the 'shock upset' category after Lester Piggott controlled the pace like the master he was to steer Commanche Run to victory by three-quarters of a length. There could be no caveats about this second reverse. Piggott had won the tactical battle. Any preconception he was bound to set a stiff gallop on a Leger winner was immediately dispelled as he did precisely the opposite along the back straight. All the while Cauthen had Oh So Sharp tailing Commanche Run like an elephant calf does its mother. With half the race gone, there was still no injection of pace: Piggott dawdled along between the six and the four poles in around 26 seconds. Only at the top of the half-mile straight did he begin to stoke Commanche Run's boilers. The colt answered him with a quarter of 22.93 that would've been exceptional had he been on rails. It was asking an awful lot for any challenger to accelerate off that speed in soft ground. When Oh So Sharp was told to go past Commanche Run the leader still had plenty of coal in reserve to repel the filly through a last quarter barely slower at 23.94. There was no two ways about it. Piggott had ridden a blinder.

> I was sitting on Lester's tail and felt that he was playing into my hands by setting such a steady pace. But when Commanche Run quickened, my filly could not go with him and I never felt

I was going to win. She couldn't handle the bottomless, knee-deep ground. It had been a long season for Oh So Sharp, she'd been on the go since spring, and she was meeting a mature colt who'd won the Leger.

Cauthen's final observation seemed particularly ominous in the aftermath of Slip Anchor's disappointing defeat on his Kempton comeback prior to running in the St Leger. Oh So Sharp would stand in for him once more and be afforded the chance of achieving the Fillies Triple Crown.

Whether Oh So Sharp winning an English Triple Crown constituted a tougher task than that accomplished by Affirmed is debatable – but, thankfully, academic. Were either easy there'd be a longer roll of honour in both. But the status of the St Leger had come under the microscope owing to an increasing lack of quality participants. The Triple Crown had every appearance of becoming extinct. It was 15 years since Nijinsky became the 15th winner of the colts Triple Crown and another 35 back to Bahram's before that; the eighth filly, Meld, to achieve the honour was 30 years ago. The fact that Shergar, the sole Derby winner to attempt the Leger since Nijinsky, performed well below his best did the final Classic no good at all. There was even sacrilegious talk of opening the Doncaster race to older horses or reducing its distance. The St Leger needed Oh So Sharp. It needed a Triple Crown attempt to lift its profile and bring spectators through the turnstiles and a Triple Crown winner to revive its standing within the racing community.

Sheikh Mohammed, however, was not so keen to run. But Cecil was stubborn. He believed the filly could deliver, albeit acknowledging the difficulties. His father-in-law had impressed upon him the view that a horse might only reach its absolute peak once in its career. That might be its defining moment in a Classic. Bringing a horse back at, or near, its peak for three Classics was a tall order – which Noel Murless never managed owing to Crepello and Royal Palace both falling by the wayside before they could complete a Triple Crown in the Leger. 'Some of the horses were going in their coats causing me to fear that my team were going over the top. Another week and it might have been too late,' confided Cecil in the winner's circle after the Leger. 'She was beginning to go and I was just hanging on to her.'

If Oh So Sharp stayed the trip, little likelihood existed of her being beaten. An injury to Petoski meant only two Derby colts stood their ground and one of those was her stable companion Lanfranco (fifth at Epsom), to be ridden by Lester Piggott in what was supposed to be his Classic swansong. Consequently, the field of six was the smallest for a Doncaster St Leger (five, three and five contested substitute wartime Legers at Newmarket in 1916, 17 and 18) since Pretty Polly also frightened off all bar five in 1904.

Piggott's sole shot at signing off with a 30th Classic success lay in forcing the pace in the hope of exposing any flaws in Oh So Sharp's stamina. He attempted to dictate proceedings as he had on Commanche Run. But in contrast to York, Cauthen this time knew all there was to know about the capabilities of his major rival and kept Lanfranco well within range. Indeed, the surprise of the race was just how early Cauthen chose to take up the running.

> It is not a good thing being tied down to a set of instructions because once the starting gates open it all changes. As long as I know the main thing about the horse I'm riding I can react to the way the race goes and still get the best out of the horse in question. Henry would just say, 'Good luck old chap.'
>
> When you're going that far, you are a little concerned about the distance. And she was taking on the colts, she'd had a tough campaign and we were worried whether she was over the top. Through the race she was always giving me confidence. I wanted to keep an eye on Lester, as we always did, and his mount Lanfranco. They were in front and I was in their slipstream. She did nothing quickly. She was lazy and dossed when she got to the front. So I was determined to let nothing come at me late and take her by surprise like Petoski did at Ascot.

> But I thought as long as she hadn't gone over the top, she had the class to win as I was pretty confident she would stay the trip. And she did. She was dossing when she got to the front, but he always had it under control. She was fantastic.

Thus did Cauthen judge it prudent to strike once Lanfranco's gallop began to drop at the three-furlong marker. With the wind in their faces, he and Oh So Sharp battled up the long Doncaster straight into the history books. They quickened through furlongs of 12.70 and 11.96 but, never benefitting from more than a length advantage as her initial attack slackened through the next furlong (12.67), the gallant filly possessed enough reserves to find a bit more. In response to six taps from Cauthen's whip, she hung on by three-quarters of a length through a final 220 yards in a resurgent 12.09.

In so doing, she'd drifted off a true line and television coverage jumped the gun by wrongly announcing there was a stewards' inquiry – which thus prompted one to be called and an anxious Cecil to lap the winner's circle. Within a few minutes justice was done and the trainer was able to relax. 'No praise too high for Cecil as star filly keeps her edge,' opined *The Sporting Life*. 'Oh So Sharp's Crowning Glory,' was the headline of choice in other papers. The filly never ran again. She was euthanised in October 2001 following the onset of laminitis. Her daughter Rosefinch won the Prix Saint-Alary in the hands of Cauthen; another daughter, Shaima, won the Long Island Handicap with Frankie Dettori on board – and he later steered her son Shantou to victory in the 1996 St Leger.

Record books were shredded. Oh So Sharp became the ninth to achieve the Fillies Triple Crown. Some aver the female version to be less meritorious than the colts; yet in order to achieve it those fillies had to beat colts; that alone renders the achievement laudable. Her partner became the first jockey to achieve a Triple Crown in both America and England; he and Cecil had collected four of the five Classics in one season, only the seventh and sixth to do so in 171 years and feats not achieved since Lester Piggott in 1970 and Fred Darling in 1942. Furthermore, as broadcast in *The Sunday Times* headline 'Sharp's Leger, Cecil's million', her trainer had become the first to win £1 million in a single season. The studious also noted that Cauthen had needed only six seasons to win each of the five Classics; it had taken Lester Piggott 17 seasons.

Horse, jockey, trainer and owner headed their respective tables at the end of the season. Oh So Sharp's total earnings reached £311,576 (well clear of Slip Anchor in second); her Triple Crown demonstrating the fiscal march of time by accounting for £299,343 compared to Meld's £38,166. Cauthen's season ended with a second championship courtesy of 195 winners (at a winning percentage of 23.84), the highest total since Gordon Richards notched 231 in 1952; nonetheless, having got so close to a double century, he was disappointed not to have achieved the feat for which bookmakers had offered odds of 7/4 in mid-summer. Cecil was leading trainer for the sixth time in ten years: his haul of 132 races was a record for a British trainer in the 20th century, beating his 1979 mark by four; his earnings topped £1m; as did Sheikh Mohammed's, the first owner so to do, whose 118 winners set a further record (three more than David Robinson's 1973 total).

> All her Classics were great, but it was special to win that Triple Crown. People were wondering if the Triple Crown would ever be won again. It takes a very special horse to win all three races. Of course there are good individual milers, mile-and-a-half, and mile-and-three-quarter horses. But to win over the three distances in the same season makes it an exceptional animal. When a horse can prove itself over the three distances it shows it has speed, stamina and courage, which make for a great thoroughbred.
>
> It was 37 years before another American Triple Crown winner followed Affirmed. And it's 35 years and counting since Oh So Sharp did it in England, which tells you all you need to know. It shows how tough it is to have a horse who is special enough, and have the good fortune for that horse to stay in top form. Part of it revolves around them winning when they're not

110 per cent. Like champions in any sport, even when they're not right, they gut it out. The will to win is so strong. The Triple Crown doesn't happen very often – on either side of the Atlantic – and that's what makes the achievement so memorable. It's a feat worth waiting for and means so much to racing and its public.

Cauthen has no hesitation in naming Oh So Sharp as the best filly he ever rode. Even when pressed, and benefitting from almost 30 years of reflective retirement, he remains adamant.

> Oh So Sharp should probably have gone through her career unbeaten. In the King George, on rock hard ground she hated, I was forced to kick on sooner than I wanted after the horse I was tracking carried me wide into the straight. Then it was bottomless at York. She had a great attitude, a great desire to win and a wonderful stride, so much power – she just enjoyed running – a lot of talent and a lot of heart. When you look at the fillies she beat in the One Thousand Guineas – Al Bahathri, Bella Colora as well as Triptych – that tells you how tough a filly she was, racing on ground firmer than she liked.
>
> I rode some outstanding fillies. The likes of Pebbles, Indian Skimmer and even Triptych, who Oh So Sharp beat in two Classics, were rated higher by *Timeform*, for example. But if they all ran against each other on good ground I'd still choose to ride Oh So Sharp over the others – and Slip Anchor as well. Oh So Sharp was the best filly I ever rode because she was so versatile.

As the 1985 season drew to its record-breaking close, Cauthen had more on his mind than the identity of the best filly he ever rode. When he got back to Kentucky he entered a three-week chemical dependency programme at Christ Hospital in Cincinnati. Alcohol, it's often been said, is the curse of the weighing room; on a jockey's empty stomach its effects can be sudden and turn Jekyll into Hyde. Although Cauthen had quit drinking three months earlier, he wanted, in typical forthright fashion, to tackle the issue head-on.

> Newmarket was kinda cool; but it got me drinking! By the end of the year I was in a drying-out joint. There's a point where you realise, although you like alcohol, it's messing up your life. I got the balance wrong. I wasn't happy the way I was dealing with alcohol and I decided to do something about it. None of my friends thought I had a problem. It was pretty much within myself. And drinking is not necessarily good for your weight. You don't sleep as well. Basically, you're not happy. And sometimes you can't stop things on your own.

Cauthen attacked the new season of 1986 with renewed vigour. By its end he'd partnered for the first time a filly whose career caused some to dispute his award of the palm for the best filly he rode to Oh So Sharp. During the Warren Place seasons he'd swing a leg across four more Classic-winning fillies. And one of them, without a shadow of doubt, held strong claims to be Oh So Sharp's superior. She made her debut just over a year after Oh So Sharp sealed her Triple Crown. Her name was Indian Skimmer. Aside from their indisputable quality, the two were as different as chianti and frascati. Where Oh So Sharp had moved with feline stealth, Indian Skimmer was a freight train in a hurry.

There is something about a champion race-mare that generates devotion, adoration and, yes, an affection that borders on love, which the male of the species can never approach. If that female has the odd kink in her personality and if, furthermore, she's blessed with the eye-catching bonus of a grey coat, that female can imprint herself on the public consciousness like no other. Three decades before Indian Skimmer won the hearts of English racegoers, another equally charismatic grey diva bestrode Warren Place. Noel Murless trained Petite Etoile to carry off the Guineas, Oaks, Sussex Stakes, Yorkshire Oaks, Champion Stakes and a brace of Coronation Cups between 1959 and 1961, exploits earning a *Timeform* rating of 134 – the highest accorded an older female at the time. That's seven races later granted Group One status. In a career of similar length but dogged by a persistent back injury, Indian Skimmer would win six (if one includes the Sun Chariot upgraded to Group One in 2004) and be rated 133 by *Timeform* – 2lb higher than Oh So Sharp. 'The Little Star' lost some races and on occasions lost her rag, but she never lost her band of devoted followers. Indian Skimmer would prove no different.

Indian Skimmer had it in her to be a champion from the outset. She was a tall, deep-bodied grey, with dapples fore and aft, by 1984's champion two-year-old Storm Bird out of the unraced Vaguely Noble mare Nobiliare, a close relation to the champion American three-year-old filly Dark Mirage. She cost Sheikh Mohammed 350,000 guineas. However, unlike her Asian aquatic bird namesake, she didn't skim over the turf so much as pound it with a rounded action clearly more suited to give in the ground. Accordingly, the one race Cecil gave her as a juvenile came at the back end of 1986 over seven furlongs at Newmarket in which Cauthen gave her an educational introduction to finish a 'running-on' fourth.

Indian Skimmer's three-year-old campaign lasted just three months before the back problem that was to blight her entire career forced her onto the sidelines. Fortunately for us, she crammed five races into that restricted period during which she went from strength to strength as her experience and confidence grew. Of equal significance was the prevailing ease in the ground.

A routine introduction at lowly Wolverhampton (a ten-length romp) prefaced a rapid climb up the fillies' ranks via the Pretty Polly Stakes and the Musidora Stakes at York instead of competing in either the English or Irish Guineas on account of the ground. She'd shown herself well up to Oaks standard: no fewer than 11 Oaks entries languished four lengths or more behind her in the Pretty Polly and at York she trounced the Oaks second favourite Bourbon Girl by four lengths. Next time up Bourbon finished second in the Oaks. Indian Skimmer would've been a very warm favourite had she gone to Epsom. But she didn't hold an entry: 'She was so backward and unimpressive that I decided against entering her,' explained Cecil. 'I've still got some useless fillies left in the Classic so I must have made a mistake.'

Of course, how well Indian Skimmer's back would've withstood Epsom's irregular topography is questionable. Her Classic destiny lay across the Channel where French ground may be counted upon to ride softer. She was supplemented into the Prix de Diane and warmed up for a Classic showdown with dual Guineas winner Miesque by competing in the traditional Diane trial, the Prix Saint-Alary (Group One) over a mile and a quarter on 24 May. Indian Skimmer treated the French fillies with as much disdain as she'd shown the English, winning as she liked.

In the opinion of many, the French Classic that matters most is the Prix de Diane. Compared with the Prix du Jockey-Club run the previous Sunday at Chantilly, the ambiance of the Diane is distinctly more upper crust. The highborn monsieur will promenade with an elegant lady dressed by Chanel draped on his arm; the handsome couple at one with the Prince de Conde's resplendent chateau overlooking the back straight that is nothing more than a sumptuous stable block, Les Grandes Ecuries, built by the dotty aristocrat who believed he was to be reincarnated as a horse. Traditionally, the English had shown scant interest in the Prix de Diane; the Duke of Hamilton's Little Agnes won in 1872 but she was trained in France. Of late, however, the English had made a point of visiting Chantilly on Diane Sunday. Madam Gay, Mrs Penny and the Queen's Highclere all re-crossed La Manche with the spoils – yet none of them as majestically as Indian Skimmer.

Thus far in Indian Skimmer's four-race streak, Cauthen had sat in the driving seat with not a care in the world. To ensure Indian Skimmer got the gallop she wanted in the Diane, Cecil took no chances and ran her stable-mate Laluche, whom Cauthen had partnered as an unbeaten Group-winning juvenile. If Miesque failed to stay a strongly run ten and a half furlongs on her first effort beyond a mile, there seemed nothing to prevent Indian Skimmer obtaining her Classic due. The ground was soft and Indian Skimmer went off at shades of odds-on with Miesque at evens. One should be in no doubt as to how outstanding a filly was Miesque. She'd already bagged a quartet of Group Ones: the Prix de la Salmandre and Prix Marcel Boussac at two and the English and French Guineas at three. However, her one loss came on soft ground and she was unproven at the Diane distance. The Diane would prove she was an out-and-out miler: only once was she asked to race beyond a mile subsequently during a glorious career in which she added a further six wins at the highest level in the Jacques le Marois (twice), Moulin, d'Ispahan and the Breeders' Cup Mile (twice).

But as the 11 fillies entered the Chantilly stalls for the Diane, no one knew that for certain and had Miesque proved the better filly it would've hardly been earth shattering. Providing Miesque with a pacemaker suggested her trainer, Francois Boutin, planned to offset any stamina doubts by engineering a slow gallop. If that was the reason for Microcosme's participation it was a wasted entry fee because the Diane worked out like a morning on the Newmarket gallops. Indian Skimmer followed Laluche's healthy lead (with Microcosme dividing them) until passing the chateau at the end of the back straight when she moved easily into second. Then, passing the 400-metre cones, a nudge or two from Cauthen's elbows shot Indian Skimmer four lengths clear with the alacrity of a gendarme chasing a pickpocket through the Metro. Miesque, by contrast, had nothing much to offer once she set off in pursuit, and struggled to hold on to second place at the line.

'Indian Skimmer storms in', stated the headline in *The Times*; *The Sporting Life* was its usual bellicose self with 'Indian Massacre! Skimmer humbles Miesque to join all-time Greats. Given a champion ride by Steve Cauthen, she proved herself the Queen of Europe when annihilating the double Classic heroine Miesque.' Figuring prominently was the Cecil quote: 'I don't like comparisons, but Indian Skimmer is very good indeed.' Cauthen was not about to disagree.

> In the Pretty Polly she was rather headstrong. But in the Musidora she relaxed beautifully and in the race she did it so quickly I didn't have to ask her a question at all. She was learning fast and proved she was a real racehorse. But I wasn't sure she'd stay a mile and a half.

In the Diane we were always well placed and travelling strongly as the two pacemakers set a six-furlong gallop, which enabled me to get her settled. When I picked her up and took her to the front two furlongs out she produced a fantastic burst of acceleration and quickly sprinted four lengths clear.

Oh So Sharp was a triple Classic winner and a great filly, but Indian Skimmer had the better turn of foot and was just that little bit special. She is entitled to be compared with the all-time greats, but I feel she was a mile and-a-quarter specialist and I would not have wanted to have gone a yard further. But over ten furlongs Indian Skimmer was something else.

It would be folly to say her Prix de Diane coronation signalled the high water mark in Indian Skimmer's career given that she'd win another three Group Ones. But the air of invincibility that once clung to her gave way subsequently to an air of will-she-won't-she. In 1987 she'd won five from five by an aggregate of 24¼ lengths; afterwards she won five from ten by an aggregate of just 7½ lengths. A combination of back and shoulder problems and underfoot conditions were at the root of this reversal in fortune. In late July Cecil announced she'd miss her scheduled re-appearance in the Matchmaker International at York (the former Benson and Hedges Gold Cup) owing to her old problems resurfacing: 'She tends to lose her action and stiffen up behind and I'll be giving her some back treatment and letting her down before sending her for two weeks rest at Dalham Hall.'

That was the last seen of Indian Skimmer on the racecourse for 362 days. She returned to action at Sandown to lock horns with colts for the first time in the Brigadier Gerard Stakes. In truth, Indian Skimmer had nothing to fear physically; intimidation was an unlikely prospect. She was one of those fillies who gave every indication she could handle herself in a donnybrook: she exuded toughness bordering on the epithet 'butch'. Nevertheless, she found both Highland Chieftain and Media Starguest, neither of whom held pretensions of Group One class, too good on a day when she never appeared to be happy in herself. A second trip to Sandown for the Eclipse promised a sterner test of her current mettle. The field was headed by the previous year's winner Mtoto, fresh from a second win at Royal Ascot in the Prince of Wales's Stakes, plus a supporting cast featuring the Group One fixture that was Triptych (on whom Cauthen had just won the Coronation Cup) and the useful four-year-old Shady Heights, who'd won the Tattersalls Rogers Gold Cup over the distance at the Curragh. Cauthen could get her no nearer than fourth, beaten some three and a half lengths by Mtoto – who later added the King George before finishing an unlucky second in the Arc. In other words, though unsuccessful, Indian Skimmer's form was improving as the rustiness was being rubbed away. York's International signified further progress. Promoted to second on the disqualification of first past the post Persian Heights (he'd edged into her ground just as Cauthen was launching his challenge), she narrowed the gap to the 'winner' Shady Heights from three and a half lengths in the Eclipse to a mere neck despite that interrupted challenge. And the fast ground (evidenced by a new track record for the distance) had not been in her favour.

Just over two weeks later, the real Indian Skimmer turned up at Phoenix Park for the Phoenix (Irish) Champion Stakes. Autumn was fast approaching and firmer ground fast departing. The filly duly turned earlier form with Shady Heights, Persian Heights and Triptych on its head, brushing them aside more comprehensively than the official margins of three-quarters of a length, one length, and two and a half lengths may suggest. A routine demolition of Infamy and Percy's Lass when tackling fillies only in the Sun Chariot at Newmarket set the stage nicely for the Champion Stakes in which she'd renew rivalry with Shady Heights, Persian Heights and Percy's Lass plus the Guineas winner Doyoun in a field of five. Indian Skimmer was sent off an odds-on favourite to win her second Group One of the season.

The outcome was a resounding four-length rout of Persian Heights with no fewer than 19 lengths separating her from Percy's Lass in rear. The victory had not come without the odd nervy moment – in this instance prior to the race when Indian Skimmer dug her toes in during the parade. But just when it seemed she'd not budge an inch, out onto the track walks the suited figure of Henry Cecil, risking sodden Gucci loafers to whisper endearments in his becalmed filly's ear. A pat here and a word there; and, suitably reassured, off she went to the gate as if something had been made of nothing. 'She can be a right cow-bag. But on the right ground I have never had anything like her and I think she is still improving,' said her besotted handler. 'I have trained some very good animals, but she is brilliant. It would be unfair to her not to say she is the best I have ever had – and that includes the colts.' Frankel was yet to come, of course. But the likes of Reference Point, Slip Anchor, Kris, Wollow, Ardross, Le Moss and Oh So Sharp – outstanding milers, middle-distance horses and stayers – were, 'pound-for-pound' as they say in boxing, all inferior to Indian Skimmer in the eyes of their Warren Place custodian.

The growing kudos of the Breeders' Cup even tempted Cecil to America. The trainer accompanied Indian Skimmer to Churchill Downs where she contested the Turf over one and a half miles. This was her first attempt at the distance, but if she was going to get the trip anywhere it would surely be on a tight American oval where speed and adaptability take precedence over pure stamina. The ground came up on the easy side and she started favourite. After giving her jockey a hard time early on, she was in with a fighting chance coming off the final bend four wide into the short finishing straight; she got past Triptych but couldn't catch the home side's Great Communicator and Sunshine Forever.

Those last four races came with the assistance of Michael Roberts, the 11-times South African champion and future English champ of 1992. He'd been called-up by Cecil because Cauthen had experienced one of those potentially life-threatening falls that Eddie Arcaro reckoned tested the resolve of even the strongest. It was the category of accident often referred to by jockeys and journalists alike as being 'buried'. That may register high on the scale from euphemism to hyperbole – but it leaves the right impression. The track was Goodwood – where bunching on the downhill run to the winning post often leads to problems. The race was of little importance, the County Club Hotels Handicap. His mount was a three-year-old filly called Preziosa; an outside ride, trained by Gavin Pritchard-Gordon. She was a big angular filly who took a firm hold. Cauthen had fallen on no fewer than three occasions at Goodwood in the past. He suffered the fourth when Preziosa clipped heels at the start of the dangerous descent three furlongs out. He was ambulanced to St Richard's Hospital in Chichester, concussed but with no bones broken, where he stayed for three days. The statutory lay-off for concussion was three weeks – which would've enabled him to be back for the Prix de l'Arc de Triomphe. He didn't make it. There was a problem with his neck. He wrote off the remainder of the season and went home to Walton to recuperate through the winter.

Cauthen returned to England on 2 March. The next day he worked two horses for Cecil on the Waterhall gallop.

> I never ever considered not riding again. But it was good to get the legs back on each side of a horse. I felt very comfortable, like I was back home and driving a car. I don't remember much about the accident. They found it had shattered my sixth vertebra. It mended pretty quickly, but the specialist advised me not to risk it again that season. It was in a bad place and I might have damaged it seriously if anything had happened. I had no pain, just discomfort and stiffness. It was back to full mobility a month and a half before I returned to England.
>
> I spent a lot of time during the winter building myself up, running, swimming, cycling, playing tennis and gym workouts. Then I rode a few horses around the farm. The intention was to ease myself into it gradually, not bust myself trying to do 8st 7lb straight away. I was 9st in the winter. I needed to lose 7lb in three weeks when I resumed riding and it was tricky. The problem was trying to get fit and lose weight at the same time. I needed to build muscle tone but not to gain weight – and muscle is heavier than fat. It was a thin line. And very hard to do in the cold weather.

THE WARREN PLACE HAREM

I'd often ride somewhere during the English off-season. In the spring of 1988 I had a spell in Hong Kong. I think I rode a dozen winners out there. Another year I went to Japan and won seven. In Australia one winter I won three; and during a trip to South Africa in 1980 I recall winning at Turffontein on a sprinter called Fats Domino. Well, I wanted to race in Hong Kong again in 1989 but I had a lot of trouble with my mouth. I got an abscess and had to have my wisdom teeth removed.

Regaining peak fitness would take time. Nothing prepares a jockey for the real thing but the real thing.

I wasn't quite 100 per cent for race-riding. The only gateway to get race-riding fit is in races, basically to get your wind right. There's no doubt that most jockeys won't be at their 110 per cent peak fitness for the first few races, just like a horse. You can't just snap your fingers. I wouldn't know how fit I really was until I'd actually race-ridden and had a few strong finishes. But I wasn't as unfit as I thought. I thought I might get to the two-furlong marker and need an oxygen mask! It took me until the Dante meeting at York to be right back to 100 per cent.

The wait for the first winner was short: Monday, 27 March at Kempton. Nor was the test of his nerve. Three days later, riding Sandmoor Cotton at Doncaster, his stirrup leather broke 50 yards from the winning post. The tack malfunction couldn't have come at a worse point in the race. The gods gave Cauthen a free pass on this occasion.

The buckle on my own leather snapped on the way to the start. They gave me a spare leather at the start, but it must have been 200 years old as it broke in two places. It happened pretty close to home. I nearly fell as I was halfway out of the saddle. It was subsequently recommended that there should be a full set of serviceable equipment at the start. So something good came out of bad.

Given his calamitous experience seven months earlier, it was no wonder Cauthen was so indignant. Now that he was one of the senior voices in the weighing room, this wouldn't be the last issue where he'd find himself speaking out on behalf of less articulate colleagues. On the positive side, there was no doubting the horse with whom he was itching to be reunited: Indian Skimmer. Cecil reported the mare in tip-top shape: 'If I can keep her like this she'll be unbelievable. At the moment she's definitely better than she's ever been in her life.'

Indian Skimmer's huge fan club couldn't wait for their idol's reappearance. But not without a few degrees of trepidation. Those with memories of Petite Etoile's disappointing five-year-old career couldn't bear to think this might be another case of 'the old grey mare ain't what she used to be'. Henry Cecil needed no reminding what his father-in-law maintained about getting high-class females to show their true form after the mid-summer of their fourth year: it was extremely difficult: 'A five-year-old mare is not any easy proposition,' stated Noel Murless. He continued: 'I found that top-class, three-year-old fillies will hold their form until about the next June. They did not come on at all afterwards. You've got to string mares up if you're going to keep them on at four and if you're going to take on the colts. I think it's against the run of nature.' Nevertheless, there are always exceptions to the rule. The great ones can defy the march of time. But even though Allez France, Dahlia and Time Charter, for instance, had won good races at five – as would Triptych under Cauthen – they were, like Petite Etoile, nowhere near their best. Mares such as Zenyatta and Winx would confound the Murless law in the future. How would Indian Skimmer fare?

The partnership resumed at Sandown on 29 April in the Gordon Richards Stakes. The odds-on favourite made comfortable progress on her preferred soft surface until reaching the Sandown hill, but then found things a mite tougher and only just got home by a head from the race-fit colt Per Quod in receipt of 4lb. The last quarter had been a 29-second slog. This wasn't Indian Skimmer at her imperious Diane or Champion Stakes best, but Cauthen had nursed her all the way and been at his most tender. As for the merits of the performance, Indian Skimmer's old adversary Shady Heights was well beaten off; and in third place, a further head behind, was Carroll House, who went on to win the Phoenix Champion and the Arc.

A month later Indian Skimmer was sent to Longchamp for her first Group One target of the season, the Prix d'Ispahan. 'Indian Skimmer in majestic form despite the firm going,' announced *The Times* in a headline conveying a certain degree of relief. Cauthen bided his time, five lengths behind the pace-setter, In Extremis, until deep into the straight before closing him down and going on; he did not touch his partner with the whip in holding off Gabina by half a length.

> It was nice to see Indian Skimmer come back so well. She seemed better than ever, though she would've liked softer ground. She was saving herself the whole way.

To Cauthen and Cecil's disappointment, the ensuing months proved dry ones. That old bugbear, firm ground, prevented Indian Skimmer from delivering the level of performance the spring had promised. She missed the Prince of Wales's Stakes at Royal Ascot and only a week before the Eclipse was she able to leave the all-weather gallop for her first work on the grass of the Limekilns – traditionally the best ground in Newmarket. Her strong work did not escape the bookmakers' notice and she was quoted at 4s behind Guineas and Derby winner Nashwan at odds-on. Until the morning of the race it remained touch and go whether she'd take her chance. Such prevarication told its tale. As soon as the pressure was applied early in the straight, it could be seen she was in trouble, hating every stride. At the line she was still a short head behind her 200/1 stable-mate Opening Verse, some five lengths adrift of Nashwan. This was not the Indian Skimmer of old. This replicated the ageing Petite Etoile who'd succumbed in the 1961 Queen Elizabeth II Stakes to Le Levanstell, who was more than a stone her inferior.

Indian Skimmer never ran again. Her wings had been clipped. She joined the ranks of five-year-old mares forced to surrender to Father Time. Her record stood at ten wins from 16 starts. Despite unions with stallions of the calibre of Mr Prospector and Danehill, only one of her six foals reached the track. But for ten glorious weeks in 1987 the 'Skimmer' had flown high, wide and handsome.

Warren Place housed a ready-made female replacement for Cauthen in the guise of Diminuendo. The term *multum in parvo* comes to mind whenever one thinks of the tiny chestnut daughter of Diesis, a full brother to Kris, the sire of Oh So Sharp. She'd been picked out by Sheikh Mohammed himself at the Keeneland Sales, at a cost of $125,000, and stood just 15 hands. But within that diminutive frame was a purring V8 engine and a willing attitude; according to Cecil, Diminuendo was so sociable she'd 'chat away to all the crocks at the back of the string.'

Diminuendo won four from four in her first season: a Leicester maiden followed by the Ewar Stud Farm Stakes and Group Two Cherry Hinton Stakes (setting a new track record) at Newmarket preceding a crack at replicating Oh So Sharp's victory in the Hoover Fillies Mile. Though taking her time to close on the leader, once hitting her stride inside the last furlong, she unleashed a withering turn of foot to pass the post two lengths in front of Ashayer – who franked the performance by winning the Prix Marcel Boussac on her next start. Diminuendo was given 9st 2lb in the Free Handicap, 5lb below the French filly Ravinella at the head of the list.

The formbook suggested Diminuendo would have to improve some to trouble Ravinella in the One Thousand Guineas; and after succumbing to Ghariba in the Nell Gwyn Stakes, it seemed highly unlikely she'd do so during the fortnight to the Classic. Although Diminuendo showed sufficient progress to turn the tables on Ghariba, she proved no match for Ravinella, who beat her by three lengths, with Dabaweyaa splitting them. However, she'd raced up the Newmarket hill with the elan of a cheetah chasing a springbok, which held out high hopes of the Oaks being the Classic to suit her talents.

If falling short of the exalted standard set by Indian Skimmer 12 months earlier, Diminuendo demonstrated which filly ruled the middle-distance roost in the summer of 1988 by stringing together four displays culminating in a Yorkshire Oaks victory that was as scintillating on the watch as it was on the eye. This streak began as it ended – on York's Knavesmire. Diminuendo demolished her field in the Musidora, much as Indian Skimmer did. 'Diminuendo new Oaks favourite after brilliant win,' declared *The Times* after Cauthen had shot her clear up the straight to win by four lengths and five from Asl and Princess Genista. 'Afterwards bookmakers who had the temerity to offer 9/2 about the impressive winner for the Oaks were nearly trampled underfoot in the rush to be accommodated, and she was backed down at all rates to 5/2 favourite in front of Dabaweyaa.'

> She quickened and won her race in three strides. She relaxed and enjoyed herself. There was no reason why she shouldn't stay a mile and a half, but I thought she should go to France as she won over the Diane distance at York.

Cecil thought otherwise. He tended toward Epsom. The trainer got his way. Diminuendo would not follow the Indian Skimmer route to Chantilly and instead took her chance in the Oaks. Cauthen became increasingly enthusiastic about his filly's chances, particularly if there was a drop of rain. And so he should've been. 'Diminuendo demolition job in the Oaks,' reported *The Sporting Life* in the aftermath of a display from the favourite every inch as impressive as Oh So Sharp's.

> I'm not sure if the runner-up Sudden Love was a Triptych but my filly could hardly have won more easily. Just as in the Musidora,

she killed them in two strides and had the race won. She needed less bustling along than Oh So Sharp and proved herself in the same class. I did not want to get involved in any traffic problems, so I pulled her out coming down the Hill to avoid trouble. When I asked her to quicken before the two-furlong pole she went and won her race.

She stayed the trip well. I had my doubts after York, but since then we worked her at home and she showed herself so relaxed that we were all fairly confident. Henry told me to ride her as if she stayed. He was more confident beforehand than he had been with Oh So Sharp and Diminuendo proved herself a great little filly.

Cauthen had kept Diminuendo tucked away in midfield as Atropa led the 11 runners to the top of Tattenham Hill at nothing more than a sedate gallop almost three seconds down on the Derby. Such crawls are always liable to spark a chaotic sprint finish. Cauthen needed no reminder of something so blindingly obvious to a rider spoon-fed on the clock. By the time the field had rounded Tattenham Corner and straightened up, he'd manoeuvred Diminuendo out ready to attack. Passing the two marker he uncorked the bottle – and she fairly exploded away from the remainder. Diminuendo clocked the fastest final quarter of the week's races over the distance at 23.65, largely owing to a scintillating 11.45 penultimate furlong that initiated her victory surge – both figures surpassing those of the Derby winner Kahyasi.

Diminuendo appeared to have a routine task in the Irish Oaks a month later at the Curragh. The Ribblesdale Stakes winner Miss Boniface (a daughter of Tap On Wood) and the Oaks d'Italia winner Melodist (in Sheikh Mohammed's second colours) seemed likeliest to fill the places. Diminuendo left the stalls a 9/2-on favourite but running inside the final quarter it was Melodist who looked like giving Sheikh Mohammed the victory. Somehow Cauthen galvanized his partner: all four limbs seemed to wrap themselves round the tiny filly and throw her at Melodist. They snatched a dead heat, the first in an Irish Classic since 1944. An explanation for this narrow – inexplicable – outcome emerged: Diminuendo had come into 'season' at some point before entering the gate.

There was nothing inexplicable about the outcome of Diminuendo's next race, the Group One Yorkshire Oaks. It turned out to be the demolition job to end all demolition jobs. Miss Boniface (beaten two lengths in Ireland) and the Oaks second Sudden Love were the best of the quintet who opposed the 100/30-on favourite. The Knavesmire's carpet of grass was as slick as a tiled floor; track records were set left, right and centre. There were no last minute worries this day: Diminuendo stripped looking a glowing picture of equine health. She was in the mood to put any doubters in their place. The 2:25.79 Diminuendo clocked for her mile-and-a-half shattered the 15-year-old record by over two seconds. It was an exhibition of sustained pace from stalls to winning post that took the breath away.

After the mile was completed in 1:37.71 (two seconds faster than the colts posted in the Great Voltigeur 24 hours later), Cauthen sent Diminuendo alongside Sudden Love. The two fillies tore through the next quarter in 23.58. But whereas Ray Cochrane was all out aboard Sudden Love, Cauthen's demeanour was relaxed in the extreme, the very antithesis of that at the Curragh. Diminuendo responded to a nudge by forging clear in a heartbeat. Five, six, seven ... the gap grew to eight lengths as she continued pouring on the speed. While the crowd began saluting this regal display, Cauthen ceased his urging. And allowed her to coast past the post five lengths to the good; the two lengths Miss Boniface was adrift at the Curragh now extended to almost 18 lengths.

The Yorkshire Oaks proved Diminuendo's zenith. She started favourite for the St Leger but was worried out of the prize by Minster Son. And in the Arc she was never seen with a chance in finishing tenth of the 24 to Tony Bin. Diminuendo headed off to the breeding paddocks and a date with Blushing Groom.

The Knavesmire also provided the backdrop for the career high-spot of the next Cecil-Cauthen filly to excel. Snow Bride was a chestnut daughter of Sheikh Mohammed's Awaasif, an outstanding middle-distance filly rated 130 by *Timeform* after winning the Yorkshire Oaks and running third in an Arc. Snow Bride, wearing the silks of Sheikh Saeed Maktoum Al-Maktoum (a close relation of Sheikh Mohammed), had lost her unbeaten record in the Pretty Polly Stakes (being in 'season' was the explanation offered) when she came to contest the Musidora Stakes of 1989. What a show Snow Bride and her partner would put on.

Cauthen's performance on Snow Bride was a classic example of what we'd come to expect from him. Not for the first occasion, the clock under his helmet operated at a subliminal level on the Knavesmire. Perhaps there was something in its flatness that provided the perfect canvas on which to execute that flawless brand of pace judgement founded on those flat dirt surfaces back home. Whatever its origin, Cauthen was ready, willing and able to dictate a pace to suit on the Knavesmire like no other jockey riding. This day he chose to establish nothing more than a brisk, yet sensible, gallop for the first four and a half furlongs that was slower, for example, than the following day's graduation race. Thereafter he gradually upped the tempo through the remaining six. Once her head was turned for home, Snow Bride burned the turf down the straight with furlongs of 12.00, 11.12, 11.06 and 11.90, a ruthless display of speed that put the heavily backed favourite Pilot to the sword – and fully redeemed her tarnished reputation. 'Cauthen excels,' stated *The Times*, 'riding a brilliantly opportunist race.'

> My mount in the first race had dropped me at the start and I landed on my arm. It hurt and I was very shaken. But I regrouped and carried on. I kind of planned to make all the running on Snow Bride. I thought my only chance of beating Pilot was to try and outstay her. Snow Bride reminded me of Diminuendo. She wasn't very big but she was active and agile and sure to handle Epsom.

Despite Snow Bride's scintillating display, her trainer remained unconvinced about her having recovered condition sufficiently to contest the Oaks for which he had a second live contender in Tessla, the leading juvenile filly of 1988 following wins in the May Hill Stakes and the Hoover Fillies Mile. Both fillies made it to Epsom, Cauthen sticking with Snow Bride. Neither struck a blow at Aliysa, who beat Snow Bride by three lengths. Cauthen had just burgled second place on the line by a short head. As well he did manage to pinch second place, because Aliysa was disqualified subsequently after camphor was detected in her routine urine sample. Some months passed before this amended result was confirmed; by which time Snow Bride had retired following a fourth place in the Prix Vermeille and victory in the Princess Royal Stakes.

The 'gift' of this Oaks success compensated for the 'forfeiture' of another. Snow Bride was meant to be Cauthen's intended mount in the Irish Oaks, but he cried off in order to attend the wedding of his brother Doug back home in Kentucky. John Reid was booked as his replacement. In the event, Snow Bride was withdrawn owing to the ground, leaving stable second string Alydaress, on whom Cauthen had won the Ribblesdale at Royal Ascot, technically his to partner instead. Alydaress was a half-sister to one of Cauthen's first decent fillies, Desirable, and another yearling cherry-picked by Sheikh Mohammed himself. She caused a major upset in the Irish Classic by toppling the odds-on favourite Aliysa. Had Cauthen stayed at home for Snow Bride he'd have switched to Alydaress and won another Classic.

It was expected either Chimes of Freedom or Rafha would pick up where Oh So Sharp, Indian Skimmer, Diminuendo, Snow Bride and Alydaress left off. But for all their juvenile promise, neither filly stamped her presence on the 1990 Classics. Chimes of Freedom at least provided Cauthen with a pair of Group One successes by winning the Moyglare Stud Stakes at the Curragh at two before adding the Coronation Stakes and the Child Stakes at three. But she didn't enter the stalls for any Classic. Rafha did line up for a Classic – and won it. However, Cauthen had elected to ride Moon Cactus, a decisive winner of Goodwood's Lupe Stakes on her seasonal debut, in the

Prix de Diane, leaving Willie Carson to bring Rafha home two and a half lengths in front of the stable's number one.

In point of fact, even the Group One-winning Chimes of Freedom probably couldn't claim to be the best juvenile filly Cauthen rode for Cecil during his six seasons as retained jockey. That laurel might go to Bluebook, a chestnut filly by no less a legend than Secretariat, on whom Cauthen won the 1987 Princess Margaret Stakes at Ascot and finished fourth in the Lowther at York to earn a *Timeform* rating of 115 – 3lb more than Chimes of Freedom. And Bluebook came nowhere near the best two-year-old filly Cauthen partnered in his entire English odyssey. This particular Ian Balding-trained female was ridden by Cauthen in 1986 to win a Newbury maiden by three lengths from future Yorkshire Oaks and Prix Vermaille winner Bint Pasha. He was unable to ride the pint-sized 14.3 hands filly again. At the end of the season Forest Flower, since that's who she was, had added the Queen Mary Stakes, Cherry Hinton Stakes and Mill Reef Stakes and been controversially disqualified from first place in the Cheveley Park Stakes. She was placed joint second in the Free Handicap (2lb below Reference Point) and rated by *Timeform* at a whopping 127 seldom exceeded by a juvenile filly. A year later Forest Flower short-headed Milligram for the Irish One Thousand Guineas.

Partnering this production line of Cecil-trained fillies brought Cauthen more than transient glory. It enabled him to appreciate he was working alongside some sort of genius, because the languid Cecil manner disguised an alchemist capable of turning base metal into gold as far as training thoroughbreds was concerned.

> Henry had something of the mad genius about him. He was born with an innate talent, a God-given talent. No question. He was very different, eccentric in his ways, but a lovely guy. We got along from the start. He intrigued me and we had a good relationship because we understood and accommodated each other.

THE WARREN PLACE HAREM

He was a very intelligent guy and very quick to recognise different characteristics in horses: he didn't train horses as a block, he was very individualistic; he could spot talent at a very early stage of horses arriving at Warren Place, but also he was very sensitive to one that was nervous or lazy. He had this incredible eye for detail and missed nothing. He knew where a horse was, how they were doing, mentally and physically. He knew when to race them and give them confidence, and when they were ready to step up and take a challenge. He liked what he did and he had that genius for it but he was very guarded. When you have something special, you don't want everyone else to know how it's done. But Henry's thing was so unique that most people could be with him for 24 hours a day and not grasp what it was.

His mind was active all the time. You could be talking to him and suddenly he would be overcome with that vague look and be miles away, almost certainly thinking about one of his horses. He put a lot of strong canters and ground work into his horses so when they got to the races they knew their job and continued to thrive. Henry gave a lot of thought to which races suited them best and placed them very well. He tried to give his horses confidence, just like he tried to give everyone around the stable confidence that they're doing a good job. For instance, Henry would say before a big race 'you're the best in the world, do what you want,' – which made you feel ten feet tall. And with regard to my weight, he'd tell me he'd rather I be 2lb over and be strong.

But above and beyond all that, he grafted, like most people who are successful. You see a lot of gifted people who don't use their talent, and eventually they fall by the wayside. If you don't work at it, you're going to end up hitting a brick wall.

Warren Place was a happy place to be and a very special time for me. I thoroughly enjoyed my six years as stable jockey. I felt like I was part of the place and always would be. Maybe I was used to being treated like an equal. They were happy to have me around and I was happy to be there.

The sentiment was mutual. The overwhelming consensus among the people who made Warren Place the most successful yard in the land was that Steve Cauthen was the best stable jockey they ever had.

FOUR

PACE MAKES THE RACE

ACCORDING TO Laz Barrera, 'Pace makes the Race.' And in Steve Cauthen there was no better exponent of exploiting that dictum to the maximum. His great rival Pat Eddery did not give praise lightly, but on this score he was emphatic: 'Steve had marvellous timing. He used to jump off and go like hell on some horses and you'd think he couldn't last up there for too long. But he didn't half take some pegging back. He'd learned to ride by the clock and it made him very hard to beat.' A second champion jockey, Joe Mercer, was bang on the money: 'If Steve sets off in front and you're behind you've got to be worried.'

Instances of Steve Cauthen putting the above philosophy into practice during his 'English Odyssey' come no more apposite than his Derby successes on the Warren Place colts Slip Anchor, Reference Point and Old Vic. Not for them the kind of tender handling adopted with their female stable companions. Cauthen pressed their big engines for every cubic centimetre of pace in an effort to burn off the opposition from the front. The two Derby victories at Epsom on Slip Anchor and Reference Point, in particular, paid homage to that aforementioned American maxim because on a track as tricky as Epsom mistakes lurk beneath every blade of grass and only faultless rides prevail. Each race proved to be a Cauthen masterclass in pace judgement.

> Early on in my career I really didn't know much about the Derby. I knew there was racing in England – but not much more

about it than that! The only Derby that mattered to me was the Kentucky Derby. Then, in 1978, Robert Sangster offered me the ride on Hawaiian Sound. But it was only two days before the Belmont, so I turned it down. I didn't think it would be fair to Affirmed's connections if I flew all the way over to England and back so soon before the last leg of the Triple Crown and I didn't want there to be any accusations if I got beat. But because 'Shoe' then got to ride him they showed that Derby on television in America. All of a sudden I knew what the Epsom Derby was – and seeing it really opened my eyes. It's a great occasion. For a professional jockey those sort of days are what makes it for you. It's marvellous to be in a race like the Derby and to be involved in the day.

To have a chance is even better!

The pinnacle of a Flat-race jockey's career is to win the Derby. It assures immortality – much as victory in the Grand National does for a jump-jockey. However, whereas the National annually offers dozens of mounts and the resultant fusion of fences and mayhem often presents the laurel to an outsider and its partner, similar largesse seldom occurs at the Derby. Prized mounts on one of the favourites was the norm for success at Epsom. Cauthen shared the weighing room with past or future champion jockeys in Joe Mercer, Michael Roberts, Kevin Darley, Seb Sanders and Jamie Spencer, all of whom never won the Classic. Yet John Parsons, last seen leading up a yearling at the Newmarket Sales, will forever be remembered as the 16-year-old who won the 1862 Derby on his solitary ride in the race, the 40/1 shot, Caractacus. One way or another, any jockey, whatever brilliance he possessed, needed a slice of luck to win the Derby.

Cauthen had experienced the role luck can play prior to and during the Derby. In 1983 he actually rode the Derby winner but his win on Teenoso came in the Lingfield Derby Trial. In the main event he was obliged to partner The Noble Player for Barry Hills and had to endure a distant view of the Piggott posterior riding Teenoso to an effortless success. Twelve months later it was his turn to inherit a ride from Piggott, whose rift with owner Daniel Wildenstein enabled him to ride Claude Monet for Henry Cecil. His new mount was bred for the job, being a chestnut son of Cauthen's Triple Crown buddy Affirmed while his dam, Madelia, had landed the double of French Guineas and Oaks. Having won traditionally the premier Derby trial, the Dante at York, the pair went off joint-third favourites and led passing the three-furlong marker. Then Claude Monet stopped as if he'd had his throat slit – apparently he choked on a clod of turf. He never ran again.

Then there was the track itself. The Epsom maze challenged to the full a rider's horsemanship and his jockeyship. As a test of a rider's intelligence, the Derby course demanded the equivalent of an Oxford degree. Split-second decisions were the norm not the exception. Victory went to the smartest, the alert and the quick-witted. Willie Carson once said that jockeys leave their brains in the weighing room when they go out to ride in the Derby. 'Epsom is dreadful, the last course in the world you'd choose to run a Classic for three-year-olds in June,' he's on record as saying. 'Tattenham Hill can be a dream if you are going well on a high-class horse, but if they can't handle the descent it's like pushing a wheelbarrow with square wheels. You cannot take the openings you need and the others can do what they like with you. It's a nightmare.' The four-time winner had a point: in the white heat of the 'Blue Riband' it requires a cool head but all too often a rush of blood ensures such reason goes west. Not for nothing had it gained the reputation of being the 'rough-house Classic.' The contributory factors were obvious: sheer weight of numbers leads to overcrowding on a track where gradients, bends, paths and cambers are ready to ambush the unwary or unlucky. Putting it succinctly, Epsom was, in the colourful opinion of Derby-winning jockey Ray Cochrane, 'a real bitch to ride'.

John Reid, a third Derby-winning jockey, has described the trouble spots. 'The first five furlongs are quite steep and once they come back to you from the outside towards the inside rail you can get a lot of trouble. By the top of Tattenham Hill the pace is getting hot and that's a danger area.

If you're stuck on the fence you cannot manoeuvre, as a lot of horses that have been up there early start cracking. They can come back very fast, just as others are trying to move up to mount a challenge. It can get a bit rough. Then, in the straight, you don't want to be on the fence. It's rare that you'll get a run there because the camber causes horses to roll down onto the far rail. Steve was the first jockey in my lifetime to make all the running in the Derby. Before it was the bad horses up front to show themselves off, going too fast, and there was no point taking them on. And there's no doubt that the pressure gets to you. It's the one race in the year when no quarter is given. It's every man for himself. If you get tightened up, that's tough. It's not a race for an inexperienced jockey. I got wiped out on my first two rides.'

Cauthen had been warned. But he could still barely believe his eyes on making his acquaintance with Epsom Downs.

> Lester's dad Keith sent me a bunch of old Derby videos to watch but seeing Epsom for the first time was quite a shock. It was so different from what I was used to. It's one of the trickiest courses there is. And wasn't the easiest for me to get used to. Even the five-furlong course is a problem: you're flying downhill, crossing roads and mats – the sort of things that can make a horse do crazy things.
>
> On the horseshoe, the descent to Tattenham Corner is very steep – much steeper than it looks on television. And all the way up the straight you're riding on the side of a hill, there's a substantial difference between the height at the outside rail and the inside rail, which is why there's an incident at nearly every meeting. Green or unbalanced horses slide off the camber toward the far rails. You find you have to balance and re-balance them six times up the straight. It's very easy to get it wrong, yet it's the one place in the world you don't want to.
>
> We all felt very sorry for Greville Starkey on Dancing Brave. Dancing Brave was probably unlucky to lose that Derby in 1986. I happened to be back there with him when he was getting knocked

over early on and there was nothing Greville could do. His only option once he was stuck at the back was to sit there and make one run. And four furlongs out in the straight is as early as you can do it. If he'd pulled out earlier on Tattenham Hill he would have been stupid, no jockey would do that in a million years.

But if you're sitting on a Derby favourite and you get it wrong you're there to be shot at by the critics.

'Unlucky losers' litter Derby history like so much confetti. In 1909 the magnificent Bayardo, subsequent winner of the St Leger, Eclipse and Gold Cup, suffered one of his only two defeats in 16 starts, losing all chance when Sir Martin fell in front of him approaching Tattenham Corner. Twenty years later Kopi came down during a scrimmage on the descent before going on to gain compensation in the Irish Derby. In 1948 another future Leger victor in Black Tarquin ran wide at the Corner, carrying with him the Two Thousand Guineas winner and favourite My Babu. French challengers Shantung and Prince Regent would probably have won instead of finishing third in 1959 and 1969 had each not met problems in running. Some mishaps, like Sir Martin's, proved fatal: Marsyad and Angers (another French favourite) broke legs in 1952 and 1960. But 1962 witnessed the greatest catalogue of woe: seven of the 26-strong field fell near the top of the Hill following the stumble of King Canute II. Among the casualties was the favourite, Hethersett, who later demonstrated his ill fortune by taking the St Leger by four easy lengths. The Stewards endorsed the opinion of the jockeys that poor horses dropping back had caused the melee, and regretted the fact that 'horses not up to Classic standard were allowed to start.' Or as the *Daily Mirror* informed its readers with tabloid aplomb, 'Derby Duds get the blame.'

The manner of riding the Derby has been a slave to fashion. In the 20th century that fashion was invariably shaped by the two outstanding Derby jockeys, Steve Donoghue and Lester Piggott. Donoghue claimed that he owed his four successes in five years during the 1920s, on Humorist, Captain Cuttle, Papyrus and Manna, to being in the first three at the top of Tattenham

Hill. Thus enlightened, embryonic stars like Gordon Richards and Charlie Elliott went hell for leather in a spate of subsequent renewals in an almighty scramble for those perceived best positions near the front. Even Joe Childs, the irascible master of the waiting race, was ordered to make all on the headstrong Coronach in 1926, although his typically sardonic explanation for their five-length success implied otherwise: 'The bastard ran away with me.'

Yet no position could be more imprudent in the event of a stiff early gallop than one near the front. It's far preferable to languish in rear, conserving energy, while those up ahead squander theirs. A jockey with 'brains' could easily exploit that situation to his advantage. Such a jockey was Harry Wragg, dubbed the 'Head Waiter' for his patience and apparent anonymity during a race. While others cut their own and each other's throats by engaging in suicidal early gallops, Wragg hovered in the background, biding his time, to pounce late in the Derbies of 1928 and 1930 aboard Felstead and Blenheim respectively. 'Drop in on somebody's heels,' he explained. 'You can do it in athletics, you can do it in racing. Slip-streaming is the name of the game, and at the last minute, whoosh!'

Then along came Lester Keith Piggott. A jockey whose genius was, like the weather, a phenomenon one experienced but could not define; so magnetic was Lester's hold over the racing public that had he donned wellington boots to cross the English Channel many would've seized the chance to back him at short odds. Yet as a man he was a flawed individual to whom the rustle of banknotes would drown any irritating criticisms. The 'Long Fellow' won the Derby on ten occasions and he cast a long shadow. His methods must be right: 'You need a horse that can lay up handy, a few places behind the leaders. Getting too far back can be disastrous as there is no part of the course where you can readily make up ground forfeited early on. You have to get into a reasonable place and keep out of trouble as beaten horses fall back on the downhill run.'

Thus, if the two supreme Derby jockeys, Piggott and Donoghue, reckoned to be worth 7lb round the Derby course, were of one accord, their strategy must be right. Position, not pace, became the mantra: 'Tattenham

Corner taken in fourth place, two off the rail, just like Lester.' However, the majority of Piggott's wins came during a phase when the early gallop had noticeably slowed again: jockeys had to be among the leaders in readiness for the inevitable sprint up the straight. On Nijinsky, for example, Piggott prevailed with a blistering final quarter of 22.40 seconds; Sir Ivor's speed was unleashed even later – a final furlong timed at 10.68 to scythe down Connaught as if he were summer hay.

When approaching his Derby debut on Tap On Wood in 1979, Cauthen was able to draw on the wisdom of Jimmy Lindley. 'I think I rode in 14 Derbies myself, the first on Scipio in the Coronation Derby won by Sir Gordon on Pinza and the last in 1972. You can't ride to a set pattern in the big races. The key in the Derby, like most of the big races, is to get a good start and then control how fast you're going. It's much easier then to drop back – you're still in control. Trouble happens when you get a poor start. You don't want to kick up that first hill just after the start at Epsom. And you must think ahead. At the seven furlong marker you need to be thinking where you want to be at the five. I liked to be fifth or sixth at the top of Tattenham Hill because then I'd be in charge of where I wanted to go. If, for example, they drifted wide coming round Tattenham Corner – which often happened – I could make a dart up the fence. With all the undulations you must use the descents to make up your ground and save yourself uphill. Also, you must do lots of homework the night before: fix in your mind the colours of each horse and how they liked to race – which colours to follow and which ones to avoid getting stuck behind because they were likely to be dropping back at this point and would take me out of the race. But you can't win if you're not going the pace that you want. The great thing with Steve was you seldom had to tell him anything twice. He had a great tactical brain and grasped things straight away.'

One thing agreed by all was that pillar-to-post successes were as rare as pink elephants: just five since 1780: Whalebone (1810); Tiresias (1819); St Amant (1904); Tagalie (1912); and Coronach (1926). Both Call Boy (1927) and Nimbus (1949) led from the gate but were briefly headed in the closing stages before fighting back to win. In more recent memory, Moon Mountain and Yves Saint-Martin were collared a furlong out in Blakeney's Derby of 1969 and beaten around two lengths into fourth; the Sangster-Hills runner Hawaiian Sound nearly made it in 1978 under an inspired ride from Shoemaker, only succumbing to Shirley Heights in the shadow of the post by a head. 'He imposed his authority on them and had them stacked up behind him like a pack of cards coming round Tattenham Corner,' said Hills afterwards. It was Shoemaker's very first ride in England, let alone an introduction to Tattenham Hill that he likened to 'coming down a ski slope without any skis.' However, in 1974 Brian Taylor rode Snow Knight very much to the Lindley plan, breaking fast and then dropping in behind the leader before making the best of his way home from five furlongs out at the top of Tattenham Hill. The first three to finish that year, moreover, were the first three round Tattenham Corner.

Thus, while it's true to say 'Pace makes the Race' one should add a significant codicil: different kinds of pace demand riding a different kind of race. When it's slow, be near the front because every top-class horse is capable of launching an even-time sprint; if it's too quick, shelter in rear waiting to ambush tiring leaders. In short: if a jockey sets out to make the pace he'd better judge it to perfection or his horse will run out of steam close to home and be nailed. If need be, could Steve Cauthen go one better than 'The Shoe'?

> I had never consciously thought about forcing the pace or making sure that races were run faster than before. But I knew I was as good a judge of pace as anyone and was prepared to back that judgement in a race. In the States, day in, day out, we did nothing else but ride to the clock. If you were two-fifths of a second out over five furlongs you got a rollicking.
>
> But time means nothing. I focused on the pace not the time. The time taken isn't the important thing. It's how I was doing it that mattered. Was the pace within the horse's comfort zone.

'What is he capable of? When I choose to kick, will we get to the end and not hit the wall at the half-furlong mark? And I'd consider the track: can I nick a length by cutting a corner or dropping onto the fence? And what am I up against? How do I beat them? If I'm on an out-and-out stayer, I've got to kick on to stretch the rest. If I'm on the front end with a turn of foot I'd try to be first off the mark to get the chasers off balance and leave them scrambling.

A world-class jockey can ride any horse the way he needs to be ridden. As long as I knew the main thing about the horse I'm riding, I can react to the way the race goes and still get the best out of the horse in question. You have to take races and horses as you find them.

But with Henry's horses I knew they'd be fit and know their job. If I was given what I needed to pace the race the way I wanted, and determine the way the race was run, I knew a Stoute or a Dunlop or a Harwood horse following me would struggle, nine times out of ten, to reach me and then have something left to get past me.

At this juncture it's worth studying the Derby course and the distribution of pace its peculiarly unique topography instigates. What does the clock tell us when the race is run on typically decent summer ground? The first half mile is uphill and rarely produces anything approaching even time. Naturally the quarter from the five to the two poles down Tattenham Hill proves the fastest portion of the race (as quick as 20.75 seconds in 1974) and, as the runners take a while to balance themselves in the three-furlong straight, it is often the penultimate furlong, from two to the one pole, which yields the quicker, race-winning furlong of the final three.

Although times must be considered in the light of conditions underfoot, the conclusion to be drawn from numerous sets of Derby fractions is emphatic: a running time of 2:10 at the two-furlong pole is the absolute limit for any front-runner hoping to hang on for victory. Go faster and the door is open for any 'closer' who has been hiding off the pace and still has some running left in him. Go slower and the door opens for all and sundry in a last-ditch sprint.

Those were the many factors for Cauthen to sift. And the particular challenge on the front-running Slip Anchor and Reference Point: how accurate would the clock in his head be? Would it be fool proof under the weight of expectation? That he got it exactly right on both colts must surely go down as two of his finest performances – and two of the finest in Derby history.

Slip Anchor was bred for the task. He had a Derby winner in Shirley Heights for a father and a mother who ran second in the German Oaks and came from a family that included winners of both German Oaks and Derby. He belonged to a member of an equally blue-blooded human family in Lord Howard de Walden, whose ancestor earned his title after helping to thwart the Spanish Armada in 1588. At two, Slip Anchor looked big and rangy; and often exhibited a frightening oxygen deficiency that made him wobble about as if on the verge of collapse. Cecil's vet likened these attacks to a 'teenage fainting fit'. He was crying out for time in which to fill out and mature. Once that transformation was complete the bay colt turned into a flying machine.

> At the start of the season he was just another horse. I was told Lester had got off him at the back end of his two-year-old season and said he was shit. But at that point he was just a big, weak, backward horse and all he did by the end of the season was win a little race at Nottingham. When he went up to Newcastle for his first race of 1985, Paul Eddery rode him and he finished third and showed a little more, so I rode him in the Heathorn Stakes next time and he won nicely. He was my style of horse, with a beautiful long stride, so I just let him get out and bowl along and he ran so well that day that Henry could see he was improving

and he decided to run him in the Lingfield Derby Trial. It was a case of how well he handled the track, and he galloped them into the ground. I never even picked up my whip. I could've won by 20 lengths not ten if I'd wished. I started easing him up a furlong out when I was clear. The big issue, the reason we went to Lingfield, was to find out how he'd handle coming down a hill and he went round like a ring in a barrel. He was so athletic and clearly wasn't going to have a problem with Epsom, so this was when we really started thinking we had a proper Derby horse. He'd improved out of all recognition.

Cauthen was not alone in his estimation. Slip Anchor also sensed a transformation.

He'd just started to realise he could be a really great horse: he got a noticeable swagger about him, a confidence from winning races. When he saw how he pulverized his work horses by 25 lengths without doing a stroke, you could see him thinking: 'Well, I am pretty good.' And the horses he was beating were no slouches. They were winners. I remember how well he was progressing because I rode him out each morning for about two or three weeks before the Derby – I didn't want anything to go wrong with him – and each time he gave me more confidence. He had a lovely temperament with no kinks of any kind. I was able to take it the way it came in the Derby. He stayed well, acted on any ground and would handle Epsom without any problem. Even between Lingfield and Epsom he improved a stone.

Physically he was starting to fill out and strengthen, and we were having a grand run, our horses were in great form and there was a real buzz in the yard. Everybody was happy with the horse, but I think I had the most confidence in him and asked my Dad to come over for the race. Everyone else, the owner in particular, was getting worried about just how certain I was. Lord Howard so badly wanted to win the Derby that my confidence frightened him, but I felt the horse getting better by the day.

Henry Cecil hardly dared to hope that Slip Anchor would bring him his first Derby: after all, he'd not even had a placed runner in his 16 seasons holding a licence. Cauthen's sky-high confidence in Slip Anchor's ability to win the Derby prompted a line uttered to the colt's lad that entered Derby folklore: 'This horse is a f***ing certainty!' George Robinson, Newmarket Heath's legendary work-watcher, agreed: 'By making all when he won at Newmarket, Slip Anchor proved he had the hallmark of a very good horse. The Heath finds out any weaknesses in a horse's courage. He goes a relentless gallop and has the ability to finish his races well, something that so many front-runners fail to do. By making his own running he is sure to keep out of trouble and I think he will gallop the others into the ground.'

Cauthen had no reservations about accomplishing just that. He'd implicit trust in the accuracy of his mental timepiece. Nor had he any qualms about reviving the Donoghue strategy. And he knew Henry Cecil had implicit trust in his ability to choose the right option once the gates clanged open.

> Slip Anchor broke clean, although it took him a stride or two to find his rhythm. Doing it from the front was not something many people ever considered. A lot said that wasn't the way to do it but it's effective when you've the right type of horse. That's how Slip Anchor had to be ridden. My plan was to get to the front and use his stride, make all, but well within himself, and that's what we managed to do. He was long legged but agile – and he went round Epsom like a cat. After 50 yards it was obvious nothing was going my pace. I just had to let him go. And I never saw another horse in the race until I had a look around in the straight.

PACE MAKES THE RACE

When we got to the top of Tattenham Hill, I gave him a breather, and as we started to come down the Hill I felt he was going so good I let him free-wheel for a while and he just started opening up. Petoski was right behind me and he stopped at that same point and carried a couple of horses back with him, which helped me get away, and coming into Tattenham Corner I started to let him really roll. I had a peep over my shoulder early in the straight and saw that I was about 15 lengths clear. I was surprised how far I was in front. Because of the camber, it's like running down the side of a mountain into the rail, horses tend to lean that way and it's hard to get a sustained run out of a horse in the straight. Pegging back ten lengths or more is tough. I knew it was an insurmountable gap.

It was pretty amazing watching the replay to see how far clear he was by the time he got into the stretch. I was sitting quietly and feeling good about everything. From then on I knew I couldn't get beat, and then started to ask him to go for home. After that it was a question of keeping him together up the last incline. He did start to get a little bit tired but there was never really any threat to us.

The greatest threat to Cauthen had lain with Slip Anchor's draw (aside from arriving late after his helicopter was initially grounded by fog). The stalls were positioned toward the far side and Slip Anchor was in box three toward the centre of the track. After a furlong there's a right-handed kink in the course. He needed to break fast and grab an instant lead before that point in order to avoid any possibility of being boxed-in by runners then tacking from right to left toward the inside rail.

'Steve committed to making all the running,' says Jimmy Lindley. 'But he knew how fast he was travelling. He would've given up the lead if he'd been going too fast and dropped back. He had the confidence in his ability to judge how fast his horse was going and what he was capable of. That confidence is what top jockeys are paid for. People say there's not much difference between jockeys. That's wrong. There's a vast difference between jockeys on the big days. That's why the best ones are paid a lot of money. That's why they ride for the top trainers. The trainer feeds them all the information they need and then leaves it to them to get on with the job.'

Cauthen 'got on with the job'. Slip Anchor did his bidding and was five lengths clear at the top of Tattenham Hill. The rest was a walk in the park.

Cauthen was in perfect sync with the stopwatch. Slip Anchor completed one and a quarter miles (on going officially declared as good) in 2:09.71 – bang on target. The key fraction to this point was the lightning 22.17 quarter down Tattenham Hill when Cauthen let his mount 'really roll' and left the field toiling in his wake. For those watching on television Graham Goode endorsed the images on the screen: 'This is a sparkling performance! We know the horse stays and Steve has surely stolen it!' Goode never uttered truer words. A referee would've stopped a boxing match to prevent further punishment. Slip Anchor had no need to produce the kind of sub-23-seconds final quarter with which the likes of Nijinsky won his Derby: 26.06 was enough to ward off any danger. Law Society (who won the Irish Derby on his next start) was beaten seven lengths; and the distance of 13 lengths between Slip Anchor and the third horse was a record margin.

> We came back in and Henry patted me on the leg and said, 'Well done, old fruit.' That was Henry all over. But it was obvious he was delighted by it and it's something I'll never forget.

Relentless Slip Anchor in a Different League,' insisted *The Times*. 'Cauthen rode with the supreme confidence that he has been showing all season.' Another headline declared, 'Housewives' Darling wins Derby'. Lord Howard de Walden was beside himself with joy: 'I used to dream about it at school and I can hardly believe it's happened at last. Cauthen has always been supremely confident, and it absolutely terrified one.' His only anxiety on the day emanated from the muggy overcast skies that delayed the helicopter ferrying his jockey (and Piggott) from Newmarket and caused him to miss the opening race. Fortunately no such inconvenience had prevented Tex Cauthen from jetting across the Atlantic to witness his son making history by becoming the first American to ride a winner of the Derby since Frank O'Neill triumphed on Spion Kop in 1920. And Cauthen trod virgin territory: he became the only jockey ever to ride the winner of the Kentucky Derby and *the* Derby.

Slip Anchor never won again. His fall from grace began with a jarred near-fore joint forcing him to miss planned engagements in both the King George and St Leger.

> Slip Anchor was the best he ever was on Derby Day. Brilliant! I got off him thinking he could be the best horse I'd ever sat on. He loved Epsom. He flew down the Hill and handled everything well. It was a freakish performance that put him up there with anything I'd ridden in the States, including Affirmed. I'd never ridden a horse with such a stride on him, and I thought at the time he was bound to improve and might be as good as Affirmed. He and Affirmed were two different types as Affirmed like to come from behind. But he was never the same horse after he was injured in his box.

When Slip Anchor returned to action in September he was beaten by Shernazar at Kempton and then by Pebbles in the Champion Stakes; both four-year-olds followed his lead and trumped him for finishing speed. On his reappearance in 1986 he was again defeated, in the Jockey Club Stakes by Phardante – whom he'd thrashed by 25 lengths in the Derby. He was retired to Lord Howard's stud where he proved a charming and amenable resident who sired the Oaks and Leger-winning filly User Friendly before his death in 2011. Although his farewell to the racetrack was a muted affair, during those four weeks in the summer of 1985 Steve Cauthen had thrust Slip Anchor into the history books by enabling him to run like the wind.

And Cauthen would soon be presented with another colt on which he might mimic the mistral: Reference Point.

> Slip Anchor was a great Derby winner. Reference Point was a great champion.
> We knew Reference Point had enough talent to win the Derby. He'd proved himself previously as an out-and-out galloper; he liked to grind them into the ground just like Slip Anchor. The main difference was that Slip Anchor used to show us what he could do at home, but Reference Point was so lazy. We will never know how good Slip Anchor could have been, but, for me, Reference Point was the better horse, easily one of the best four I've ridden, because he went on and proved how good he was.

For a jockey entirely happy backing his pace judgement at the front of a race to be united with a gallant and resolute galloper like Reference Point promised a coupling made in horological heaven. The clock was always under threat when Cauthen climbed aboard the strong and compact bay colt for a quintet of top middle-distance events in 1987.

The union, however, was not the instant love match beloved of romantic novelists. Despite the colt being backed for the 1987 Derby at 66/1 before even seeing a racecourse, Cecil was initially unimpressed because he showed little enthusiasm on the gallops. And even after the Mill Reef colt had broken his maiden at Sandown (where Cauthen paid a stall handler to whack the dozy colt's backside to ensure he broke smartly), Cecil's jockey opted to partner stable-mate Suhailie, who boasted an unbeaten record in three starts, in the Group One William Hill Futurity over a mile at Doncaster four weeks later. Cauthen was soon in trouble on the favourite and had the uncomfortable sight of Pat Eddery's rear aboard Reference Point disappearing further into the distance all the way down the Doncaster straight. There could be no carping about the authority of Reference Point's five-length victory (some thought it as much as seven) over the Royal Lodge winner Bengal Fire – or the dozen lengths he had over Suhailie. On ground officially described as good to soft, the colt made every yard of the running – the first ever to do so since the race's inception as the Observer Gold Cup in 1966. 'First-class Reference,' said *The Sporting Life*, adding, 'His big bay frame is still a long way from being sculpted into the hard-muscled racing machine it promises to be next season.' Louis Freedman's colt topped the Free Handicap with 9st 7lb, 2lb clear of Ajdal and 8lb ahead of Suhailie, and left his owner-breeder, former deputy senior steward of the Jockey Club and self-made property millionaire, entertaining thoughts of grander things: 'I've dreamed of winning the Triple Crown since my school days. It would put the seal on my racing career.'

Reference Point went into winter quarters with the Triple Crown well within his compass. Mill Reef had already sired a Derby winner in Shirley Heights and a French Derby winner in Acamas, plus a Guineas winner in Fairy Footsteps; and Cecil had trained his dam, Home On The Range, to win the Sun Chariot in the Freedman colours. Reference Point's style of running at Doncaster suggested the St Leger might be the easiest of the three legs to accomplish and the Guineas the hardest: he seemed a relentless galloper in the Slip Anchor mould. Freedman's dream was not to be. On 12 March his colt was found to be suffering from a sinus infection; 11 days later he was placed under a local anaesthetic so that Cecil's vet, Richard Greenwood, might drill a hole one-eighth of an inch in diameter into his nose through which plastic tubes would be inserted in order to flush out the pus every day. This ordeal Reference Point would endure for 12 days.

Reference Point's Derby prep became the Dante over York's extended one mile and a quarter on 13 May, three weeks before the Classic. He made all to win by a length from Ascot Knight. Cecil and Cauthen could look forward to Epsom with growing confidence even though a nasal spray to alleviate any discomfort was still being used on Reference Point up to five days before the Derby

I wanted to let him stretch his rivals in the Dante but I also wanted to give him as easy a time as possible because he'd been ill for five weeks. I gave him a backhander over a furlong from home but even when Ascot Knight got to my girths I still thought I'd win.

Before the race none of us was very confident that he'd done enough to win that day. But Reference Point did it quite easily in the end and I was very pleased with him. The way Henry trained his horses was they got plenty of basic ground-work but Reference Point hadn't done that much fast work, which is why we thought he'd come on a lot for the race.

Cauthen was then faced with the dilemma that frequently arises in a stable packed with talent when a big race comes along. In 1985 he'd correctly chosen Slip Anchor over the Predominate Stakes winner Lanfranco as his Derby mount; Warren Place again housed not one but two Derby colts in Reference Point and Legal Bid, whom Cauthen had steered to a course-record time in the Lingfield Derby Trial. The two Cecil colts occupied first and second in the Derby market. Cauthen had abandoned Reference Point once to his cost. Would he make the same mistake a second time?

When I rode Slip Anchor I was quite confident he was better than Lanfranco, so I made my choice early. I knew he was good from his home work even before he showed it on the racecourse.

But these two were both very nice horses. Both were very relaxed at home and there wasn't all that great a form guide to what they'd done on the track. They'd both done what we asked, but they hadn't done it in the obvious style that Slip Anchor did. When I got on Reference Point's back in the morning, he'd plod along with his head down.

He'd laze around with anyone, he was so docile. And he was hard work. I got more tired riding him in the morning than I did in the afternoon at the races. Legal Bid was lazy at home too, although he did tend to jig-jog at first. He may've look flashy, with all that white on him, but he was as genuine as they come. It was a very game performance at Lingfield.

It was a very difficult decision and not one taken lightly. They were both good horses. I had to decide as soon as possible which one to ride but I didn't have too much difficulty in making up my mind.

Despite this anxiety, Reference Point won his fourth race in a row by what was fast becoming his *modus operandi*: taking command out of the gate and letting his jockey dictate the pace. Or, as *The Times* put it following the Derby, 'Relentless Reference Point reigns.' It continued: 'The mantle of Lester Piggott has now settled firmly on Cauthen's shoulders and the invisible clock in his head has never worked better than on this brilliant occasion.'

Reference Point didn't have to make the running but he was a galloper so I wanted to be somewhere near the pace. I wouldn't have been frightened to be behind one or two. It was the same with Slip Anchor. If something had gone rabbiting off I would've sat in behind. As it was, I wanted a strong pace and had to make it myself. I rode him to the front because it suited us to do that. I did not want to get caught in behind inferior horses. I wanted to keep clear of trouble and give the horse every chance.

Nothing scared us going into the race. The only thing that worried us was whether he'd act on the course. My first preoccupation was to keep him balanced racing down Tattenham Hill. Slip Anchor was a very balanced horse. Reference Point tended to change his legs a bit and I just wanted to get him down the Hill and into the straight without getting him unbalanced, before I started kicking; then to let him find his stride.

Reference Point's Derby was quite possibly the fastest on record. Mahmoud's hand-timed record of 1936 was 2:33.80. The hand-time for 1987 was 0.38 seconds lower viz 2:33.42. Moreover, back in the 1930s hand-timings were less reliable than today owing to the distance from the clocker in the grandstand to the gate and the vagaries of the rising tape; the advent of VHS or DVD recordings has lent far greater accuracy. And the value of the performance was arguably greater. Even without the aid of Mother Nature, modern watering systems and the lush carpet of grass they stimulate, create going which is never likely to equal the rock-hard surfaces often found in the first half of the 20th century whenever dry weather prevailed. Bustino's official track record for Epsom's mile and a half of 2:33.31 was set in the 1975 Coronation Cup but the hand-timed record stands to Apelle at 2:33 flat in the 1928 Coronation Cup.

Reference Point's time resulted in no small measure from the punishing gallop dictated by Cauthen. He was drawn in the middle of the 19 runners; knew his horse might be tardy out of the gate; and knew they might easily be 'cut up' when the field swung right to reduce the first kink in the course and then left again toward the inside running rail. Cauthen took no chances and gave Reference Point a kick in the belly that brought him to the head of affairs through an opening half a mile that was two seconds faster than Slip Anchor's time and quicker than anything on record at 52.66 seconds. The first quarter caught the eye: 24.60 from a standing start and gradually running uphill was three seconds faster than the norm – as posted in the meeting's other races over the distance. A foolhardy pace to some, but Cauthen could not risk his notoriously idle partner switching off behind a wall of horses. Reference Point had no need to match Slip Anchor's accelerating split along the top of the hill, but his quarter down Tattenham Hill to the three pole was barely slower at 22.90.

Then we witnessed the hallmark of a class horse and a class jockey. Cauthen quickly got his mount on an even keel with an unflustered dexterity he'd have sold his granny for in 1979, but which had now become second nature to him. Despite his exertions thus far, Reference Point responded gamely to his jockey's elbow-pumping beat to complete the ten furlongs in 2:09.20 – replicating almost to the last pip the running time posted by Slip Anchor. For the second time in three years Steve Cauthen was right on the money.

What followed rekindled memories of Affirmed's stretch run in the Belmont – except on this occasion there was more than one moment of truth. Reference Point was either going to cry enough owing to his efforts through those initial ten furlongs or he was going to tap sufficient reserves with which to repel every boarder. His jockey found the appropriate response like he had for Affirmed on that glorious June afternoon nine years ago. It was arguably Cauthen's finest sleight of hand of the entire 'English Odyssey'.

Each time anything got near his partner's quarters thereafter, Cauthen challenged Reference Point for more by resorting to the American ruse of getting a horse to switch its leading leg: one crack; reins gathered; two more cracks; reins re-gathered; three more cracks. Each time Reference Point responded. His last two-furlong fractions were faster than the norm, a staggering display of guts and determination given his earlier exertions. A penultimate furlong in 11.90 seconds acted like a dagger to the throat of any pursuer; another in 12.32 completed a taxing final quarter of 24.22, bettered just three times in the last ten renewals. The 6/4 favourite passed the post with one and a half lengths to spare over Most Welcome. Those privileged enough to watch the 1987 Derby as it unfolded, in the flesh or on television, had been gifted some idea of what it was like to view the 1978 Belmont as it happened. A sense of awe prevailed. When rational thought returned, one could only applaud horse and jockey. For we had witnessed something special. Something outstanding made to look effortless. All of 59 years had elapsed since Joe Childs's 'involuntary' pillar-to-post win on Coronach before Slip Anchor's swaggering saunter of 1985. Yet this day we'd watched Cauthen execute this arduous feat for the second time in three years. Had Cauthen not achieved anything else during the 'English Odyssey', these two bravura displays of consummate skill alone would have ensured immortality. It would be another 33 years before Emmet McNamara and Serpentine managed to follow suit after passing the two pole in 2:09.77.

Bookmakers had taken a hammering. William Hill alone had ante-post liabilities of £750,000. But on this occasion there'd been no Suhailie moment for Cauthen to endure: Legal Bid finished 14th, some 13 lengths in arrears.

> You had to keep at him as he was aware of everything going on around him. He was even looking at the crowd at the top of the Hill. He was totally unsuited to the course. He had to be 'babied' all the way round. Everything was fine until he came down the Hill and round the Corner into the stretch. I really had to try and keep him together because he didn't come down the Hill as well as Slip Anchor, and was still idling turning into the straight. He didn't act on the track at all. He hated the cambers. I kept on asking him and it was not until Most Welcome got upside that he truly got balanced and found his stride. He only really got on top in the last furlong.
>
> He was much better suited to a galloping track. Many horses had been beaten there because of the circuit but Reference Point had so much courage, and his class got him home.
>
> It was a ride I was proud of because keeping him balanced was the key: once you start pushing the heads of one around there you're pretty much sunk.

It was decided to forego the Irish Derby option in favour of the two-furlongs shorter Eclipse Stakes: Louis Freedman wished to demonstrate his colt, now worth an estimated £15m, had the speed to attract commercial breeders and wasn't just a resolute galloper. Then it would be on to the King George; and finally the St Leger. The one target virtually ruled out completely was the Prix de l'Arc de Triomphe: 'He loves to run from the front, and that may not be his kind of race,' said Henry Cecil.

PACE MAKES THE RACE

The Derby winner, however, would have a far deadlier assassin skulking in the Sandown shadows than any pursuing him at Epsom. If any animal was capable of lying in Reference Point's slipstream, the possibility always existed that he might be beaten for speed at the death. The four-year-old Mtoto possessed a potent kick-finish that had brought him success in the Prince of Wales's Stakes at Royal Ascot. This stiletto would need blunting.

It was accepted that the Derby winner would make the pace but the ploy of Triptych's connections in running a pacemaker of their own to 'worry' him early on backfired as Cauthen tore through the first half-mile in 48.93, some three seconds faster than the handicappers 24 hours earlier. The even-money favourite reached the two pole to complete the mile in 1:37.43 – he was slowing but still over a second up on the handicappers. Cauthen had done his darndest to get Reference Point into a winning position. As the man who jumped from a ten-storey building was heard to mutter passing the fourth floor, 'So far, so good'. Victory looked in safe keeping. Until a combination of Mtoto's speed and Sandown's hill decided the issue. Driven upsides the leader by Michael Roberts, Mtoto skewered Reference Point by three-quarters of a length. The final quarter of 26.28 may sound slow but the Sandown hill seldom permits anything below 26 seconds. Reference Point had not surrendered without a fight. The time of 2:04.33 was a new record for the race. Cecil had gone easy on Reference Point for 12 days following his hard race at Epsom and the colt blew for 40 minutes after the Eclipse, suggesting he may not have been back to peak fitness.

Three weeks later Reference Point proved himself in the pink for the King George VI and Queen Elizabeth Diamond Stakes; back at his preferred trip but faced by even fiercer competition. In 1987 the King George went some way to restoring its prestige as Europe's mid-summer, all-aged championship for middle-distance horses. Reference Point would need to beat six others who had enjoyed Group One success in Europe, namely the five-year-olds Triptych (England, Ireland and France) and Acatenango (Germany and France); the four-year-olds Moon Madness (England and France) and Tony Bin (Italy); and three-year-olds Sir Harry Lewis (Ireland)

and Unite (England and Ireland). Between them the septet had accumulated 22 Group Ones that included six Classics in addition to Reference Point's Derby: Irish Two Thousand Guineas (Triptych); Irish Derby (Sir Harry Lewis – following his fourth at Epsom); English and Irish Oaks (Unite); Acatenango (German Derby). In due course, Reference Point, Triptych, Acatenango and Tony Bin would add more – notably the latter's Arc of 1988. Rounding out a truly competitive nine-horse field were Celestial Storm (second in the St Leger) and Bourbon Girl (runner-up in both the English and Irish Oaks). The main absentee was Mtoto owing to the soft ground. Thus, pretty much all dues were paid to age, sex and nationality at the highest level – albeit with the notable exception of any French challengers.

Cauthen's task was to go where few had gone before. The number of King George winners who'd led from start to finish was no more encouraging than the number of all-the-way Derby winners. The roll call numbered just three, ironically all French, Match, Nasram and Pawneese. And despite being caught by Mtoto in the Eclipse, Cauthen set out with the same front-running, catch-me-if-you-can intentions. To beat this clutch of proven Group One rivals, Reference Point had to put them under the knife as early as possible.

Although the ground and the longer distance were unlikely to inconvenience Reference Point, the sight of him powering down the initial quarters to Swinley Bottom in 25.10 and 23.38 nevertheless appeared distinctly courageous on Cauthen's part given that Acatenango, Triptych, Sir Harry Lewis and Unite (the first meeting of current Derby and Oaks winners in England for 20 years and the first ever in a King George) were in close proximity and still on the bridle raised the possibility that Reference Point might pay for his pilot's gung-ho attitude. Yet quite the reverse ensued.

Reference Point had broken his opponents' hearts not his own. Having been given a breather through Swinley Bottom, the colt responded with a quarter in 24.30 when Cauthen asked for renewed effort between the six and four poles. Suddenly every opponent was under pressure. Finding acceleration in the mud is difficult enough without having that extra surge of energy drained in trying to keep up with Reference Point for a mile completed in an astonishing 1:38.92 – nearly four seconds faster than posted in Mtoto's victory on better ground 12 months later.

Acatenango was the first to run up the white flag; then Triptych. Every horse floundered when asked to attack the leader, who galloped on in tremendously game style to hold Celestial Storm by three lengths with the ultra-consistent Triptych a neck behind. The slow final quarter of 27.56 confirmed the Derby winner's gallantry; his last furlong exceeding 14 seconds was the slowest in recorded memory. The colt had met his moment of truth and passed it: the older generation had been humbled.

> I was a lot more confident than in the Eclipse. Ascot was a more suitable course: he needed some rising ground to shine, and the going was that much easier. With the trip being a mile and a half I was not chasing him up from the start. He was often on the 'wrong' leg in the Eclipse and I had to keep on getting at him. I'm not taking anything away from Mtoto because he was obviously a very good horse indeed. But Reference Point had taken a long time to get over the Derby and had only ten days' work beforehand. But at Ascot he was always bowling along happily and it was there every time I asked for it. They tried to lay up with me but couldn't. He jinked at something and became unbalanced early in the straight, but he soon got going again. When I gradually let him lengthen, he picked up and left them for dead. They just couldn't get near me.

'A breathtaking all-the-way blitz', enthused *The Life*. 'Bookies concede Point on St Leger,' it continued, as one spokesman for the industry was quoted as saying, 'We don't bet on potential disasters though we might open a market on how far he wins nearer the day.'

> It was great to see him show everybody what a great horse he was. He proved he was in the Dancing Brave class. That was

evident on a line through Triptych who was beaten into third by Dancing Brave the previous year and there was no better yardstick than her.

A routine victory from two opponents in York's traditional St Leger trial, the Great Voltigeur, brought 'Herbie', as he was known at Warren Place, to Doncaster a scalding odds-on favourite to collect his second Classic. Perhaps of greater significance to the sport than seeing a hot pot go through the motions was the fact that a very good Derby winner was bothering to turn up. Long ago someone coined one of the Turf's most enduring aphorisms: 'The fittest horse wins the Guineas, the luckiest horse wins the Derby, but the best horse wins the St Leger.'

However, had the anonymous sage been alive in the 1980s he might've felt obliged to revise his thinking because latterly it was more a case of the Leger being won by the horse closest to Derby calibre who deigned to show up. Since Nijinsky secured the Triple Crown in 1970, the only Derby winner to contest the Leger was Shergar in 1981; the fact that this great horse suffered defeat hammered another nail in the Doncaster Classic's coffin. There were a number of alternatives for animals being prepared for a tilt at the Arc or the autumn's increasing portfolio of lucrative middle-distance events: the Irish Champion Stakes; Preis von Europa; not to mention the three Arc trials run on the same weekend as the Leger. Moreover, perceived wisdom insisted modern breeders, commercial breeders governed by market trends rather than traditional owner–breeders, demanded speed not stamina. Winning the Leger, ran the canard, was the kiss of death for a colt's stallion prospects. To frank the point, Oaks winners with less to lose did participate: Dunfermline (1977) and Sun Princess (1983) completed the double between Meld and Oh So Sharp. There was even talk of reducing the Leger's distance or opening it to older horses in an effort to court the best Classic colts. Despite these assorted pressures, the 'Old Man of Doncaster' refused to die. It had received one boost from the Triple Crown-winning Oh So Sharp.

Now it needed the shot in the arm from a Derby winner of Reference Point's calibre.

On Doncaster's flat and sweeping track, the clock was always going to be in danger from a jockey like Cauthen on a runner like Reference Point – especially if the prevailing wind was behind the runners down the long back straight, as was usually the case when one blew. On Leger afternoon it proved to be a tent-ripper. The 11/4-on favourite was propelled to record early fractions as he led Dry Dock, King of Mercia and Mountain Kingdom that put him on target to better the electronically timed 3:03.53 race best set by Touching Wood in 1982. That's until a wind like a steam-hammer struck him as he turned back into the home straight. As it was, he still completed the final half a mile faster than the fillies in the Park Hill Stakes or the Mallard Handicap over the Leger trip.

> The St Leger was a comparatively easy race that put Reference Point spot on for the Arc. My biggest concern was the bits of newspaper everywhere and two or three times I had to duck and dive and pull him out of the various bits of trash. I picked him up three furlongs out and gave him a couple of slaps to make sure. I had a peep two furlongs out and saw Pat coming on Mountain Kingdom but I just kept squeezing. It was just a case of keeping him up to his work. If I'd really got at him, he'd have won by four lengths instead of one and a half. But with the Arc only three weeks away we were obviously anxious to give him as easy a race as possible.

The Leger marked winner number 147 of the season for Cecil, beating the record of John Day set in 1867; it rose to 180 by season's close at a phenomenal success rate of 40.4 per cent; and prize-money little short of £2m gave him his seventh trainer's title in 12 years. Reference Point was already earmarked for a place at Sheikh Mohammed's Dalham Hall Stud, which meant there was now only one conceivable target left for him: the Prix de l'Arc de Triomphe. Only

Mill Reef and Sea-Bird had won the Derby and Arc in the same season; but, tellingly perhaps, no St Leger winner had gone on to claim the Arc that same season. Nijinsky, most famously, was beaten a head; Crow and Sun Princess were other runners-up. Ironically, had the sinus problem not cropped up and Reference Point had gone to the Guineas and then achieved the Triple Crown, it was more than likely his season would've stopped at Doncaster. Victory in Paris, however, would seal the colt's place alongside the immortals. Hills and Corals installed him an even-money favourite.

Unlike several of his peers, Henry Cecil had no reputation for foreign piracy. Not even in the shallower waters of Germany or Italy. In a training career of 19 seasons, Cecil had won just 11 races outside his homeland by the afternoon of Reference Point's Arc – and then often owing to special circumstances. It was only thanks to their Italian owner Carlo d'Alessio, for instance, that Irvine annexed the Group One Premio Roma in 1972, Frassino the Gran Premio Citta di Napoli six years later, or Panjandrum the Premio Tevere in 1980. Even Ireland got the cold shoulder: only Cloonagh's victory in the 1973 One Thousand Guineas announced an interest – or, in truth, more the interest of his half brother Arthur Boyd-Rochfort, the filly's owner. However, even Cecil couldn't ignore France altogether. In 1981 Ardross, his prolific collector of Cup races, finished fifth in the Arc before following up with victory in the French St Leger, the Prix Royal Oak; and he only just went under by a head to Akiyda in the 1982 Arc. But perhaps Cecil was beginning to relax his strategy with encouragement from Sheikh Mohammed, now one of his biggest patrons and an avid fan of global competition. Only the previous year the Sheikh's El Cuite achieved double Group One success in the Premio d'Italia in Milan and the Prix Royal-Oak while Indian Skimmer had twice left her mark earlier in 1987; and Orban would give Cecil another Premio Roma a month hence.

Cauthen wasn't slow to appreciate Cecil's mild case of xenophobia:

> Henry was not a great one for travel; he'd rather stay at home and win the championship here. He didn't even want to run in

France. I'm not sure he grew to love travelling his horses but he did it because that is the way ahead. Travelling horses got so much easier that the barriers came down.

I love international racing for its ability to bring all the great people together in competition. With most races, the excitement is in the build-up, the mystique of the characters and then you've really got something. Everyone was very wary of the Breeders' Cup at first but anything that gives us a better idea of the true champions is worth a shot.

The Prix de l'Arc de Triomphe, however, tended to remain uncharted waters. It might be argued that prior to Reference Point Cecil simply lacked suitable Arc candidates beyond Ardross. Louis Freedman had already fielded one Arc hopeful in Attica Meli, sent over by Noel Murless back in 1973. If Cecil hadn't the ammunition to fire at the Arc before 1987, Freedman now armed him with an exocet in the form of Reference Point.

French distance races are infamous for being run at a crawl concluded by a sprint. The Arc bucked this trend. One or more of the leading lights were invariably aided by a pacemaker – and not one with the deliberate intention of acting as a tortoise. Reference Point's running profile was known well enough. Why gift him a 'soft' lead whereby Cauthen could orchestrate the rhythm he wished? Once it was announced the Aga Khan was running Sharaniya and Tabayaan besides his Prix du Jockey-Club winner Natroun the thought occurred that Reference Point might have company at the head of affairs, viz a 'spoiler' to provoke him into running too freely and expending energy too soon. But if Cauthen was presented with a blank canvas, how would he wield the brush? Few winners had ever made every metre to win an Arc: the nearest being Ribot, in the leading pair all the way, and Alleged, who took up the running after three furlongs in 1977.

To the English who flocked to Longchamp, there was little cause for any such reservations. Although recent trends in quality and prize-money had seen the Arc outstrip the King George in prestige, such was Reference Point's perceived superiority that the 1987 field of ten was the smallest since 1946 and he entered the stalls at 10/7-on. He'd soundly beaten his nearest market rivals, Triptych and Tony Bin, in the King George. Mtoto had missed Ascot because of the soft ground. Now it was firm. Could his renowned finishing kick outweigh Reference Point's relentless galloping as it had in the Eclipse? Odds of around 6/1 seemed a fair bet. The 'King of Lonchamp', Yves Saint-Martin, partnered the Prix du Jockey-Club winner Natroun at 5s; the colt he beat at Chantilly was on offer at 20/1 – but Trempolino, who'd turned the tables on Natroun when winning the traditional Arc trial for three-year-old colts, the Prix Niel, would benefit from the assistance of three-time Arc winner Pat Eddery.

Longchamp on Arc Sunday offers sharp contrast to Chantilly on Prix de Diane Sunday. The hardened turfistes of the Parisian suburbs are out in force for this race via buses departing at noon from every *arrondisement*. And freed by the low cost of entry to the 'posh' enclosures, these Parisians from the lower orders give loud vent to any owner, trainer or jockey who comes within range – before a race to warn what'll transpire if the said target doesn't do his bit to multiply their hard-earned cash and after the race if the warning goes unheeded. Even President Mitterrand received his fair share of heckling as soon as he was spotted. This riotous cacophony mingles with the pungent aroma of *touloussain* sausage to concoct a unique atmosphere once sampled never forgotten. Even the ever-growing influx of English *rosbif* weekenders fails to dilute the Gallic atmosphere. Cauthen, too, found Arc Sunday an intoxicating date in the Turf calendar.

> My favourite course was York, a big sweeping track, and I loved the atmosphere there. And in Europe it had to be Chantilly. But I loved Arc day at Longchamp the best: the atmosphere, the whole occasion.

Cauthen did not find much about this particular Arc day to remember fondly. The headline in the following morning's *Sporting Life* summed up his thoughts perfectly: 'Point Blank! Reference Point bows out so tamely.' The first paragraph of Geoff Lester's report went: 'Even the bravest soldiers can go to war once too often and sadly British champion Reference Point was gunned down on his farewell appearance.'

Cauthen had dragged the field along as was his wont. But entering the final straight the flame that always seemed to burn in Reference Point was extinguished like a candle in a wind tunnel. He was swallowed up in the manner of Pharaoh's chariots crossing the Red Sea, passed by horse after horse, including previous victims Tony Bin and Triptych and his own stable-mate Orban. But, most notably, by Trempolino, whom Pat Eddery shot four lengths clear in a matter of half a furlong to claim his fourth Arc with a new track record of 2:26.30.

How could this shattering upset have happened? It might be argued Reference Point's catch-me-if-you-can attitude was bound to take its toll eventually: his season got to the bottom of him and he just got dog-tired – pure and simple. Conversely, it might be argued, why change a winning gambit? But the official electrically recorded sectional times do suggest the fractions he and Cauthen reeled off in the Arc were verging on the superhuman: metric quarters of 27.10, 24.30, 23.00, 23.60 and 23.20 for ten metric furlongs in 2:01.20 had never before been clocked in an Arc. Track records were set in the Arcs of 1969, 1971, 1980 and 1986; the equivalent ten-furlong times in those four races were up to four seconds slower. More pertinently, none of those times was the work of an eventual winner. What we can say with certainty: if Cauthen had got it right and Reference Point had stretched away up the Longchamp straight in the manner of his racing profile their fractions would've raised the bar to heights beyond the reach of 99 out of 100 Arc winners.

Reference Point's fifth quarter looked the key fraction: 23.20 for the penultimate race quarter which passes through Lonchamp's so-called 'false straight'. According to Yves Saint-Martin (winner of four Arcs), the pace through this section of the race carries as much significance in determining the winner as the final quarter. 'Never ask your horse for an effort here or he'll crack halfway up the straight. It's here that visiting riders make a catastrophic error. It's because they start forcing their horses at this moment.' This lesson was soon learnt by French-based Cash Asmussen: 'If you go for home too quickly you are dead meat. In the false straight the good horses are trying to get a breather to get lucky for the finishing run.' Reference Point didn't get one. And just as Saint-Martin warned, Reference Point cracked.

Thus, Cauthen was in the rare position of having his pace judgement open to criticism. Yes, the ground was quick and exceptional fractions might be expected: Ashayer set a new juvenile track record for the mile in the Prix Marcel Boussac. And Reference Point had proved in the past he could still muster a finish off a strong pace. But in the Arc he couldn't. Usually fast Arc times epitomise a close Arc finish: less than five lengths covering the first six. In 1987 the figure was almost 11 lengths. Quite simply, Cauthen and Reference Point had burnt most of them to a frazzle: the final quarter of 25.10 was the slowest quarter of the race bar that from the gate. The Reference Point of Derby Day might well have repelled all boarders. But the cutlass was not there on Arc Sunday.

Some 32 years later Cauthen acknowledges the points hiding within those Arc fractions. But he's unrepentant. It was a question of needs-must.

> I'd not beat these good horses without setting the pace I did. I'd got done for foot in the Eclipse and I had to try and test them all. I was happy enough early on. We were going better than Natroun's pacemaker, Sharaniya, and I was able to dictate the pace. But as soon as we straightened up we had trouble fighting off the Aga Khan's second string Tabayaan, let alone the good horses, and we had nothing left.

André Fabre, Trempolino's trainer winning the first of a record eight Arcs by 2019, confessed to being unsurprised at Reference Point's demise: 'He's a great horse. But the Arc is the Arc and you cannot cram too much into one season. You cannot beat the horses every day.' In other words, to be sure of winning an Arc in the autumn one must make it the season's number-one target and not the post-script to a tough campaign that began in the spring. Mill Reef and Dancing Brave got away with it. But they'd not contested a St Leger three weeks beforehand.

> Maybe horses I rode that had a chance, like him, were always running in the Arc as a bit of an afterthought. You have to train for that race specifically. It has to be the aim from about half-way through the season. And you do need a lot of luck in the Arc, particularly if it's an open year. It's only different when you get a horse of class and speed like Dancing Brave who can take a handy position anywhere the jockey wants. But not winning an Arc was my greatest disappointment in Europe.

Whether or not Cauthen had erred in setting too fast a pace on Reference Point was a debate rendered null and void following a post-race examination of his mount by veterinary surgeons: it looked as if he'd cracked a bone in his near fore; subsequently the colt was found to have an abscess in his foot that had triggered an infection extending into his leg. Whether before or during the race was impossible to say. A fighting fit Reference Point may well have justified Cauthen's pacemaking. As it was, he'd gone out on his shield.

Whatever the precise cause of Reference Point's disappointing display, his early gallop had set up another track record following that in the Eclipse and the record hand-time for the Derby. One suspects only the adverse conditions prevented Reference Point clocking track records at Ascot and Doncaster. Even so, he retired having recorded the fastest-ever opening six furlongs in an Arc (1:14.40); one mile in the Eclipse (1:37.43) and Arc (1:38.00); and the fastest ten furlongs in a Derby (2:09.20) and the Arc (2:01.20); plus the quickest extended ten furlongs in the St Leger (2:14.28). The clock certainly took a bashing when Cauthen got Reference Point on a roll. Unfortunately, the colt's zest in the stallion shed never replicated his vim and vigour on the track: his only Classic winner being Ivyanna in the

1992 Oaks d'Italia. However, some honour was salvaged: Reference Point still headed the 1987 International Classification 1lb above Trempolino; *Timeform* put the difference at 4lb and awarded him a rating of 139.

> The only race Reference Point struggled in was the Arc, when he wasn't right. Other than that he never ran a bad race. In the Eclipse he met Mtoto, a damned good horse, an older horse, and at that stage of the season an older horse has an advantage. The King George field was very strong and he proved that day that on the right track over the right distance he was a very talented horse. He was a real superstar horse. He was one of the best I rode, no doubt.

Cauthen's 1987 season concluded with a race every bit as fascinating, and enervating, as the Arc. He and Pat Eddery engaged in a see-saw struggle for the jockeys' championship. In mid-September they were still locked together like a pair of mating adders. By the end of the month Eddery had inched ahead; a fortnight later Cauthen was three to the good. The duel would go right down to the last afternoon at Doncaster on 7 November. Willie Carson put his own unique twist on their exhausting scrap: 'Whoever comes out on top, both men will be winners. They have played their replay and even some extra time. It is now down to penalties. And even then it will probably go to sudden death!'

> There was a real rivalry but only because we both wanted to win and Pat was the main guy because he was a great rider, had the Abdulla stable behind him and he could do just about any weight. His agent was getting him all the outside mounts he could, so if you wanted to try and do it, he was the guy you had to beat.
>
> I'd done it once when I was still with Barry, then sailed away with it in 1985 riding for Henry. And in 1986 I finished second

to Pat, so I was determined to get back on top. It was different from what I'd been used to in the States, in terms of the driving, but I'd been over for a few years by then and I was used to it and the two countries were the same in that you ended up taking rides from people you didn't know on horses you didn't know at weights you wouldn't normally do. You push yourself and it wears on you because it's a long season. Pat could do 8.3 or 8.4 whereas I was struggling to do 8.7, so he had a few more opportunities than I did and it was obviously a bit more of a struggle for me than it was for him. I was riding all of Henry's and going everywhere for spares. I remember one day going up to Edinburgh where I'd only been a couple of times in my life and I couldn't find a sauna. I was running around trying to find a hotel where I might least be able to get a hot bath and lose a couple of pounds and finally found one and got it done. But it was a crazy summer.

At the start of the last week Cauthen still led by three; the bookies made him 2/1-on, with a tie, replicating that between Steve Donoghue and Charlie Elliott in 1923, on offer at 4/1.

Both men rode a winner at Lingfield to make the score 192 to 189 in Cauthen's favour, but an Eddery treble to Cauthen's single at Leicester on the Tuesday reduced the gap to just one. The action then switched to Edinburgh, where Eddery struck on Hopping Around to level the scores and Valtaki in the last to nose ahead for the first time in three weeks as Cauthen's four mounts all ran unplaced. Thursday involved the comparatively short journey westward to Hamilton. The pendulum swung back to Cauthen: a double for him; no joy for Eddery from six rides. Friday meant the long haul down to Doncaster for the final, debilitating two days of a campaign which had sprung into life on the self-same Town Moor over seven months earlier. Cauthen won the sixth race on Cecil's Proud Crest but a frustrating second and third is all Eddery could accumulate and he went into the last day lagging by two.

The battle leaps from the racing pages to the front page as the two 'knights of the pigskin' prepare for the deciding joust. Once Cauthen brought the 11/1 shot Vague Discretion from last to first to win the nursery by a head the pressure on the defending champion begins to soar. Neither man features in the next two finishes. Eddery now needs to win on all last three chances to force a draw. He rides the favourite in the three o'clock; and romps home on Night Pass. In the next he's on the little Irish filly Vilushi, while Cauthen partners the grey Padre Pio. Two furlongs out, Vilushi moves into the lead but the Eddery body is not at a confident angle. For half a furlong or so Eddery holds the pack at bay. Then it brushes Eddery's championship hopes aside. It's Cauthen's title: 197 to 195.

> At the end of 1987, I was 'cooked', absolutely knackered. I'd literally lived horses 24 hours a day, seven days a week, for eight months. And no matter how much you enjoy it, too much of a good thing can be bad for you.
>
> You must have tunnel vision to become champion jockey. You must almost block everything else out. I not only had to battle with Pat but also with my weight and myself. I won that battle. This was the hardest battle I had ever been through. I learnt a great deal about myself. I am a fighter and a survivor. I guess I'd always vaguely known this. You never know what you can do until you do it. It was a great time but it was the season that stopped me from going for the championship ever again. It took me three months to recover. I had too much of a weight disadvantage to do it all over again; I was likely to kill myself if I tried. I decided it was better for me to be as right as I could be for the big races.
>
> It was fun, like any good rivalry or any great race, and sometimes, even if you don't win, it's very satisfying. Pat really did me a favour, though. With him challenging so hard, I never let up and never stopped thinking about racing. Reference Point

winning the Derby gave me a thrill but this was a really great moment for me.

It was the tightest margin of victory to the championship since Scobie Breasley beat Lester Piggott by one in 1963 and Freddy Fox rode two winners to Gordon Richards's single on the last afternoon to snatch the title by a similar wafer-thin margin in 1930. How tight the duel had been may be gleaned from one October day when Newmarket was abandoned owing to high winds and Cauthen hit the road to Catterick for two rides while Eddery stayed put: Cauthen notched a double that proved to be his margin of victory on 7 November.

'Cauthen takes crown from weary Eddery,' ran a typical headline. 'A beaming grin that spread from ear to ear broke out on the boyish American face,' continued the report in *The Times*. 'Beside that, Irish eyes were not smiling but betraying the effects of a vain attempt to come first in a contest that had sapped every ounce of energy from his drawn body over the longest eight months of his and his conqueror's lives; nearly a thousand rides each – and the whole issue was settled with just one race left of a season neither will forget.'

The dethroned champ was a man of few words; riding thoroughbreds to win races they had no right to was his preferred means of expression. But on this occasion he proved quite effusive: 'Steve's a great guy but that stopped once you got on the track. I've never been bitter with anyone in my life, but when I was out there it didn't matter who it was against. There's no friendship when you're out to win. I did miss a couple of days most weeks by riding in Ireland but I still had 150 more rides than Steve. And travelling was easier for me. I was lucky because I was able to afford my own plane and be home for dinner. Steve usually had to drive. I gave Steve a lift in the plane lots of times. We went to Edinburgh, stayed in a hotel and had dinner together that night – and the next day he came out and done me! That's the way it was all year.'

Cauthen's respect for the champion he'd usurped was palpable – both as a jockey and a man.

Pat was without question the best jockey I rode against. He was a natural. He couldn't tell you how he did it, but he just knew how to do it. The kind of guy who you could beat in a Group One and he'd be happy for you but be figuring out how to beat you in the next race.

It's hard to say what made him so good, but horses just seemed to run for him. He could ride horses in all kinds of ways. I don't think he over-thought things, he just had a talent to work out how to ride a horse, whether that was from the front or dropping them in. It was all feel to him, a natural feeling He always seemed to be in the right place, gave them plenty of chances and got them to finish well. He was also a strong finisher, had good hands, great timing and they ran like crazy for him.

I felt somewhat fortunate because I had a lot of ammunition, but after that Pat rode a double hundred and he was champion 11 times – and that says it all. I felt so sorry for Pat. After such a long battle, after such a tight fight, one of us had to win. It could so easily have been him and I appreciated his sportsmanship. Neither of us would've liked the idea of finishing second but it wouldn't have been the end of the world. One title does not mean a thing. You have to judge over a longer period than that. All it proves is that a guy rode maybe one more than the other and that does not necessarily make him any better.

The season had proved beyond wildest dreams for Warren Place. The stable won more than £2m in stakes, 27 Group races of which seven were at the highest level, and a new domestic record of 180 winners at a staggering success rate of 40 per cent. Delight was tinged with disappointment for Cauthen. He regretted not to have passed the magical 200 mark which had proved such an insuperable barrier to every champion jockey in the post-Gordon Richards era. Doug Smith (168), Scobie Breasley (179), Piggott

(191), Carson (182), Eddery (176), Mercer (164) and now his own 197 constituted the highest championship-winning total of the seven individuals concerned – although Smith recorded 173 when second to Richards in 1947 and Eddery had just got within five of the double ton. However, racing's ever-increasing internationalism insisted both Eddery and Cauthen had breached the 200 barrier by making up the shortfall with victories abroad – Cauthen via three Group One successes in France alone. This was nothing new: Piggott achieved a global 200 in 1966 and again in 1970 when he added no fewer than 43 wins in France to the 162 in England.

The days of a purely English-oriented champion like Richards had long gone. Nevertheless, a domestic double-century remained a coveted prize. With helicopters increasing a jockey's ability to ride the two meetings a day that evening fixtures had introduced, the 200 barrier was brought within reach. When Eddery finally joined the 200 Club in 1990 he became only the fourth to do so in 130 years; in the ensuing 29 years a feat for so long viewed as beyond the reach of all bar the exceptional would be achieved by no fewer than six jockeys – one of whom (Jason Weaver) did not head the list. In truth, the jockeys' championship seemed to become something of an anachronism owing to tinkering with its criteria: the traditional season bookended by the Lincoln and Manchester November Handicaps, for instance, was replaced by a shortened season beginning at the Guineas meeting and concluding at a newly instituted PR venture called 'British Champions Day' at Ascot in October.

The marriage of Cauthen's pace judgement and Cecil's training methods ensured we'd not have long to wait before another galloping machine appeared on the scene. As a juvenile, this colt was a 'sleeper' like Slip Anchor rather than a champion in the Reference Point mould. His dam was a two-miler called Cockade, a sister to the Two Thousand Guineas winner High Top. His sire was Sadler's Wells, a son of the outstanding sire Northern Dancer and winner of an Eclipse and Irish Two Thousand Guineas, who was on course to become the stallion sensation of the 20th century as its final decade unfolded. He'd eventually be leading sire on no fewer than 14 occasions and overtake the 18th century's Highflyer at the top of the all-time list; among his 12 English and 14 Irish Classic winners were the champion filly Salsabil and the Derby winner Galileo – destined to continue his father's dominance as a stallion in the 21st century. Cecil ran the strapping bay son of Sadler's Wells twice as a two-year-old, winning a mile maiden at Haydock by six lengths in the second of them. The sight of this colt pounding his rivals into submission became commonplace once he commenced his three-year-old campaign in 1989. This colt was Old Vic.

It's fair to say the emergence of Old Vic as the champion middle-distance colt of 1989 caught both Cauthen and Cecil by surprise. Even after Old Vic had begun to show his hand in 1989, Cecil was still talking of him as nothing more than 'an improving horse with quite a good future' who might possibly take in the Derby Italiano, very much toward the bottom of the totem pole when it came to European Derbies. Warren Place reckoned it housed a handful of colts holding superior Classic prospects. Old Vic quickly kicked such negativity out of the window by stringing together an unbeaten sequence of five races by 2 July by an aggregate of 27½ lengths. And this quintet did not include the Derby Italiano but did include both the French and Irish Derbies.

The first couple of victories that had failed to enthuse trainer and jockey came in a minor event at Newbury and the Guardian Classic Trial at Sandown. The third arrived in another traditional Derby trial, the Chester Vase. Here we saw a different Old Vic. At Sandown he'd been held up and ridden to win from a furlong out. At Chester, wearing Sheikh Mohammed's second colours in deference to the Stoute-trained favourite Warrshan, he'd take the lead fully five furlongs from home. Judging pace around the Roodeye's flat one-mile bowl amounted to fried chicken and gravy to an American jockey. Cauthen allowed Child of the Mist to cut out an early gallop two seconds up on handicap pace before unleashing Old Vic. The colt responded with one of only two mid-race quarters in a middle-distance race at the three-day meeting below even time to settle the outcome. A further quarter at around even time allowed Old Vic to cruise the final furlong yet still break the track record. The runner-up, Golden Pheasant, was beaten two and a half lengths – months later he deprived Nashwan, the Guineas, Derby, Eclipse and King George victor, of his unbeaten record in the Prix Niel.

> Old Vic wasn't that big but he was well-balanced and he handled Chester really well. He was a real out-and-out tough stayer who needed a good pace and I got a nice lead. But when he tried to take a breather, I decided to go. We thought he'd be right for one of the lesser Derbies and then the St Leger.

As Old Vic's stable-mates with Derby pretensions fell by the wayside, it was clearly time for a re-think. Chester spelt out two things: without question, Old Vic was up to Derby standard; but, second, he'd sustained sore shins on the fast ground and shouldn't be risked unless there was some give in the ground. The colt's training regime as the Classic neared consisted of swimming in the BBA pool at Newmarket. A spell of dry weather cast the deciding vote. Epsom had to be missed. Instead, Sheikh Mohammed paid £18,500 to supplement Old Vic into the Prix du Jockey-Club where the ground held greater promise of being easier. Nevertheless, it needed considerable overnight rain to transform the Chantilly ground from firm to good to soft by Sunday afternoon for Cecil to finally commit Old Vic. English punters could not believe their good fortune when they saw Old Vic available at a generous 47/10 in a field of 12, with Galetto (favourite on account of his five-length win in the Prix Lupin), the unbeaten Dancehall and Louis Cyphre all preferred in the betting.

Anyone prophesying another one-horse race like the Lupin was correct so long as they didn't identify Galetto as the animal in question. Old Vic put his rivals to the sword in the manner of King Hal thanks to as clinical a display of front-running jockeyship from Cauthen seldom witnessed – not just in the Prix du Jockey-Club but in any European Derby. No English-trained colt had ever returned with the French Derby. If the French-bred and owned Gladiateur had been the 'Avenger of Waterloo' when winning the 1865 Derby, Old Vic most certainly redressed the balance in 1989. He vanquished the French as ruthlessly as Henry's band of brothers at Agincourt. 'Cecil and Cauthen mastermind the Chantilly revolution: Old Vic brings the house down as French heads roll,' trumpeted the front page of *The Sporting Life*. Daniel Lahalle continued: 'Old Vic and Steve Cauthen broke the French monopoly in the Prix du Jockey-Club in a style which left their rivals shell-shocked.'

Cauthen's mental chronometer had operated to the nano second. After disputing the lead for a metric furlong, he'd edged Old Vic across towards the rail from his wide draw by the time they passed the chateau at the end of the back straight. Cauthen then proceeded to wind up the pace. The first kick came off the final bend and it left his pursuers struggling. The severity of the examination Old Vic was setting may be assessed from the sectional times. He completed the metric ten furlongs into the home straight in 2:03.37, which was up to five seconds faster than other marks for the Classic on similar ground. Cauthen wasn't finished. He gave the screw one more turn. Old Vic quickened away through a penultimate furlong of 12.14, which amounted to the *coup de grace* in the soft ground. Dancehall and Galetto were left gasping in vain pursuit. Old Vic could afford to admire the scenery as he galloped out the last 200 metres. Despite his early pace he still completed the last quarter faster than recent winners Mouktar and Natroun. The margins of victory were seven lengths and eight lengths; and for Dancehall, good enough to take the Group One Grand Prix de Paris on his next start, this constituted a sole career defeat. We'd just witnessed a Derby annihilation to rank alongside those of Shergar and Troy at Epsom or Shahrastani and Assert at the Curragh – and even evoke O'Kelly's tribute to Eclipse: 'Eclipse first, and the rest nowhere.'

> We went to France thinking we had a chance. But that was the day he showed what he was. We had luck with the rain. The horse liked the ground and was in perfect condition. I thought

'Bug Boy'. (Getty)

The image of 'Stevie Wonder' destined for the cover of *Sports Illustrated*. (Getty)

The 'Six Million Dollar Man' and his 'Two Million Dollar Horse'. (Getty)

Homage to Walton's favourite son: a mural in 'Steve's Pub'. (Author)

Rene Williams's bronze captures perfectly the aerodynamic Cauthen seat on Affirmed in full cry. (Steve Cauthen)

Barry Hills and his new jockey dogged by reporters. (Getty)

The first winner of the 'English Odyssey' is unsaddled at a soggy Salisbury. (Getty)

Two influential bosses confer: Sheikh Mohammed and Robert Sangster. (Getty)

Tap On Wood completes a fairy-tale start in the Guineas. (George Selywn)

A favourite Cauthen memory: Susan 'The Sheila' Sangster leads in Gildoran after his Gold Cup success. (PA)

'With master Cauthen's compliments—a mint julep and Kentucky fried chicken'

A majestic Cormorant Wood comes away in the Benson & Hedges. (George Selwyn)

Time Charter sublime in the Coronation Cup. (George Selwyn)

Old allies reunited on the Newmarket gallops in 2003. (Racing Post)

Oh So Sharp's Triple Crown starts with the narrowest of wins in the Guineas.
(George Selwyn)

But continues with a facile victory in the Oaks.

(Racing Post)

The affection of jockey for his partner is there for all to see before completing their Triple Crown at Doncaster.

(George Selwyn)

Indian Skimmer ready for the fray at Longchamp. (George Selwyn)

Slip Anchor in splendid isolation in his Derby. (George Selwyn)

Cauthen becomes the first jockey to win the Derby and the Kentucky Derby. (Getty)

Reference Point repels all borders in his Derby. (Getty)

Poetry in motion: flat back and toe-in-the-iron to the fore on the best horse Cauthen rode this side of the Atlantic. (Getty)

Cauthen and Eddery: the best of rivals. (Racing Post)

Old Vic powers away to win the Chester Vase. (George Selwyn)

Pebbles making history in the 1985 Eclipse. (Racing Post)

The 'Iron Lady' struts her stuff in the Coronation Cup. (George Selwyn)

In The Groove bags the Juddmonte International.

(George Selwyn)

Whoosh! Never So Bold spread-eagles his field in the July Cup. (George Selwyn)

The 'Cadillac Colt'.

(George Selwyn)

Arazi back to his imperious best in the Rond-Point. (George Selwyn)

A pensive jockey aboard Alnasr Alwasheek at the gate for what will be his last Derby.

(Author)

he would win but the opposition was not very good. Nobody ever wanted to make the pace over there, so I did. I was able to dictate it and he just kept quickening and quickening through the stretch and won very impressively.

All of a sudden Old Vic was a champion. I certainly never knew it before. After his first two races at Newbury and Sandown I thought he was a very nice horse but he never gave me the feel he was going to be the horse he turned out to be. If we'd gone to Epsom, we wouldn't have beaten Nashwan, not on that track. Second or third was the best we could have hoped for. But I would have had a chance of beating him with the situation in our favour not his.

That 'situation' did not materialise at the Curragh. Following his Derby victory, Nashwan went for, and achieved, the Eclipse-King George double. And as it turned out Old Vic very nearly didn't line up for the Irish Derby either. The Newmarket training grounds continued bone hard and his exercise in the four weeks between the French and Irish Derbies was restricted to swimming and the all-weather strip. For the second time Old Vic's participation in a Derby depended on the ground possessing some juice. The decision was always going to be made late – and was further complicated by the colt developing a warble on his back the day before the race. 'It's still growing,' Cecil told the Press. 'It's in the worst possible place, on the side of the tack just where the saddle goes, and won't come out for a day or two. We couldn't use medication, so we kept on poulticing it.' Sheikh Mohammed was keen to run. Victory in Europe's richest Classic (£321,491) would continue his lucrative sequence in the season's Irish Classics as he'd won both Guineas courtesy of Shaadi and Ensconce. Old Vic was declared to run just minutes before the clock ran out. The well-watered ground rode 'good'; and the warble was protected by the insertion of two circular shaped sponge pads under the saddle.

The Curragh is a bleak 12 square miles of green County Kildare grass, 25 miles south west of Dublin close to Newbridge and Naas. Many of

Ireland's premier trainers are based there, within hailing distance of its premier racecourse. Bleak it may be. But Old Vic lit up the Curragh like a firecracker as Cauthen repeated the successful tactics of Chantilly virtually to the last pip.

Opposition to the 11/4-on favourite was limited and had also crossed the Irish Sea. Isle de Nisky, fourth in Nashwan's Derby, was second best at 5s and would provide a decent form line between Nashwan and Old Vic. Supporters of Zayyani, who held out some hope on the strength of his second to the Derby third Cacoethes in Royal Ascot's King Edward VII Stakes yet was primarily of interest because his great grandam was no lesser figure than Petite Etoile, might be accommodated at twice those odds.

The contest, which in the strictest sense of the word it was not, may be best summed up by the headline in *The Life*: 'It's Old Vic all the way and earns ovation.' Cauthen allowed Old Vic to dominate and they gradually increased the tempo for a spectacular stalls-to-post display reaching its crescendo with a pulsating stretch run that saw him pass the post four lengths clear of Observation Post.

The three half-mile fractions revealed the quickening pace: 51.15 seconds; 50.94; and 48.99. The first half-mile was run nearly three seconds slower than the previous year's renewal, but the next half-mile, on the stiffest section of the track, was nearly three seconds faster as Cauthen began the process of engaging Old Vic's higher gears preparatory to opening the throttle at the top of the straight. Old Vic was motoring so smoothly as he passed the two pole that he broke 11 seconds for the ensuing furlong down the incline. Consequently, the last furlong proved no more than a procession, with Cauthen merely flicking hands and heels – and yet it still exceeded the equivalent fraction standing to recent winners Kahyasi, Sir Harry Lewis and Shahrastani.

> Every day leading up to the race was good. But we got there and he had this big boil, a warble, on his back. You almost couldn't put a saddle on him. It was touch and go if we were going to run

until somebody came up with the idea of trying really thick pads with the part over the boil cut out. The boil was niggling Old Vic when I first got on his back, as he started jogging. But the moment we went to canter to the start, he was fine. The race was pretty much the same deal as the French Derby. He controlled the race and won very impressively again.

Michael Seely observed in *The Times*, 'Another classic performance from Old Vic, showing the courage of a lion, combining speed and stamina of the highest calibre. And another superb display of front-running tactics from Steve Cauthen, who became the first jockey to win the Kentucky, Epsom, French and Irish Derbies.' It was further noted that Sheikh Mohammed's monopoly of the season's Irish Classics had now brought the Maktoum family success in seven of the 11 Classics thus far held in England, Ireland and France – which by the season's close would become eight from 15 thanks to Alydaress registering Sheikh Mohammed's fourth Irish Classic of the year in the Irish Oaks. To form students, however, the result shed some light on the respective merits of Old Vic and Nashwan. On a line through Ile de Nisky, Old Vic came out one pound inferior to Nashwan. Some, however, preferred Old Vic's Chantilly form to Nashwan's at Epsom: *Timeform* calculated him to be 1lb superior to Nashwan at 136.

> I always rated Old Vic. He was a great galloper. But I had the highest respect for Nashwan and it would've been very exciting had they met on our terms – a good track and on decent ground.
>
> The four Derbies have different appeal. But each was exciting in its own way and now that I'd won them all, my main ambition was to land the Arc.

Old Vic's attempt at achieving that ambition for Cauthen in 1989 came to nought. He missed the King George owing to a pulled muscle (though the firm ground would've scuppered that outing anyway) and a bout of coughing ruled out both the Arc and a possible transatlantic raid on Canada's Rothman's International. Cauthen picked up a spare ride on Derby third Cacoethes in the Arc but they finished way behind Carroll House.

Nor would Old Vic get to Longchamp in 1990. His seasonal debut was delayed until the Hardwicke Stakes at Royal Ascot. The best part of a year off the track could account for the rustiness that saw him finish only third to the 50/1 shot Assatis and his Irish Derby victim Ile de Nisky. The 17lb turnaround in the form with the latter signalled how much leeway Old Vic needed to recover if he was to be a viable contender for the King George. In the absence of a suitable warm-up race, he was given a racecourse gallop at Newbury to bring him on; but his greatest foe would again prove to be Mother Nature. Ascot's surface was as dry as the Karoo. Cecil agonised. He walked the track on the Saturday and five minutes before declaration time gave Old Vic the go-ahead. It's fair to say he wasn't sure if he'd made the correct decision: 'The last time I walked a course was before The Minstrel's King George in 1977,' he said lugubriously. 'I opted to let Lucky Wednesday take his chance and he broke down.'

Old Vic didn't break down. Nor did he win the King George. But the one quality he never lacked was intestinal fortitude. In losing this King George by a neck, after making all the running on ground as unhelpful to him as could be, Old Vic produced a display of guts beyond most thoroughbreds. But who knows the scars it left.

The identity of Old Vic's nemesis proved ironic: it was his own stable-mate, the three-year-old Belmez. And Belmez had come out of retirement to do so. After elevating himself into Derby contention by winning the Chester Vase on 8 May (from the eventual Derby winner Quest For Fame), Belmez was found to have injured his near-fore tendon and was 'retired'. Searching for a stallion position rather than a comeback race became the priority. Within a few days, however, the colt's future was revised. He might be able to race again. Six weeks later he ran third in the Irish Derby to Salsabil. Belmez hadn't just rolled away the stone in the manner of Lazarus, he'd now smash it to smithereens in the King George. Old Vic didn't even get to wear Sheikh Mohammed's second colours; Cauthen wore the distinguishing white cap because the Sheikh's number-one candidate was the André Fabre-trained Coronation Cup winner, and favourite, In The Wings ridden by Cash Asmusson – leaving Mick Kinane to wear the third colours on Belmez, the solitary three-year-old in the 11-horse field.

Old Vic's task appeared to be aided by the inclusion of a pacemaker running on behalf of Cacoethes. Cue Sod's Law. Limeburn missed the break entirely. Recognising the only option left open to him, Cauthen seized the initiative and pushed Old Vic into the lead. However, the tactics that had proved so successful at Chantilly and the Curragh, as well as here in the 1987 King George on Reference Point, would come unstuck.

The hand-clocked sectional times Cauthen posted on Old Vic are instructive; and, though viewed with the benefit of hindsight, suggest Cauthen was pushing his luck. A slower opening quarter was to be expected with Limeburn out of the equation: Old Vic clocked 25.80 seconds. Then Cauthen got down to business. Old Vic rattled into Swinley Bottom with a quarter of 22.70 to reach the mile post in four seconds, up on Nashwan's pacemaker the previous year on similar ground. As the hare continued to lead the hounds a merry dance, he unleashed another quarter in 23.64. The half-mile Old Vic had just completed in 46.34 likely proved critical. Even though it was covered largely on the descent, expending this amount of energy so far from home with much of the remaining six furlongs on the rise might tax the fittest of animals. Was Old Vic sufficiently battle-hardened after one run in 12 months? And, even if he was, could he do himself justice on ground he loathed?

Cauthen was pursuing the same strategy as he had aboard Reference Point in the Arc. He'd scant option. If Old Vic was going to prevail he had to run the finish out of the 'closers'. He pounded on. He completed one and a quarter miles in 2:03.14 – still two seconds ahead of Nashwan's running time. But it saw him approach the end of his tether. Cauthen had out-run everyone bar Belmez. The two Cecil animals went at it hammer and tongs, Old Vic on the rail and Belmez on his outside. Neither gave an inch. Belmez got his nose in front – only for Cauthen to switch his whip into the left hand. Sifting through the dregs of Old Vic's reserves, he found some hidden grains of true grit to grind back an advantage. But that scorching gallop had to tell. The strength drained out of every part of Old Vic's body, except his heart. It was inevitable he'd give best to his younger rival at the end of a prolonged slugging match cruelly verified by a final furlong of 14 seconds that bore comparison with the card's Ladies race. Old Vic went down, colours flying, by a neck. A shattered Cecil was reported to be disappointed that the finishing order was not the other way round.

Although Belmez went on to win the Great Voltiguer (beating the St Leger winner Snurge) en route to the Arc, Old Vic was always going to be Cauthen's choice of mount at Longchamp. However, he wasn't seen again on a racecourse until 3 September, when Cecil galloped him over ten furlongs at Nottingham in company with Shellac prior to his Arc prep in the Prix Foy ten days later.

> The ground was only just good enough for him, and with that in mind I asked as much as I could without overdoing him. But he still finished five lengths clear of his galloping companion.
>
> He'd given us a lot of thrills and was kept in training by Sheikh Mohammed specifically for the Arc and Breeders' Cup Turf in mind with the hope the ground would be good at that time of year. But it was a really dry summer and it was difficult to keep him going. He ran a brilliant race in the King George and we were hopeful things were building up for a successful autumn campaign. He was a different horse when he had his ground and half the battle is being able to train the horse day in and day out so he gets his confidence by cantering on decent ground.

Alas, Old Vic missed both prep and Arc. Moreover, Cauthen had to suffer the mortifying sight of the one race he still coveted being won by a colt that until four months before had been his ride. Charles St George sold

Saumarez in May for a reported $400,000 to an American partnership, and though Cauthen (who'd won twice on him already) was able to ride the colt to six-length success in the Group One Grand Prix de Paris for his new stable, he was obliged to partner Belmez at Longchamp – better fancied in the market despite bruising a foot two days beforehand. They finished fifth, beaten around five lengths. Belmez really had delivered Cauthen a 'double whammy'. Not content with depriving him of another King George, he denied him the opportunity of that elusive Prix de l'Arc de Triomphe. As far as Cauthen was concerned, this really was the Arc that got away.

Old Vic's racing days were done. And like Reference Point he was a disappointment at stud. That is, on the Flat. As a sire of jumpers his tenacity and sheer bloody-mindedness reaped magnificent dividends. His progeny included Gold Cup and dual King George winner Kicking King and two Grand National winners in Don't Push It and Comply Or Die. He was also champion jumps sire in 2007/08 prior to his death in 2011.

Cecil's last English Classic winner for Cauthen came from an unlikely source – and at an unlikely venue. Michelozzo won the rearranged 1989 St Leger at Ayr; and in so doing raised Cauthen's tally of English Classics to ten – passing Danny Maher's total as the leading American rider on the all-time list.

The St Leger was only the fourth race Michelozzo had run in his life. Although he was by the Champion Stakes winner Northern Baby, his stars were aligned with the St Leger. He was a first foal of a French middle-distance performer who was a half-sister to El Cuite with whom Cecil and Cauthen had won the 1986 Prix Royal-Oak – the French version of the Leger. And one member of this family, Moon Madness, had already won the Doncaster Classic in the 1980s. Michelozzo did not run at two. The handsome bay did not make his debut until April 1989 when he won a minor event over an extended mile at Nottingham by ten lengths. His owner, Charles St George, was never shy of pitching his horses into the highest company. Consequently, for Michelozzo's next race to be the Group Two Princess of Wales's Stakes at the Newmarket July meeting caused few murmurs of surprise. Ridden by Paul Eddery, he ran creditably, beaten just over three lengths into third by the future Prix de l'Arc de Triomphe winner Carroll House. Michelozzo was getting the hang of things and announced himself as a Leger contender with a decisive victory under Cauthen in Goodwood's March Stakes over the Classic's 14-furlong distance. Then fate took a hand.

On the opening day of the St Leger meeting, four horses fell in two separate incidents but at the same point in the Doncaster straight. Racing was abandoned owing to subsidence, possibly connected with the coal workings that surrounded Town Moor. The 213th St Leger was transferred to Ayr on the following Saturday. Cauthen had won two renewals of the Scottish Derby at Ayr, on Prince Roland and Jalmood. Could he add victory in the first genuine Classic ever held in Scotland?

Dame Fortune had rolled her dice in Cauthen's favour. In transit up the A1 to Doncaster, two nails had been driven into Michelozzo's foot when he spread a plate; the resultant abscess would've ruled him out of the Leger. The extra week was a reprieve – and simultaneously removed two dangerous rivals in the shape of Oaks winner Aliysa and the Derby third Cacoethes who were saved for the Arc. After the abscess was cut out and drained, Michelozzo was sound again by the Wednesday and flown up to Ayr. His exercise had been confined to swimming. A positive sign, as it transpired: it had begun raining at Ayr. One and a half inches drenched the track over the next three days, turning the ground soft; had the Leger been run at Doncaster as scheduled the ground would've been good and far less comforting for Michelozzo.

With his two main threats out of the reckoning, the principal danger to Michelozzo appeared to be the filly Roseate Tern, the only runner with Group One-winning form through the Yorkshire Oaks; she'd also beaten Michelozzo's stable companion Alydaress by one and a half lengths in the Ribblesdale – thus giving Warren Place an idea of what Michelozzo had on his plate at Ayr. The remaining six runners hadn't a prayer. An opinion not lost on the punters who piled onto Michelozzo and forced his price in from 9/4 to 6/4.

PACE MAKES THE RACE

Michelozzo proceeded to win like the 'good thing' he clearly was. The rain clouds cleared just in time for the 15,000-strong crowd to follow the runners down the back straight led by Terimon's pacemaker Skisurf. Swinging wide into the long Ayr straight, Roseate Tern, Sapience and Terimon all held as good a chance as Michelozzo. Cauthen was unflustered. Relishing the soft conditions, Michelozzo took up the running passing the two marker and a furlong inside 12 seconds was quite sufficient on the prevailing ground to put him well clear. He galloped merrily on to an emphatic success by eight lengths (whilst easing up) from Sapience, who'd won the Ebor Handicap carrying just 8st 4lb on his previous start. Poverty of opposition or its inability to act on the ground doubtless had something to do with Michelozzo's wide winning margin, yet few English Classics have been secured so categorically; one had to go back to St George's Bruni and his ten-length success in 1975 to find a Leger won by more. The colt had given Cecil his fourth St Leger and Cauthen his third.

> Michelozzo was still a bit weak. He was very lazy in the race. But he came back on the bridle turning for home. What settled it is that he could both stay and quicken in that ground. He loved that ground, and I felt he was improving.

St George quickly scotched any possibility of him stumping up £30,000 to supplement Michelozzo into the Arc. Both he and Cauthen considered the colt too immature for the inevitable dog-fight Europe's toughest race always engendered. Michelozzo was put away to await 1990. Cauthen believed Michelozzo would make up into a fine prospect at four. Unfortunately, he was wrong. Michelozzo did not take his chance in the Arc after a winless five-race campaign that yielded nothing better than second place in the Ormonde Stakes at Chester in the spring and fourth in the Prix Royal-Oak in the autumn. Michelozzo was subsequently transferred to John Hammond in France where more opportunities on his favoured easy ground might be forthcoming. After winning a couple of races he was repatriated with

Richard Hannon, winning an apprentice handicap at Chepstow in July 1992 (for a *Timeform* rating 18lb below his 1989 figure of 127) but running without success the following season at the age of six.

Michelozzo was a 'sleeper' in terms of Classic potential akin to Slip Anchor and Old Vic – one totally at odds with a juvenile champion like Reference Point. There were other Warren Place champion juvenile colts for whom Cauthen entertained stronger hopes of Classic success than the unexposed Michelozzo. The quartet of Sanquirico, High Estate, Be My Chief and Peter Davies, for instance, promised the earth yet crumbled to dust. Between them, these four colts won all 19 of their races at two years old, which included 11 Group races – two at Group One level. At three years of age, by contrast, they mustered just ten outings and scraped one misery success. Misfortune did play its part but never was Cauthen better able to rue the maxim 'some you win and some you lose'.

> The thing with two-year-olds is your opinion alters as the year goes on, simply because the young horse can change so much. It's like kids. All of a sudden they spurt up two feet seemingly overnight, and you don't even recognise them. At the outset all your geese are swans. They haven't let you down yet. So if you're not optimistic then, you never will be. Tell me a joke and I'll probably forget it in five minutes. But most things about horses I remember. And it was always interesting to look back, say five months later, and see whether I was right, wrong or way off target.

High Estate experienced the greatest misfortune. Sporting the famous 'black, red cap' colours of nonagenarian Jim Joel (son of South Africa's diamond king, JB Joel), his four-length win in the 1988 Royal Lodge Stakes followed wins in the Coventry, Champagne (the Goodwood version) and Solario Stakes to earn him top spot in the Free Handicap and a *Timeform* rating of 127. However, in gaining that Ascot success he'd split a near-hind pastern – and on recovery was never the same horse. Intended comeback after intended comeback came and went: missing the Dante and the Predominate at Goodwood put him out of the Derby picture. Victory in a three-horse minor event at Newcastle was the sum total of his three-year-old career, which ended with him running eighth of 11 in the Champion Stakes and saw his *Timeform* rating drop to 116.

While High Estate was racking up his five wins in 1988, the Classic prospects of St George's Sanquirico were brutally exposed in the Craven and Dante. His *Timeform* rating dropped 15lb from the 126 earned by five wins built around the July Stakes, Solario and Royal Lodge of 1987. In 1990 another St George runner excelled at two: the flashy white-socked chestnut Peter Davies won all three of his races, culminating in the Group-One Racing Post Trophy (formerly the William Hill Futurity) over a mile at Doncaster. *Timeform* put him on 120 – with a 'p' that denoted 'likely to make more than normal progress and improve on this rating.' Two abject displays in 1991 suggested he was rather a plodder and he was sold.

Be My Chief also had the 'p' beside his 123 rating in 1989. He was a bay son of American sire Chief's Crown out of a mare representing the highly productive female line descended from Pretty Polly. He belonged to Peter Burrell, the great nephew of Pretty Polly's owner Eustace Loder, and his six wins at two included the Champagne at Goodwood, the Solario and the Racing Post Trophy. The colt proved the kind of lazy yet resolute galloper once rousted that provided meat and drink to a jockey unafraid of making his own pace. It's worth dwelling on the fractions posted by Be My Chief in two of his Group victories because they illustrate the pivotal role played by Cauthen's pin-sharp judgement. Despite the stiff uphill nature of the half-mile from the Goodwood stalls, Be My Chief posted a sabre-rattling 49.32; a quarter of 23.01 round the bend into the straight completing six furlongs almost three seconds quicker than the fixture's two other contests at the seven-furlong distance. The race was over; the juvenile track record broken. The colt's final start came in the Racing Post Trophy which, owing to Doncaster's problem with subsidence, was moved to Newcastle. Conditions were horrendous, with storm force winds battering the track. Cauthen utilised the tail wind in the straight to spring right away from his four rivals after rounding the turn. Asked to really extend passing the three pole, Be My Chief lengthened immediately to record furlongs of 12.05, 11.55 and 11.95 which, despite the lack of challengers, amounted to a finale easily surpassing that of the card's nursery. Be My Chief appeared certain to feature in the 1990 Classics. But the only 'Classic' he contested was the Scottish version at Ayr in June; he finished out of the money. The firm ground that prevailed in 1990 was said to have made training the colt difficult. The trip to Ayr was Be My Chief's solitary outing as a three-year-old – and the last of his career.

> Be My Chief proved the biggest let-down because we were excited about him over the winter, but he never really got going as a three-year-old, nothing seemed to go right for him. With High Estate we were more excited on behalf of Jim Joel than anything else because he'd got another good horse. Peter Davies may have got lucky at that early stage in his career. He was a strong galloper who stayed on well and the Racing Post Trophy suited him more than the others. I don't think we figured out his best distance as a three-year-old; he was kinda one-paced.
>
> It's not uncommon for some juveniles to be flattered by what they achieve in the autumn. Barry had a colt called The Noble Player who earned a high rating after running placed in the Royal Lodge and Grand Criterium in testing conditions. To my mind he was never an exceptional horse – and I've good cause to forget him. I had to ride him in the Derby for Barry – which cost me the winning ride on Teenoso!
>
> None of these came close to Reference Point at two. He was the best of Henry's juvenile colts for sure. But some top three-

year-olds are never heard of at two. Slip Anchor was a perfect example of that. I did ride one wound up with a higher rating than Reference Point – Storm Bird back in 1980. But that was only a late pick-up ride at the Curragh for Vincent O'Brien. I was happy to get the chance, though, to be honest, I was more excited about the fact I was riding one for Vincent! Storm Bird didn't feel like a superstar on the day – he won easily enough but he was no jet rocket.

The best juvenile filly I got to partner was another outside ride – Forest Flower from Ian Balding's in 1986. She broke her maiden at Newbury but I was never able to get back on her afterwards. She went to the Queen Mary but there was no guarantee I'd not have to ride for Henry; same story in the Cherry Hinton. It was just one of those unfortunate things. Funnily enough, I was also offered the ride on her great rival that year, Charlie Nelson's Minstrella.

As far as Cauthen was concerned, the descendants of Pretty Polly both 'giveth and taketh Away'. The disappointment of Be My Chief was offset by the improvements with age shown by other scions of the Pretty Polly family in Paean and Shavian, half-brothers who ran in the apricot silks of Lord Howard de Walden. The pair were related to Be My Chief through their mutual grandam My Advantage. There 'endeth' the pedigree common ground. Paean was by the St Leger winner Bustino, an influence for stamina; Shavian was by Lord Howard's very own Kris, more an influence for speed.

Second on his only race as a juvenile, Paean improved to win four of his seven races in 1986, the last over the two miles-plus of Newmarket's George Stubbs Stakes in October. Testing conditions seemed to bring the best out of him. And the Royal Ascot of 1987 couldn't have turned out more to his liking than if Lord Howard himself had instructed the heavens to do his bidding. The two and a half miles of the Gold Cup would take some getting thanks to torrential rain throughout the week. Cauthen had been due to partner Bonhomie in the feature race but once he surveyed the conditions he had no hesitation in swapping Sheikh Mohammed's colt for Paean, who came into the race after finishing second on his first stab at Group company in the Sagaro Stakes. A flood of money poured on Paean, shortening his price by eight points to 6/1 at the off.

One must say the field wasn't the Gold Cup's finest: the single Group One winner was Authaal (from Shergar's only crop to race) who'd won the Irish St Leger. Cauthen's new mount loved every squelching furlong; others didn't. Cauthen brought Paean home by 15 lengths in a time 11 seconds slower than standard; his final quarter run in splendid isolation, taking almost 30 seconds. Such a crushing margin of superiority hadn't been witnessed in living memory. 'Runaway Paean is a Walden Wonder,' declared *The Sporting Life.* Hopes that Paean would go on to prove he was more than a soft-ground 'wonder' by adding the Goodwood and Doncaster Cups were dashed immediately when it was discovered he'd bowed a tendon.

By 1990 Ascot's St James's Palace Stakes had been raised to Group One, which enabled Cauthen to deliver Lord Howard a second at the Royal Meeting courtesy of Shavian. The handsome bay colt also provided Cauthen with an opportunity to demonstrate the art of winning from the front before the Queen. And just for good measure he proceeded to advertise the extent of his tactical acumen by landing the fillies Group One equivalent, the Coronation Stakes, 24 hours later by deploying the reverse – he laid off the pace.

Shavian had endured a difficult start to his second season. Training setbacks and third place in the Craven saw him miss the Guineas; fourth in the Predominate Stakes behind stable-mate Razeen ended any hopes of a campaign over middle distances. Then he began to improve at home. His opportunity of a Group One over a mile beckoned in the St James's Palace. But, on the book, he'd have his work cut out to cope with Anshan and Rock City (third and fourth in the Guineas), Royal Academy (runner-up in the Irish Guineas) and the improving Lord Florey – who went off the odds-on favourite on the strength of his recent success in the Heron Stakes at

Kempton. Cauthen immediately hustled Shavian to the head of affairs and brooked no argument. Shavian's initial half-mile of 49.15 was little below the best-ever on the Old Mile, and a third quarter in even time maintained the pressure on rivals now flying distress flags. Conversely, on Chimes of Freedom in the Coronation, Cauthen was calmly assessing the moment to slip the leash from the filly after six furlongs completed almost two seconds slower than the St James's Palace. Predictably, the respective last quarters confirm the contrasting race rhythms. Cauthen had to pull out all the stops on Shavian to hold off Rock City; the ordeal lasted 27.90 seconds. Chimes of Freedom, however, was yet to be slipped into overdrive, and when Cauthen engaged the turbo she undercut her stable-mate's fraction by 1.65 seconds. Yet it still contrived to look a doddle.

Shavian's next target was the Sussex Stakes (Group One), highlight of 'Glorious Goodwood'. Shavian started favourite but failed to cope with the pair of older horses, Distant Relative and Green Line Express. Cauthen reeled off three cracking quarters in or below even time but he couldn't shake off his main pursuers and finished a game third. Just over three weeks later, Shavian returned to Goodwood for the Celebration Mile. In the Sussex it had taken Shavian a furlong to reach the front. On this occasion Cauthen fired him out of the stalls like an ink pellet from a schoolboy's ruler. The fractions Cauthen posted, on ground stated the same good to firm as the Sussex, were within pips of those clocked in the Sussex: 23.20 versus 23.50 for the opening quarter; 24.80 v 24.34; and 22.40 v 22.14 for the next pair. There was no one of Distant Relative's class stalking Shavian this day and Cauthen was able to let Shavian coast the last quarter. This renewal of the Celebration Mile had written itself into the history books as a pace-setting masterclass from Cauthen – endorsed by *Timeform* stating Shavian's time-rating to be the best recorded by a three-year-old all season. Thanks to Shavian's application and Cauthen's 'Rolex', Lord Howard's colt had earned himself a stallion career at the Brook Stud in Newmarket.

Although the stream of top-class animals from Warren Place showed no signs of drying up, there were inklings that the old guard was changing.

Cecil's marriage was crumbling; Julie Cecil would leave Warren Place to set up her own training operation – and take a number of valued staff with her. The ranks of Cecil's owner-breeders that had supplied tailor-made Classic prospects year upon year were also thinning out. In 1990, for example, Jim Joel was 96 years old; Lord Howard was 78; Louis Freedman 73. Their interest could only begin to wane. As a result, Cecil increasingly marched to the beat of a new drum, that of the new order: Arab owners which, at Warren Place, meant Sheikh Mohammed who held the greatest numerical hand.

The Sheikh may have only been the third son of Dubai's ruler, but by 1990 he was 'King' of the English Turf, having led the owners' table for the past five seasons. He wanted the best jockey extant to be on his horses – of which there were plenty spread all over Europe. Cauthen had partnered some exceptional Cecil-trained horses for the Sheikh. Now Sheikh Mohammed wanted Steve Cauthen to be available for all his 600-odd horses that were spread amongst the likes of Cecil, Michael Stoute, John Gosden, Guy Harwood, John Dunlop and Barry Hills in England, John Oxx in Ireland and André Fabre in France. And what the Sheikh wanted he invariably got.

On 17 August 1990, Cauthen confirmed racing's rumour mill had been functioning smoothly by announcing he'd been offered the plum job of number-one European jockey to Sheikh Mohammed. The retainer was reputedly worth £750,000 per annum. Nothing was formally signed until October. The prospect of climbing aboard prime racing cavalry whose quality ensured higher weights meant he could view the scales with a Nelsonian eye, banish all thoughts of chasing the jockeys' championship and concentrate all his energies on the grand stage – and, what's more, postpone any thoughts of retirement.

As the 1991 season got underway Cauthen laid out his stall for the Press before racing at a chilly and windswept Brighton on 28 March: his weight was pretty good, at 8st 9lb, only a pound over his usual riding weight; he wouldn't be killing himself to win the championship; or riding Sheikh Mohammed's horses trained by Luca Cumani on a regular basis as Frankie Dettori was the latter's contracted rider; John Hanmer would continue trawling the form book on his behalf, but it was in his interest to familiarise himself with all the Sheikh's horses; and, lest there be any doubt, when it came to making a choice the final decision was always his alone.

Cauthen then went out to ride his first winner for his new employer, driving the Gosden-trained colt Full Cry to a hard-earned success in a humble £2,000 maiden race. The new show was on the road. The Cecil era was history.

If Benjamin Disraeli really did state 'There are three kinds of lies. Lies, damned lies and statistics' – which has been questioned – any notion of coining an eternal sound-bite wouldn't have occurred to him. However, when it comes to the view that the Cauthen years at Warren Place spawned the most successful relationship Henry Cecil enjoyed with a stable jockey, the statistics tell no lies. During Cauthen's six seasons as Warren Place's retained rider, the yard won four trainers' titles and he contributed 26 Group Ones, 14 of them Classics, at home or abroad. By contrast, Lester Piggott brought two titles and he rode nine Group Ones, including two Classics during his four seasons; Joe Mercer's four seasons saw two titles secured while he partnered two Classic winners and five other Group Ones; Pat Eddery's five-year link with Cecil coincided with one trainers' title and he rode nine Group Ones, with three of them Classics; the three Fallon years yielded two runner-up spots in the trainers' list and he mustered six Classics and five others at the top table. The nearest comparable period of success came during Tom Queally's association with the yard (2008 to 2013) when he rode 21 of the 22 Group Ones achieved but just the single Classic; with third place being the highest finish in the trainers' table. Yet, as if to prove Disraeli correct, those figures were massaged by the proliferation of Group Ones now available and the not insignificant contribution of Frankel, who provided Warren Place with ten of them.

The scope of his new retainer ensured Cauthen would still ride for Cecil on occasion. But the purple period when this marriage made in Turf heaven swept all before it was now a thing of the past. It belonged to the Ages and the historians.

FIVE

'IS STEVE AVAILABLE?'

THE MARK of Cauthen's rehabilitation and assimilation was the clamour for his services. Although plentiful acclamation came in the media, Cauthen needed no reminding how fickle praise from that source can be. Those words of Woody Stephens were a constant reminder of how suddenly a jockey may find it's 'toilet time'. But the most tell-tale expression of Cauthen's universal acclamation came in the plethora of mounts constantly being offered to John Hanmer, who must have turned down more rides than chambermaids turn down bedclothes.

Cauthen had never been starved of choice 'spare' rides from other stables. Sharpo, Time Charter, Diamond Shoal and Sun Princess, to name just four examples rated 130 or above by *Timeform*, typified the procession of equine stars requiring Cauthen's assistance before he arrived at Warren Place. With Cauthen's star constantly on the rise, the list grew longer and longer: colts of the international calibre of Never So Bold, Strawberry Road and Acatenango; and, especially, a dance card replete with fabulous females led by Pebbles, Triptych, Miesque, and In The Groove.

The impact a Cauthen ride for an outside stable might exert on a horse's future was exemplified by his association with Horage in 1983. The colt was a resident of Mattie McCormack's small yard in Lambourn; to be frank, a struggling stable that had only sent out six winners in the previous two seasons. Horage cost a paltry 8,000 guineas as a yearling but proceeded to win nine races off the reel as a juvenile, from humble beginnings at Ayr,

'IS STEVE AVAILABLE?'

Pontefract and Salisbury to the rarified heights of the Coventry Stakes at Royal Ascot, the July Stakes at Newmarket and the Gimcrack Stakes at York. Such precocity isn't always a positive augury for a successful three-year-old career. And that's what the colt's seasonal debut at Thirsk suggested when he was soundly beaten at odds-on. His entry in the St James's Palace Stakes at Royal Ascot thus appeared windmill-tilting of the most optimistic kind and he was sent off the 18/1 outsider of seven. But Cauthen was in the saddle – and he gave the huge crowd a masterclass in opportunistic jockeyship and the art of 'waiting in front'. He went for broke from the gate, quickly establishing a lead over the Guineas second and third Tolomeo and Muscatite; then he slowed the tempo to enable Horage to fill his lungs before dashing him into a four-length lead rounding the bend into the straight. Tolomeo closed but only reduced the deficit to a head. The reports were of one mind: Cauthen had 'excelled himself'. Horage ran three more times but never won again. He retired to the Ballygoran Stud. That single Group success as a three-year-old painted him as more than just a precocious juvenile and assured him of a stallion career. This lucrative future, it's fair to assert, came courtesy of some mesmeric Cauthen sleight-of-hand at Ascot.

This same scenario was played out again in 1987 with Risk Me. The colt was trained by Paul Kelleway, a man, like Clive Brittain, not noted for diffidence when it came to pitching his horses into the deep end without a life-belt. On occasion, however, Kelleway's representative proved an adept swimmer: Swiss Maid won him the 1978 Champion Stakes and three years later Madam Gay won the Prix de Diane. Kelleway adopted a typically high-flying strategy with Risk Me by running him in five Group Ones as a three-year-old (plus the Lockinge and St James's Palace Stakes that would be so designated later on). Cauthen partnered Risk Me a lot of the time; together they won the Greenham Stakes first time out in 1987. But at the highest level Risk Me was usually found wanting thereafter.

At the end of the season the colt was retired to stud at a fee of £10,000. This profitable future derived in no small measure from his success in the Group One Grand Prix de Paris, which owed everything to an inspired ride from Cauthen. Risk Me had managed to snatch the spoils in one French Group One by worrying Soviet Star out of the recently elevated Prix Jean Prat. But the colt's victory in the much more prestigious Grand Prix de Paris, for which Kelleway had to supplement him and in which he started an unconsidered outsider in a field of nine, was truly spectacular. The early pace in the ten-furlong event was typically French: pedestrian. No jockey was more dangerous in these circumstances than Cauthen. Sizing up the situation in a flash, he shot Risk Me into the lead and quickly stole a couple of lengths on the field which he increased by kicking off the final bend to win by four easy lengths. Toiling in Risk Me's wake was the Prix du Jockey-Club second and future Arc winner Trempolino. Thanks to Cauthen's masterly enterprise, Risk Me's supplementary entry fee was vindicated and his future as a stallion assured.

However, the most eye-catching outside partners in this lengthy list of 'spares' were the classy females. Cauthen was 'a ladies' man'. When he was free to escort an aristocratic filly bereft of her usual beau, John Hanmer's phone was apt to ring.

Cauthen's successful partnerships with Warren Place horses owned by Sheikh Mohammed put him in pole position to pick up the mount on one filly with credentials to surpass those of Cauthen favourite Oh So Sharp. Cauthen's citing Oh So Sharp as the best filly he rode on account of her versatility and her penchant for never doing more than was necessary to win is understandable, but in the same season as Oh So Sharp's Triple Crown he rode Pebbles, whom the formbook suggested was a mite superior.

Pebbles was trained by Clive Brittain initially for her breeder Captain Marcos Lemos, one of his oldest patrons for whom he'd won the 1978 St Leger with Julio Mariner. She was a bright chestnut with a pronounced splash of white running down her face by the sprinter Sharpen Up out of La Dolce, trained by Brittain to win a handful of races up to a mile and stay well enough to finish fifth in the Oaks. Pebbles began a relatively busy juvenile campaign of six races as a 33/1 shot in a Sandown maiden but progressed via successes at Newbury and Newmarket to running fourth in the Lowther

'IS STEVE AVAILABLE?'

Stakes and second in the Cheveley Park to the Cauthen-ridden Desirable. Pebbles exacted revenge on Desirable in the One Thousand Guineas, beating her just over three lengths into third. Then Sheikh Mohammed waved his chequebook and bought her for a reputed £3m.

The two races Pebbles was able to compete in for her new owner in 1984 went begging. The Irish Guineas winner Katies beat her in the Coronation Stakes and, following a lengthy lay-off owing to stepping on a stone which led to bruising a sesamoid, she returned to duty by running a good second to Palace Music in a track-record renewal of the Champion Stakes. Brittain assured the Sheikh he could improve Pebbles by 10lb were she kept in training. The owner agreed. And Brittain was true to his word.

Brittain had not only read the book on persuading older fillies to produce their best form, he'd also helped to write it. Like Barry Hills, he'd come into racing at the bottom; he'd spent 20 years as a stable lad with Noel Murless. Like Henry Cecil, he was aware of his old mentor's reservations concerning older fillies showing their best form after the midsummer of their fourth year. But Brittain also observed how Petite Etoile, Aunt Edith and Lupe had been kept sufficiently sweet to win Coronation Cups and a King George. 'Sir Noel's secret was to keep them in training all the time, not to let them down at all and to keep the discipline going,' he explained. 'He had a knack of understanding fillies. Petite Etoile was coltish and could be very difficult to control. Lupe, for instance, would not eat. She was the worst "doer" I have known. He knew she was not eating but he kept her going, coddled her and kidded her. You can't put pressure on a filly. They often run their best race after their worst gallop – and vice versa. A really bad gallop from a filly does not mean the same as with a colt.'

Brittain reckoned he possessed one of Angel Penna's 'great ones' in Pebbles. He set out to break the ridiculous Press talk of an Eclipse hex on fillies based on none having won the race since its inception in 1886. Nor had he forgotten how Murless tended to give fiery animals a gelding as a soothing companion. Thus it came to pass that Come On The Blues became Pebbles's paramour for the 1985 season. 'Pebbles was a very feminine type and had no coltish tendencies whatsoever. Fortunately she liked to walk so to keep her going it was just a matter of getting something with an equal stride pattern. As Come On The Blues, known as "The Minder", was also a good walker they walked together, and developed a real affection for each other.' The great Hungarian mare Kincsem, undefeated in 54 races, never went anywhere without her pet cat; Allez France bonded with a sheep; Pretty Polly with a cob. But Pebbles, like Mumtaz Mahal, the speed queen of the 1920s and ancestress of Petite Etoile, found love with a gelding. The pair became inseparable, just a grille separating their boxes through which they could keep in touch, figuratively and literally. He'd always accompany her to the races – where Brittain had other tricks up his sleeve to prevent a nervy sort like Pebbles boiling over during the preliminaries. Appearances in the paddock were avoided by resorting to various ruses such as a 'loose' shoe; and the obligatory parade for Group One events tended to be ducked – on one occasion by Brittain collapsing in a heap on the ground to let her 'escape' his clutches and canter away to the gate on her own while the rest did their duty.

'Pebbles retains her old dash,' declared *The Times* after Cauthen had ridden her to a smooth length-and-a half victory over Vacarme in the Trusthouse Forte Mile at Sandown on 26 April. 'A superb exhibition of speed and class.' Brittain had not intended she run so early in the season but reported his string to be in such good order that she was almost pleading to race. Her schedule for the first half of the campaign was to be the Prince of Wales's Stakes at Royal Ascot followed by the Eclipse and King George. The first of the three races provided one of the sensational results of the year. Pebbles went off at 5/4 behind the odds-on favourite Commanche Run in a four-horse race; she short-headed the former Leger winner but was beaten fair and square by the 33/1 'no-hoper' Bob Back. Cauthen had been confident of her ability to handle anything thrown at her: he was happy to lead or tuck in ready for a late thrust. But Pebbles was particularly fidgety going to post. And when she was driven to peg back Commanche Run, it was Bob Back who found the acceleration to sweep past them both on the outside. We'd soon know whether this was a fluke result because all three were due to contest the Eclipse – with the addition of Rainbow Quest, the winner of the Coronation Cup.

The 1985 renewal of the Eclipse Stakes signalled the passing of 100 years since Bendigo inflicted upon Derby winner St Gatien one of his only three defeats in the inaugural running of 1886. The one and a quarter miles Eclipse is the oldest of England's all-aged championships for middle-distance horses and introduced rich prizes to the calendar. It was the first 'Ten Thousand Pounder', albeit in recent years its reward being challenged and overhauled by races such as the King George VI and Queen Elizabeth Stakes. The Eclipse roll of honour read like an encyclopaedia of the turf, from Triple Crown-winning Diamond Jubilee in 1900 to modern greats Mill Reef and Brigadier Gerard. Sponsorship from Benson and Hedges and then Corals had ensured the financial bait was still sufficient to attract runners from the top drawer. Yet in all its 100-year history the race had never fallen to a female. One of the Turf's true greats in four-time Classic heroine Sceptre was run out of it by Triple Crown-winning colt Rock Sand in 1903; hot favourite Park Top was trapped on the fence to be denied victory in 1969; and in the two most recent renewals Stanerra and Time Charter both met late trouble in running that did for their chances. In truth, relatively few females had tried to win the Eclipse. Murless tried and failed; had he run Petite Etoile perhaps she'd have removed the stigma but she never ran in it. Thus was born the myth of an Eclipse 'jinx' on the fairer sex . The list of failures, as Cauthen well knew, included Cormorant Wood. But, fine female though she was, Cormorant Wood was no Pebbles.

> Pebbles won the Sandown Mile like a real star and I thought she'd take all the beating from then on. I was really looking forward to riding her. But at Ascot she didn't give the same super-charged feeling: she was found to be in season. I rode her work eight days before the Eclipse and knew we were back in business.

Drama struck the race even before the runners entered the gate. Commanche Run spread a plate and pricked his off-fore hoof in the process; although he went down to the start he was found to be lame and withdrawn. Rainbow Quest headed the re-formed market at 5/4-on with Pebbles at 7/2. However, the colt was denied the assistance of his favourite partner because Pat Eddery was claimed by Vincent O'Brien to ride at Phoenix Park. Eddery's replacement was Alain Lequeux, who'd ridden Rainbow Quest to be third in the Prix du Jockey-Club; but Rainbow Quest never had won, and never would win, in the hands of any other jockey but Eddery – and with Eddery aboard he'd later win the Arc. The colt's trainer, Jeremy Tree, who had sought permission from the stewards to have his colt mounted on the track, had to watch him behaving so unruly throughout the parade that the matter was referred to the Disciplinary Committee of the Jockey Club. Out the corner of his eye Tree doubtless spotted Brittain dipping into his box of tricks on behalf of his own potentially fractious performer. He kept her tinder dry by hiding her in the dope box on the pretext of attending to a loose shoe until the runners began cantering to the start – whereupon she tagged along at the back. 'We broke all the rules but we never defied them,' explained Brittain somewhat disingenuously. 'There's a subtle difference. If you ask for permission and they say no then you've broken them. If you don't ask for permission and you bend them, it's up to them to find you out.' Suffice to say, Jeremy Tree was not amused.

Although Rainbow Quest had a pacemaker it seemed from the stands that August's role was to slow the pace so that his stable-mate might win with the kind of late sprint that had secured the Coronation Cup. If that was the plan it was a short-sighted one. Pebbles had won a Guineas. If it came to a speed-duel there was no certainty the colt would out-sprint her. Clockwatchers know that the critical race-deciding phase of a middle-distance race at Sandown comes between the three and the two markers: the furlong after the field has straightened-up and before the Sandown hill begins to bite. After August had completed the opening half-mile in a pedestrian 53.75 (almost five seconds slower than Cauthen would clock on Reference Point on similar ground two years later) the significance of that critical furlong became instantly apparent. Which jockey would blink first?

Cauthen was ready and waiting. Tracking August into the straight, he sent the message down the reins passing the three-furlong pole and Pebbles replied in a trice. She tore through the next 220 yards in a lightning burst of speed timed at 11.17 seconds, the fastest on record for the race. She'd got first run on Rainbow Quest and it settled the outcome. Cauthen administered one precautionary tap of the whip and could then afford to sit as still as a superannuated tortoise up the rising final quarter, which Pebbles still covered in a record 25.11: a sub-26 final quarter is a rarity at Sandown. Rainbow Quest could never mount a challenge and was beaten two lengths. 'Pebbles Ends Male Domination in the Eclipse,' boomed *The Times*. 'Pebbles floors colts,' said *The Sporting Life*.

> I was always confident she'd win that day. Rainbow Quest was a strong stayer, a true mile-and-a-half horse, running with a pacemaker. I'd ridden him in the past and thought that over ten furlongs I'd have him over a barrel. I used his pacemaker for my own ends, sat where I wanted to sit. Probably I got to the front sooner than I'd planned but she was travelling so good I didn't want to wait any longer. When I kicked it was all over.

The plan for Pebbles was a trip to Chicago for the Arlington Million on 25 August – good news for Cauthen who'd be available to ride. Unfortunately for him, the enterprise failed to materialise. Something began ailing Pebbles; she went off her food. Brittain prescribed a dose of Doctor Rest and Nurse Sunshine until such time as the filly told him she was ready to come back to the fray. Pebbles convalesced for over three months. When she returned for the Champion Stakes on 17 October she required a new jockey: Cauthen would be on Slip Anchor for Cecil. Pat Eddery proved the lucky man who guided Pebbles to an imperious three-length victory over Slip Anchor. More gloom for Cauthen descended when Brittain stated

Eddery had demonstrated such a rapport with Pebbles that, harsh though it was on Cauthen, he'd keep the ride when Pebbles contested the Breeders' Cup Turf the following month. That the second running of the Breeders' Cup was scheduled for Cauthen's old stomping ground of Aqueduct only darkened the bruise. Pebbles would be negotiating no fewer than six bends on the tight seven-furlong turf track in her first attempt at one and a half miles. And no one knew those turns better than Cauthen.

Cauthen did go to Aqueduct: he picked up a more than decent spare in the Breeders' Cup Turf on Strawberry Road. Now a six-year-old, Strawberry Road had been the champion three-year-old in Australia over middle-distances with ten wins from 14 starts that included a Guineas and a Derby; at four he added a WS Cox Plate. Coming to Europe in the summer of 1983, he won a pair of Group Ones, the Grand Prix de Saint-Cloud and Grosser Preis von Baden, before running a creditable race in the Arc to finish fifth behind Sagace – well ahead of trusty yardsticks in Sun Princess and Time Charter. Cauthen was all too aware the horse he had to beat at Aqueduct was Pebbles, and he instantly gave chase when she sprinted clear along the fence coming off the last turn. Valiantly though he and his horse tried, she'd a neck more than they could pull back in the stretch he knew so well. Pebbles returned a new track record of 2:27 seconds dead. It was intended to keep Pebbles in training for another year with tilts at the 1986 King George and Arc in mind, but she damaged cartilage in her shoulder and had to be retired in July. Her *Timeform* rating of 135 stamped her the best filly Cauthen rode during his English Odyssey.

> I'd wished she'd gone to Chicago for the Million because she'd have hacked up. And, of course, I lost the ride in the Champion Stakes to Pat because I'd to ride Slip Anchor.
>
> How good was Pebbles? With a good pace in front of her she was a champion. I tried to stretch her on Slip Anchor and couldn't because she was that good. And just look at what she did in the Breeders' Cup Turf. She found three-lengths more

trouble than I did and she still won – although if Teleprompter hadn't swung wide and let her up the rail I might've won that race on Strawberry Road instead of just failing to catch her. But Pebbles was an exceptional filly.

The next female gifted with Cauthen's co-operation was already in action when Pebbles retired, but she'd not be in receipt of the gift for two more years. And, like Pebbles and Indian Skimmer (leaving aside the one-race, losing, link with Miesque), she has the credentials at least to dispute Cauthen's view that Oh So Sharp was the best filly or mare he ever rode.

Triptych may have been the greatest race-mare Cauthen ever had anything to do with. She was known throughout racing as the 'Iron Lady'. And with good reason: for to talk about a horse like Triptych one has to start with the numbers. They alone describe how great a racehorse she was without any recourse to subjective attachments. Once the latter is applied, Triptych's extraordinary, and ultimately tragic, life stirs the emotions and tugs at the heartstrings. That emotion bypasses sentimentality. Eros had reached into his quiver once more and loosed an arrow that pierced the breast of every Turf romantic. We were in love again.

Triptych's career statistics are sufficient to make Noel Murless shake his head in a mixture of wonder and admiration. She ran 41 times in six different countries over five seasons for earnings totalling more than £1.5m. Only two of her starts came out of Group company and she missed the frame on just seven of those 41 outings. She won on 14 occasions – nine of them (seven at Group One) coming beyond Murless's critical benchmark that was the June of her fourth year. All told, she accumulated nine wins at the highest level. Her dance card featured 15 different suitors: a veritable Who's Who of international greats from Yves Saint-Martin and Gérald Mossé to Shoemaker, Cordero and Pincay. It was almost a badge of honour for a jockey to display on his silks if he'd been accorded the privilege of dancing with the 'Iron Lady'. As a juvenile in France she was partnered by Alain Lequeux; as a three-year-old in Ireland it was Christy Roche who had the pleasure; once she was returned to France for her last three seasons her steady date was Hong Kong champion Tony Cruz. But that failed to stop Triptych dallying with Steve Cauthen, who rode her three times and won twice.

A cursory glance at Triptych's pedigree is enough to reveal the source of her amazing durability. Her sire may've been the French champion miler Riverman, but it's said courage and tenacity comes from the dam. Triptych's dam was Trillion, whose nine wins from 32 starts included the Group One Prix Ganay and a clutch of others in Group class. She also ran second in ten Group Ones that included an Arc and a quartet of Grade Ones across the Atlantic. Trillion's own dam, Margarethen, won 16 times in no fewer than 64 starts. Triptych raced in the colours of Alan Clore, son of retailing tycoon Sir Charles, renowned throughout the business world as a 'corporate marauder'. When Alan Clore shelled out $2.15m for the yearling to be named Triptych he could be quite sure he was getting a filly with a family tradition to live up to. She didn't disappoint.

Triptych was sent to the stables of David Smaga in France. She won two from three, the last being the Prix Marcel Boussac – the Group One that led to her being rated the top European juvenile filly of 1984. For her Classic campaign she was transferred to David O'Brien in Ireland. It amounted to an equine blitzkrieg: Triptych contested no fewer than five Classics in eight weeks. She ran seventh in the English One Thousand Guineas under Pat Eddery; with Christy Roche in the saddle she beat the colts in the Irish Two Thousand – the first filly to do so; finished fifth in the Irish One Thousand one week later; ran second to Oh So Sharp in the Oaks before taking on the colts once again in the Irish Derby, coming fifth. After a blissful eight weeks' rest she finished behind Commanche Run and Oh So Sharp in the Benson and Hedges Gold Cup, but afterwards ran her most disappointing race to date, beating only one home in the Phoenix Champion Stakes. Any suggestion of fatigue, however, was pushed aside: Triptych followed her mother's hoof-prints to North America where Bill Shoemaker rode her to be third in the Rothman's International at Woodbine.

'IS STEVE AVAILABLE?'

Triptych's path to immortality re-commenced on her return to France and the stable of Patrick Biancone. Eleven outings in 1986 brought a stunning success with Tony Cruz in the Champion Stakes following placings in almost every middle-distance Group One in Europe aided by a who's who of international jocks: Prix Ganay (Mossé); Coronation Cup (Éric Legrix); Eclipse (Legrix); King George (Yves Saint-Martin); Matchmaker International (John Reid); and finally the Phoenix Champion and the Arc with no less than Ángel Cordero in the saddle. Then she and new partner Cruz waltzed off to Santa Anita for a sixth place in the Breeders' Cup Classic on dirt before hopping aboard another jet to Tokyo for the Japan Cup when tiredness at last caught up with her and she came home 11th of 14 on ground far too hard for her liking. In the words of *Timeform*: 'The services of Jodrell Bank have at times seemed the most appropriate for keeping track of her as she has travelled almost the length and breadth of the planet to compete in big races.'

By now the racing world had accepted Triptych as a byword for resilience: like her Dam, she was clearly as tough as nails, tough as old boots – choice of metaphor was optional. And as she entered her fifth year Biancone was about to put the Murless hypothesis through the shredder. She'd developed into a big strapping mare, a poor walker and a round-actioned galloper, with a decidedly Garbo-esque personality epitomised by a haughty head carriage: she liked to be left alone in her races to do as she pleased. Unlike her front-running mother, she preferred being delivered to stage-front as late as possible to steal the applause. The same approach typified her training routine Biancone conducted on the beach at Deauville. She did her own thing. Nobody messed with Triptych. Certainly not jockeys. Whoever said 'women are to be loved, not to be understood' might've been thinking of Triptych. This, then, was the diva introduced to Steve Cauthen at York on 18 August 1987 for the Matchmaker International.

Triptych had already netted the Coronation Cup and emulated her mother by winning the Ganay in 1987; plus the usual quota of thirds in the Eclipse and King George. Cruz had earned the right to be her regular partner by now but he was *hors d'combat* with a troublesome knee. The man thought most likely to pamper Triptych and nurse her to victory was Cauthen. John Hanmer was pleased to oblige.

Noah would have run for cover on race day: one-third of an inch of rain poured on God's own county overnight and the heavens continued to cry right up to the time of the first race. With her high action, the quagmire in prospect held no fears for Triptych. She was a warm order at 13/8 to see off her nine opponents headed by the Irish Derby winner Sir Harry Lewis, the Derby second Most Welcome, the Scottish Derby winner Ascot Knight and the King Edward VII and Gordon Stakes winner Love The Groom. But odd things tended to happen when Triptych was around – and the race was delayed 20 minutes owing to a bomb scare. When it finally got underway it was Cauthen and Triptych who were packing the grenades.

The partnership was content to bide its time in rear as Most Welcome led into York's four-furlong straight. However, whereas Most Welcome stayed on the far rail, Walter Swinburn drove Ascot Knight toward the stands rail and into the lead. When the Knavesmire gets soft the near side is considered the place to go. Yet even allowing for the extra distance covered in tacking across to the near side and the exceptionally soft going, the quarter at the top of the straight was completed in 23.58, which was quicker than the median for the track's three principal races at the Matchmaker distance (the Musidora and Dante being the others) on better ground. Swinburn's move should have sealed the race for Ascot Knight. But we reckoned without Triptych. Cauthen eased her into Ascot Knight's slipstream, with him giving the impression he might as well get out a novel and read it until such time as Triptych told him to fetch a hot drink. Once satisfied, Triptych sprang two lengths clear in as many strides, skimming over the puddles seemingly without leaving a trace; she could've doubled the margin had she so desired – which, judging by the way she cocked her head, was never an option. She'd put the race to bed with another exceptional furlong split for the conditions of 12.34. After twice being the 'bridesmaid' in this Group One, *The Sporting Life* was pleased to announce: 'Now she's the bride! Mud-loving Triptych is the star at last.'

'IS STEVE AVAILABLE?'

She quickened remarkably well in the ground. She was off the bridle until half-way and had her head on one side. But when the race went over toward the stands in the straight, she suddenly picked up her bit again and started enjoying herself.

By the afternoon Cauthen sat on Triptych for a second time in May of 1988. For the Prix Ganay the mare had changed ownership after completing a hat-trick of Group Ones at ten furlongs in the latter part of 1987 by adding the Phoenix Champion and a second Champion Stakes in the hands of Cruz. Unfortunately for all concerned, the $1m bonus was no longer on the table. In between she'd come third in the Arc to Trempolino. She ran out the year on 29 November by finishing fourth in the Japan Cup on rock-hard ground – having added another country (and continent) to her tally of victorious locations by winning her Japan Cup prep, the Fuji Stakes. That 1987 season saw Triptych in her pomp: she'd won six races, five at the highest level in four different countries; *Timeform* upped her rating to 133.

Alan Clore, however, had seen his fortunes slide the other way thanks to the stock market crash of 'Black Monday', and in March 1988 he was obliged to sell his bloodstock to settle debts. The American paper manufacturer and art connoisseur Peter Brant (he once commissioned Andy Warhol to paint his pet cocker spaniel), a partner in Kentucky Derby and Belmont winner Swale and instrumental in standing Mr Prospector at Claiborne Farm, bought Triptych for $3.4m. Hanmer was soon on the phone for the Ganay ride. Brant, a fiery character who once challenged a polo umpire to a fist fight when a decision didn't go his way, would soon take a 'ride' of his own – to prison for tax evasion.

Triptych could only finish third in her quest to match her mother's second victory in the Ganay. Cauthen shouldered the blame: in a slowly run race he'd ridden her to beat the disappointing favourite, Prix d'Harcourt winner Village Star, and allowed Saint Andrews to poach an unassailable lead. Triptych's bid for a second Coronation Cup would prove equally dramatic. But Cauthen had nothing to reproach himself about at Epsom.

As was often the case, the field for the Coronation Cup was a small one and, in truth, not the strongest ever to compete. The St Leger winner Moon Madness and the Yorkshire Oaks and Prix Vermeille winner Bint Pasha were joined by another filly, Infamy, who'd begun her season by narrowly defeating Most Welcome in the Gordon Richards Stakes. Triptych was made favourite to see them off. That she eventually did so by three-quarters of a length and two lengths from Infamy and Moon Madness was a blend of Cauthen's patience and artistry and her own whimsy. 'Madam' was barely adequate terminology to describe the Iron Lady's behaviour during her fifth and final English victory for it would've taxed the patience of John Solomon Rarey himself.

> She was a bit of an enigma and did what she wanted, did things her own way. She lost interest early on, was struggling, and dropped further and further back and I began to get a bit worried. But as we came down the Hill she started to get interested and came back on the bridle. When I moved up to track Infamy, the pace quickened up and she woke up and became involved, and decided to go. I followed Infamy because I knew that Moon Madness would only run on at one pace. Then it was a case of not hitting the front too soon.

Who was the more influential partner in gaining this second Coronation Cup that placed Triptych alongside previous female dual winners Petite Etoile and Pretty Polly is hard to fathom. Press allegiance was split. 'Triptych hits top gear for Super Steve,' said *The Sporting Life*. 'Even by Cauthen's remarkable standards this performance of jockeyship was extra Special.' *The Times* opted for the mare: 'Triptych the enigmatic completes rare double.' John Oaksey's summation in *Horse and Hound* was headlined, 'Triptych changes her mind.' He continued: 'Triptych showed no sign whatever of wanting to take any active part. Sulking along at the back, she looked like a member of some radical teaching union refusing, on grounds of principle, to supervise a children's game of "Follow My Leader." To his eternal credit, Steve Cauthen sat like a mouse, humouring Triptych's every whim. He must have been starting to despair when, suddenly, for no recognisable reason, the great mare changed her mind. The moment Triptych overhauled Infamy and Moon Madness, she immediately began to pull up. "That's enough for today, young man," you could hear her saying.'

It's a moot point whether the erstwhile 'Kid' kidded Triptych or whether the mare 'carried' Cauthen in more senses of the word than the obvious. Cauthen was wise enough to let Triptych get on with it. Attempts at coercion would've been folly. Up would go her head and down would go the tools.

It took Triptych some time to pick them up in the first place. Going up Tattenham Hill, she was stone last, detached by five or six lengths from the others. The slow pace that had irritated her through the early stages now played into Cauthen's hands and Triptych's renowned kick-finish – if she could be bothered. The penultimate furlong of 11.16 triggered by Infamy – quicker than either that week's Derby or Oaks and seldom bettered at Epsom – succeeded in keeping Triptych in the mood without her own kick being compromised. The finale was the equivalent of the carriage drive back to Buckingham Palace after the coronation; Cauthen never once lifting his whip from her withers. Whoever contributed the most to Triptych's second Coronation Cup, the outcome was memorable.

Cauthen never rode Triptych again. Indian Skimmer, naturally, was his conveyance in the Eclipse; and would've been in the Phoenix Champion and Breeders' Cup Turf but for his accident at Goodwood. Triptych notched her 14th and final victory in the Prix de Prince d'Orange and ran her last race at Churchill Downs in the Turf.

Triptych's highest *Timeform* rating of 133 was the equal of Indian Skimmer at her best. However, Triptych at five years in 1987 was some 12lb better than Indian Skimmer at five years in 1989. The three occasions they clashed came in 1988 when the six-year-old Triptych was past her best: neither could be said to have been at their peak in the Eclipse and Triptych prevailed by a head; in the Phoenix Champion Stakes, with Indian Skimmer now firing on all her exceptional cylinders, the Cecil filly came out on top by a length and three-quarters; at the Breeders' Cup, Triptych's farewell, the margin in Indian Skimmer's favour was a yawning nine lengths. As for Triptych's career standing vis-a-vis Oh So Sharp, no one will ever know whether Oh So Sharp would've improved with age, as Triptych did, and maintained her marked three-year-old superiority. But, if there's more to a truly great racehorse than the contents of the formbook, Triptych must surely qualify as one of the three greatest race-mares Cauthen ever rode; she occupies the podium alongside Pebbles and Indian Skimmer. And, all things considered, anyone who suggests Triptych merits the gold medal would meet very limited opposition.

It was nothing short of a tragedy that Triptych was unable to enjoy a happy life of motherhood in the breeding paddocks nor pass on her unique genes to a next generation. Following the Breeders' Cup at Churchill Downs, she stayed in Kentucky to be covered by Mr Prospector, but on the night of 24 February 1989 she sustained mortal wounds in a freak accident. While a night-watchman was inspecting the paddock in which Triptych and several mares were lodged, some of them spooked. One crashed into the front of his lorry. Only later was it discovered that Triptych had smashed into the back of the lorry. The horse who'd withstood circumventing the globe and everything thrown at her by trainers and jockeys alike was too gravely injured to survive.

Triptych's natural brilliance and her idiosyncrasies constantly squabbled for ascendency in her behaviour. But unlike Longfellow's little girl with the little curl, who when she was bad was utterly 'horrid', Triptych was not the type to throw a tantrum. She'd merely shrug inwardly and resolve to do things the way she wanted. Perhaps we might applaud this unique and contradictory individual by remembering her as the first equine feminist.

On the same day Triptych took her last bow at Churchill Downs so too did a second female French legend. But Miesque left the stage on a high after winning her second Breeders' Cup Mile under Freddy Head. The Frenchman only missed partnering Miesque once in her 16-race career that encompassed victory in 10 Group Ones. But owing to suspension an able substitute was required for the Queen Elizabeth II Stakes of 1987. When it came to booking a jockey to ride a classy filly deprived of her regular partner, connections soon enquired about Cauthen's availability. Accordingly, another privileged opportunity came his way. He went over to Chantilly to get acquainted in a seven-furlong workout. 'That was tremendous,' he told reporters afterwards. 'She felt like the tip-top filly she clearly is. It's a marvellous spare ride.' Head rode in the work-out and passed on valuable advice about Miesque. Alas, Cauthen suffered the anguish of being aboard Miesque on one of her rare defeats as Milligram (whom she'd beat once and would again) beat her by two and a half lengths.

The last link in the chain of female gems decorating Cauthen's 'English Odyssey' that began with Cormorant Wood and Time Charter was to be In The Groove. She was trained by David Elsworth, who had assumed the mantle of England's foremost dual-purpose trainer from Ryan Price. Whenever Elsworth's name crops up in conversation between racing fans one can be sure the name of Desert Orchid will be raised within seconds. The charismatic grey known to all and sundry as 'Dessie' was arguably the last of a line of chasers stretching back to Arkle and beyond who won their spurs by contesting and winning handicaps as well as conditions races like the King George VI Chase and the Gold Cup. Desert Orchid won a Gold Cup and four King Georges; but he won as many plaudits and as many hearts by humping 12 stone and conceding lumps of weight when winning such as the Irish Grand National, Tingle Creek, Gainsborough and Victor Chandler to name just four. His dashing, front-running, gigantic-leaping persona was memorably likened to the dapper moustachioed gent in cravat and gold-buttoned double-breasted blazer who drives his open-topped sports car at devilish speed down winding country lanes. That was Dessie all right.

David Raymond Cecil Elsworth came from the Hills-Brittain mould. If anything, his ascent was even more remarkable. Raised in Wiltshire by his farm-working grandparents, he soon befriended a pair of the work-horses into doing his bidding whilst capitalising on his lurcher, ferret and air rifle to augment his paper round by making a few bob with rabbit kills. He entered racing straight from school, cycling over to the Herridge yard of Alex Kilpatrick with suitcase balanced on the handlebars at the beginning of January 1955. His first day involved sorting and washing thousands of carrots in freezing conditions that left him with terrible chilblains. He managed to ride 50 or so winners over obstacles before retiring to join Colonel Ricky Vallance as his assistant. Two years later, Vallance lost his licence owing to the 'improvement' shown by one of his horses. The jobless Elsworth took to selling dress material on Salisbury, Wantage and Devizes markets to make ends meet. In 1976 he opened a livery yard at Durrington on Salisbury Plain and two years later applied for a training licence. He began with half a dozen hurdlers. Fortune Cookie opened the Elsworth account at Devon & Exeter in March 1979; he started at 33/1. Elsworth knew the time of day – and never lost the art.

By the time In The Groove made her debut in 1989 Elsworth had moved to Whitsbury Manor Stables in Hampshire and won a Grand National with Rhyme 'N' Reason, the Two Mile Champion Chase at Cheltenham with Barnbrook Again and 'Dessie' had won his Gold Cup and two of his four King Georges. And, significantly for the story of In The Groove, he'd made his mark on the Flat through the success of Mighty Fly in the 1983 Lincoln Handicap and Royal Hunt Cup in the hands of Steve Cauthen. In the 1989 season the Elsworth-Cauthen team graduated from handicaps to Pattern races. Indian Ridge won the King's Stand at Royal Ascot where Dead Certain took the Queen Mary; later on she and Cauthen added the Lowther – and in October the filly won Elsworth his first Group One in the Cheveley Park Stakes with Cash Asmusson replacing Cauthen who rode the favourite, Cecil's Chimes of Freedom. By now Desert Orchid's fame was transcending racing: he was, said one journalist, 'the Esperanto horse, the horse than makes horsiness comprehensible.' And Elsworth had to handle being the custodian of a public idol. Now, his public relations would be taxed in both summer and winter. In The Groove turned out to be the Flat-race star he'd been waiting for.

'IS STEVE AVAILABLE?'

In The Groove was the 'macho' type of female akin to Time Charter. At 20,000 guineas she'd prove a snip. Being a daughter of Night Shift, whose record of one minor success from seven suggested mediocrity, undoubtedly reduced her appeal; but, on the other hand, her sire was the purveyor of Northern Dancer blood. Nonetheless, she was such a gross yearling Elsworth initially struggled to find her an owner, causing his wife to dub the filly 'Can't Shift'. Eventually Brian Cooper wrote the cheque he'd have no reason to regret.

The deep-bodied In The Groove radiated strength from every pore that was suggestive of speed – and she would prove blessed with oodles of the thoroughbred's most valuable asset. Her powerful ground-devouring stride also left the impression she'd welcome some cut in the ground, a view endorsed by Elsworth withdrawing her from her intended debut owing to firm going. When she did contest a Newbury maiden in June, Cauthen guided her into second spot but Pat Eddery was aboard when she failed to justify favouritism in the Windsor maiden that followed. Elsworth's fears were realised: the filly had jarred herself. After seven weeks off she resumed in one of the season's hottest maidens, the six-furlong Convivial at York's high-profile August meeting. Her display was an eye-opener. Cauthen was little more than a passenger as she thrashed her field by six lengths in a time that stood comparison with Dead Certain's in the Lowther – and her closing quarter, eased down, was still one second faster than her stable-mate's.

In The Groove was ready to compete at Group level. That much was clear. The choice of race to advertise the fact appeared less so: in the end she was sent to Ireland for the CL Weld EBF Park Stakes over seven furlongs at Phoenix Park. But Elsworth hadn't been able to work her at home as hard as he'd have liked owing to unsuitable ground on his Whitsbury gallops; at least the easier ground in Ireland, he consoled himself, wouldn't compound the issue. The foray was a chapter of disappointments. In The Groove got to the front with two furlongs to run but never looked comfortable in so doing; Cauthen dropped his whip; and she was relegated to third place by the post. Apart from the chagrin at losing his whip, Cauthen unsaddled with one other thought in mind: In The Groove needed to be waited with and brought late. He was adamant. She was a 'closer'.

The One Thousand Guineas of 1990 became In The Groove's target. But after a satisfactory second in her prep race, the Nell Gwyn, she ran abysmally in the Classic, beating only two of her nine opponents after pulling too hard and refusing to settle; Cauthen virtually ceased riding her in the last two furlongs. If those huge Cauthen hands couldn't restrain her sufficiently to harness her speed for later on, the filly's prospects seemed limited. But there are occasions when no feasible explanation for a surprisingly below par effort may be found – and, in her case, the Guineas was one such. Cauthen was obliged to watch from a respectable distance when Ray Cochrane showed off In The Groove to advantage on her next start, York's Musidora Stakes. Cauthen rode the favourite Sardegna, but the Cecil filly had no answer when Cochrane unleashed In The Groove from the back of the field. For the first time In The Groove's blinding speed was advertised. Off the back of decent early fractions she settled the outcome with a penultimate furlong in the scarcely credible split for a York middle-distance race of 10.29. And then she cruised to the line to complete the last quarter in 23.39. There'd be few fillies capable of living with that speed – and precious few colts.

In The Groove crossed the Irish Sea for another crack at Guineas glory. She'd worked well since the Musidora but to win she'd have to reverse form with Heart of Joy (hot favourite at 6/4-on), who'd beaten her by a short head in the Nell Gwyn and was all of 21 lengths ahead of her when running second to Salsabil in the One Thousand Guineas, plus Wedding Bouquet, comfortably her superior in the Park Stakes. In The Groove put up a stunning display back in Cauthen's hands. Bringing up the rear into the straight, he drove down the outside of the field to collar the favourite. One slap saw her win, going away by three lengths. The turnaround in Guineas form with Heart of Joy amounted to 24 lengths or 12lb.

> I made much of the running on In The Groove when she was beaten at Phoenix Park. This time I decided to switch her off

and bring her with one run. Even when Walter Swinburn pulled Heart of Joy back, I still decided to settle in behind him. When he moved, I followed him through. But once I picked mine up, I knew I would win.

The clock put her last quarter at 23.06 and the race-winning penultimate furlong (on the descent) at an attention-grabbing sub-11. These figures easily outstripped Tirol's in the Irish Two Thousand Guineas on faster ground and fuelled speculation she could be better than the colts. Before that hypothesis might be tested, Elsworth had to decide whether to run her in the Oaks or the Prix de Diane. She'd given him his first Classic; where would the better ground be to help her gain a second?

Epsom came up good to soft and she took her chance. However, she'd be denied Cauthen's assistance in faintly controversial circumstances. Cecil had two fillies in the Oaks, Moon Cactus and Rafha, for whom Cauthen would obviously be claimed. Prevailing opinion was one or other of the pair would go for the Prix de Diane the following afternoon. But on Thursday afternoon it was announced both fillies would compete at Chantilly – by which time Elsworth had engaged Cash Asmussen for In The Groove. 'I hung on for Steve as long as I could,' explained Elsworth, 'but I wanted to get things sewn up. If you've got a good horse, you're never any problem getting a rider – but Steve is always my first choice.' Cauthen had to sit in the weighing room watching the Oaks on television and saw In The Groove beaten a long way from home, finding little extra for Cash Asmussen's hard riding in the final quarter. She finished fourth, some six lengths behind Salsabil; Asmussen drew a suspension for misuse of the whip. This fourth tough outing inside five weeks gained In The Groove a holiday. Cauthen's mood may only be imagined when after electing to ride Moon Cactus in the Diane she was soundly beaten by the Willie Carson-ridden Rafha.

The filly's comeback saw her return to York for the shorter trip of the Juddmonte International. The race proved an action replay of the Musidora – albeit with Cauthen wearing the goggles instead of Cochrane. 'Groove back with a bang!' reported *The Sporting Life*. 'She came from last to first with a blistering change of pace and her lightning burst quickly sealed the prize.' Once in front In The Groove idled but still had one and a half lengths to spare over the Eclipse winner Elmaamul with Batshoof, favourite owing to his victory in the Prince of Wales's Stakes, a further two lengths in arrears. And she confounded those who thought her dazzling acceleration to secure the Musidora and Irish Guineas owed everything to tawdry early pace. The running times throughout the International were consistently three seconds faster than the Musidora. Yet, with the tiring leaders falling back making things very tight for room passing the two-marker, Cauthen somehow located a gap and fired In The Groove through like a sling shot bound for Goliath. So devastating was the ensuing furlong that Cauthen needed only to ride hands-and-heels to the line.

> She was inclined to stop when hitting the front so the secret was to get In The Groove relaxed. She reminded me of Indian Skimmer. She had a brilliant turn of foot and, while she just got a mile and a half, she was definitely better at ten furlongs. I'd stayed with David Elsworth after Salisbury the previous Wednesday, and when I saw the filly in her box she looked a million dollars. The trainer had her spot on.

With decent ground assured by a French autumn, Elsworth sent In The Groove to Longchamp for the one-and-a-half-mile Group One Prix Vermeille to judge whether a crack at the Arc was a viable option. She faced Salsabil, winner of the Irish Derby since the Oaks and off the track subsequently with a view to leading an Arc campaign in the manner of French-trained contenders. Salsabil struggled to beat Miss Alleged by a neck with In The Groove half a length back in third. Last early on, Cauthen had his filly rolling at the death but she'd too much to do. He switched to Belmez in the Arc and finished fifth, four places in front of In The Groove, who at least had the satisfaction of beating Salsabil by a short head.

'IS STEVE AVAILABLE?'

Once upon a time, defeat in the Arc, especially after a long season begun with a Classic preparation, would've meant retirement for the year. But in 1986 and 1987 Triptych had proved nothing was impossible for an indefatigable female by winning the Champion Stakes after a mere fortnight's rest and recuperation. Certainly Elsworth was of that belief, persuading In The Groove's owners to pay the £17,000 to supplement her into the contest. And, with Cauthen available again, In The Groove would vindicate him. 'Steve Cauthen succeeded in producing In The Groove's peerless acceleration,' applauded Michael Seely in *The Times*. 'Never has the invisible clock in Steve Cauthen's head worked better than in the immaculate timing he displayed.'

Here was another example to sit beside that on Cormorant Wood seven years earlier that demonstrated how astutely Cauthen could judge, and ride, a waiting race. Albadr had set a scorching pace for Elmaamul which Cauthen avoided by sheltering In The Groove at the rear of the ten runners who included the favourite, the Sun Chariot winner Kartajana. The pace-setter covered the initial six furlongs on a par with the mark posted during the track record performance of Palace Music in 1984; the mile passed in a Guineas-winning mark of 1:39.94. Every horse was now feeling the effects of the early speed. That is, except In The Groove, whose petrol gauge showed plenty in the tank. Cauthen administered two cracks right-handed and a few more from the left. His filly responded to each one and moved smoothly into the lead going down into the Dip. At the post she'd one and a half lengths to spare over Linamix.

In The Groove's four victories containing three Group Ones, two of them against colts, testified to her durability and the deadly acceleration that contributed to such an enviable record. Her three English wins gave her top spot in the domestic earnings table and she was crowned Europe's champion filly in the International Classifications, 1lb ahead of Salsabil. Thanks to her efforts, Night Shift headed the sires' table; and both her owner and trainer finished fourth in their lists. The best news of all was that In The Groove would stay in training as a four-year-old.

When the 1991 season got underway, Elsworth had encouraging words for Cauthen. 'As a four-year-old In The Groove is now a professional. She is very willing and works very hard. She does carry plenty of condition, but they must have the right attitude and she has. She doesn't need keeping sweet, though she can be quite demonstrative and aggressive in her behaviour sometimes. She is practically invincible on the gallops when she is on form, so you can tell when she's not at her peak.'

In early exchanges In The Groove gave every sign she was 'at her peak'; indeed, her exceptional speed even prompted Elsworth to give her an entry in the five-furlong King's Stand at Royal Ascot. But thereafter the trainer got first-hand experience of Noel Murless's reservations about the task of keeping an elder filly on song. She won two of her first three starts with Cauthen in the saddle but a further five, in which she was partnered by Ray Cochrane, Cash Asmussen and even Lester Piggott in addition to Cauthen, yielded nary a one.

Doubts had crept into Elsworth's mind, however, as In The Groove's seasonal bow in the Trusthouse Forte Mile neared. His string was not in good form and he worried she might not be forward enough to do herself justice. His fears were unfounded. 'In The Groove mightier than the sword,' declared *The Times* after Cauthen had ridden her 'to perfection'. Lester Piggott dashed Aldbourne to the front intent on drawing the sting from In The Groove's sprint finish: his calculated ploy verified by the opening half-mile completed two seconds faster than the card's other race over the mile. Cauthen waited on Aldbourne and Zoman as they tussled for supremacy between the two and the one poles before nudging his filly to a one-length victory over the much-touted Zoman.

> I could feel In The Groove beginning to tire, but when I gave her one crack with the whip she responded most gamely and found the decisive burst of speed which was her hallmark. One and a quarter miles was her best trip. You couldn't say she'd not stay a mile and a half but she was absolutely brilliant at a mile and

a quarter. If a race was run to suit her and she got switched off, she'd be okay over a mile and a half.

The opportunity to judge the validity of Cauthen's closing remark would come in the Coronation Cup. But before that Epsom date, In The Groove was dropped back to a mile for the Lockinge Stakes. At Newbury, however, the wheels fell off the cart. Starting 2/1-on to beat three rivals she went under by two lengths to the Piggott-ridden and French-trained Polar Falcon in a farcical contest that matched the grim overcast afternoon. The first half was run at a crawl and the race disintegrated into a two-furlong burn-up. In The Groove was not short of acceleration and she assumed the lead quite readily at the one pole, but any whim of competing against crack sprinters in the King's Stand was emphatically blasted to kingdom come by the raw speed of Polar Falcon, whom Piggott had brought up the near rail where he suspected the faster ground lay. Whatever the case, Polar Falcon demonstrated the speed he'd later use to put Group One sprinters in their place when adding the six-furlong Ladbrokes Sprint Cup.

Atonement for In The Groove might yet arrive in the Coronation Cup. The Lockinge setback and the fact that In The Groove had yet to win over the distance of one and a half miles convinced the bookmakers that she faced two opponents with superior credentials. Michael Stoute had once again advertised his reputation as a master at improving older middle-distance horses by bringing back last year's one-time ante post Derby favourite Rock Hopper from a hairline fracture of a cannon bone to rattle off a quick-fire Group-race double in the John Porter Stakes and the Jockey Club Stakes. And it wouldn't have escaped Cauthen's notice that the four-year-old was a son of his former sweetheart Cormorant Wood. Second favourite was the 1990 Derby winner Quest For Fame, who'd not been seen on the track for 11 months owing to the injured near-fore sustained when finishing fifth in the Irish Derby. Among the remaining four runners were Derby runner-up Terimon and the St Leger second Sapience from the Classic generation of 1989.

Could Cauthen keep In The Groove's nitro from imploding before a display of explosive speed in the closing stages? Could she add her name to that select list of female winners headed by Pretty Polly, Petite Etoile and Park Top and augmented recently by Time Charter and Triptych? Elsworth's current slump had not been lost on the Ring and with his filly sweating ominously beforehand she'd drifted in the betting on entering the stalls.

The role of pacemaker fell to Pat Eddery on Quest For Fame: a truly run race was the Derby winner's only chance of recording a win on his comeback. Eddery tapped out a sedate pace almost five seconds slower over the first four furlongs than Mystiko's in the previous afternoon's Derby before considering any increase in the tempo. Rounding Tattenham Corner, Quest For Fame was still two seconds down on the Derby running time. Binocular holders knew what to expect. There was going to be a three-furlong sprint. Michael Roberts seized the initiative on Terimon and plumped for an early strike in hope of catching Cauthen napping. The first furlong in the straight flashed past in 11.95; the next was even faster at 11.20 as In The Groove counter-attacked. This sprint came at the end of 12 furlongs not the eight of the Lockinge and the extra distance accentuated her speed advantage; it was electric enough to propel her a length and a half clear of Terimon in the twinkling of an eye. Pursued all the way to the winning post by Terimon on her outside and Rock Hopper on her inner, she held on by half a length and a neck. A stewards' inquiry into In The Groove and Rock Hopper tightening up Quest For Fame a furlong or so out was attributed to Epsom's notorious camber rather than jockey error and the result was allowed to stand.

'Groove crowned Queen,' declared the front page of *The Life*. 'In The Groove, who has the frame of a broodmare but the engine of a Ferrari, finally clinched that elusive first mile-and-a-half success when winning a memorable three-cornered Coronation Cup.' Despite this breakthrough success, Cauthen remained less than enthusiastic about her chances of staying a truly run race over the distance. But he could rest content with winning his third Coronation Cup – each one on a different filly.

'IS STEVE AVAILABLE?'

Although contesting a further four Group One events, In The Groove couldn't add to her quartet of victories at this level. In fact, she franked the wisdom of Murless's words by never winning after the June of her fourth year: fourth in the Eclipse (partnered by Cochrane as Cauthen was on Cecil's Stagecraft); a fast-finishing third in her Arc prep, the Select Stakes under Piggott; sixth in a strongly run Arc (the best of the English runners) and seventh in the Breeders' Cup Turf with Cauthen; and another fast-finishing third in the Champion (after an unimpressive ride from Asmussen) rounded out her 21-race career. She'd been aided by Cauthen in two-thirds of those races and six of her seven wins were the result; notably the four Group Ones. Sheikh Mohammed acknowledged her merit by adding her to his band of broodmares at a reputed cost of £750,000.

If there was one division that Henry Cecil never plundered on Cauthen's behalf it was that of the sprinters. This often freed Cauthen to pick and choose. Sharpo and Committed were two fortuitous links. Never So Bold would be another. And a case may be argued for him being the best sprinter Cauthen ever rode.

The burly bay colt was the spitting image of his father, the champion Irish juvenile of 1966 Bold Lad. Trained by Robert Armstrong in Newmarket, he was also the perfect advert for an improving animal being kept in training until reaching its peak as a mature five-year-old. Never So Bold improved a whopping two stone from being a decent handicapper at three years (winning three from eight) to stamping his presence in Pattern-race company with a trio of Group successes at four; and then a further 7lb when he secured what might be termed the sprinters' Triple Crown in 1985 by winning all three of the Group One events available to speedsters, viz the King's Stand at Royal Ascot, the July Cup at Newmarket and York's William Hill Sprint Championship – the Nunthorpe as traditionalists preferred calling it. Though the latter name and the Group status of the first and last legs had been prone to change, only four horses had achieved this treble in the same season during the 63 years since the Nunthorpe ceased being a humble selling race. Unfortunately, Cauthen was claimed

237

to ride the unbeaten Cecil filly Abha at Ascot, but was reunited with Never So Bold thereafter.

He and Cauthen struck first in Group company over the seven furlongs of the Prix de la Porte Maillot at Longchamp in late June of 1984. But after the pair had finished a shock second (33/1) to Chief Singer in the July Cup over a furlong less and followed up with a cosy victory in Deauville's Prix Maurice de Gheest (Group Two), the colt's handicapping days were instantly consigned to the past. His third in the Vernons Sprint Cup (minus Cauthen) behind top-notchers Petong and Habibti was reversed in the Diadem Stakes later in September with the American back in the saddle. Clearly, Never So Bold was on an upward curve but any suggestion it might be of the exponential type would've received scant support. That he was able to plot this curve had more than a dash of luck about it. He was booked for stallion duties in 1985 but had to miss the required veterinary checks owing to a pulled muscle – and was kept in training. One might resort to calling the exhibitions of raw speed delivered by Never So Bold in 1985 as a 'purple patch' or a 'rich seam'. But, in truth, there's no alternative to saying Never So Bold became the epitome of a bay bullet.

Armstrong gave him his seasonal debut in the Temple Stakes at Sandown, the colt's first-ever run at the minimum trip of five furlongs after 17 races. Cauthen quickened him clear to hold Primo Dominie and Jonacris without concern. Lester Piggott had the pleasure of sitting atop Never So Bold as he annihilated the King's Stand field by three lengths, easing up. Primo Dominie was second again; the previous season's William Hill Sprint Championship heroine Committed was a head further back. Abha's balloon, fortunately for Cauthen, had burst: she finished fourth. Though both she and Never So Bold went on to the July Cup, Cauthen was released to resume his partnership with the colt.

Like many a star of the human variety, Never So Bold was blessed with idiosyncrasy besides talent. After running the second furlong of the King's Stand in no less than 10.69 and completing the race at an average speed of 36mph like an express train, he hobbled into the winner's circle like Long

John Silver. His near-fore knee was inclined to bleed after any exertion and the joint seize up. The affliction looked awful but disappeared almost as rapidly as it developed.

This same tableau was re-enacted after the July Cup which Never So Bold completed at an even faster average of 38mph. 'An exhilarating display of speed to prove himself the best sprinter in Europe,' announced *The Times*. 'There's none so Bold!' exclaimed *The Sporting Life* headline following a second annihilation of the finest sprinters in the business. Cauthen loaded the chamber with two furlongs to run and when the trigger was pulled it needed just 100 yards for the bay bullet to convert a two-length deficit into a two-and-a-half-length advantage over Dafayna by the winning post. Once down to a walk, however, the lameness again manifested itself and Cauthen immediately dismounted. 'Armstrong ace in pain again after dazzling display,' continued the report. The trainer was quick to ease any anxieties: 'We injected his kneecap with joint fluid at Ascot but I don't think it'll be necessary this time. He'll be sound by tea-time. We've been slowly learning about it. We hose his legs a lot and put him on the Magnetopulse machine daily.'

If the July Cup had been the main course to Royal Ascot's *hors d'oeuvre*, Never So Bold served up the queen of puddings in York's William Hill Sprint Championship. 'A devastating exhibition,' was the headline to Michael Seely's report in *The Times*. 'Never So Bold's acceleration places him in a class apart.' On good ground he broke the magical barrier of one minute for five furlongs with 59.81 (averaging 38mph again). And this in spite of Cauthen easing him down once he'd cruised into the lead at the one pole following a race-securing furlong in 11.10.

Never So Bold left the visual impression that Cauthen could never have gone much faster in his life than he had on this tank of a sprinter. But therein lies the joy of sectional times: they lend race analysts an objective bonus. The Prix de l'Abbaye de Longchamp benefits from electronically timed fractions and in winning that Group One in 1991 Cauthen's mount Keen Hunter clocked a metric furlong in 10.1 – equating to 42mph. But from his privileged position in the saddle, Cauthen has no reservations.

Keen Hunter never gave me the same feeling of speed as Sharpo or Never So Bold. The better one? On soft ground I'd probably opt to ride Sharpo; on any other surface it would be Never So Bold. When I pulled Never So Bold to the outside to go past Lester's horse at York he just went whoosh!

Whether a horse is going five furlongs or a mile and a quarter they need to have speed. But they also have to have an element of stamina to carry the speed. It's a very fine balance.

And a time can be misleading. A $25,000 claimer can run six furlongs at Belmont in 69 flat if he's allowed to pop out the gate and is put under no pressure; while a better horse might run up to a second slower in a stakes race later on.

As it transpired, the Abbaye was Never So Bold's next race. And he was well beaten by the best part of two lengths into fourth. The fact that the winner was Committed, whom he'd trounced at Newmarket and Ascot, made the result harder to fathom. The filly may have taken to Longchamp and the time of year because she'd won the Abbaye 12 months previously in the Sangster silks under Cauthen himself before she was bought by Allen Paulson. Never So Bold couldn't get near enough to her to land a blow.

There was nothing left for Never So Bold to prove. This last reverse notwithstanding, he was acknowledged as Europe's champion sprinter, 8lb higher than Committed on the International Classification, with a *Timeform* rating of 135 that put him up with the best-ever speed merchants. And it insisted he was the fourth-best animal Cauthen rode during his English odyssey; only Reference Point (139), Slip Anchor and Old Vic (both 136) boast higher *Timeform* ratings. For some months Cauthen had counselled the colt's American owner to run him in the Mile at the Breeders' Cup, the series inaugurated 12 months earlier at Santa Anita. The concept aimed to bring together the best of America and Europe, which meant Europeans were inconvenienced by running at the end of their season and, bar a few races, being obliged to run on unfamiliar dirt. The Mile, however, was contested on grass; and the event was nomadic with the 1985 venue chosen as Cauthen's former patch, Aqueduct. He felt Never So Bold would suit the longer distance on the tight turning track. But Never So Bold proved all at sea and beat only four of his 13 opponents. Now Never So Bold did head off to stud.

Cauthen enjoyed no luck whatsoever at the Breeders' Cup. In eight rides spread over the 1985, 1987 and 1991 events the closest he got to a win came shortly after the ride on Never So Bold when he partnered the globe-trotting Australasian star Strawberry Road in the Breeders' Cup Turf.

Although Cauthen was fated never to land a race at the Breeders' Cup, he did win on one horse who wrote his name into Turf history by his astonishing performance at the eighth Breeders' Cup of 1991 held at Churchill Downs. His name, of course, was Arazi.

SIX
THE CADILLAC COLT

IN WHAT would prove to be his final season in the saddle, Cauthen rode quite possibly one of the best racehorses of his entire career. The bare statistics of the horse in question's races in 1992 would suggest otherwise. But like the rest of the racing world, Cauthen had seen what the horse had done the previous season as a two-year-old and could not help but be impressed; perhaps even as awestruck as the majority of witnesses to the colt's exploits. And on the Chantilly gallops Cauthen had got a 'feel' from the horse that made him wonder whether he might be as good as Affirmed – if not better. The horse was dubbed 'The Cadillac Colt' by *Time* magazine. This was Arazi.

Arazi's juvenile career in 1991 that Cauthen watched from afar was as sensational as any seen in Europe since The Tetrarch stormed through 1913 with seven wins from seven starts. In the eyes of many, not even 'Champion the Wonder Horse' displayed the awesome panache of Arazi. Although he may have resembled the television icon in performance, Arazi paled in appearance, being a somewhat lightly made chestnut whose three white socks and crooked blaze would still not have made him an attractive subject for Stubbs or Herring. Fortunately, once set alight he possessed a wonderful stride and was a most impressive mover. He was a son of French Guineas winner and Derby third Blushing Groom who became an equally noteworthy sire with horses the calibre of Rainbow Quest and Nashwan to his name. Arazi's dam failed to win; though his maternal grandam was a half-sister to a champion sprinter in Ajdal.

THE CADILLAC COLT

Arazi belonged to Gulfstream Aerospace Corporation's CEO Allen E Paulson, who named him after an aeronautical navigational checkpoint in the Arizona desert. Paulson owned 650 thoroughbreds, mostly stabled in America. Arazi, however, was housed at Lamorlaye, just north of Paris near Chantilly, in the care of François Boutin. Although the trainer may have looked the kind of aristocratic silver fox to make any lady swoon, he was a farmer's son from Dieppe who'd fought in the Algerian war. But he'd acquired the art of training the thoroughbred at the knee of a master – Etienne Pollet, custodian of the great Sea-Bird II and a man who regarded his horses in the same way as an artist did his paintings. Boutin emulated his mentor by sending out the winners of umpteen French, Irish and English Classics with the likes of Caracolero, Malacate, Zino, Northern Trick, Linamix and the marvellous Miesque – who also landed the Breeders' Cup Mile two years in a row. Assisting Arazi from the saddle was Gérald Mossé, no stranger to top-class horses having partnered Restless Kara to win the 1988 Prix de Diane and Saumarez to win the 1990 Arc.

Unlike The Tetrarch, Arazi did not go through his two-year-old career unbeaten. Like another French titan, Sea-Bird, he lost his first start. But thereafter it amounted to an imperious progress through the French calendar to equal anything Napoleon might've enjoyed. He emulated his sire by sweeping the Prix Robert Papin, Prix Morny, Prix de Salamandre and Grand Criterium – the last three all Group Ones. Among his victims were Seattle Rhyme, who'd go on to win the Racing Post Trophy, and the hitherto unbeaten St Jovite, who went on to win an Irish Derby and King George. Arazi handled the mile of the Criterium without the semblance of trouble and the Breeders' Cup Juvenile over an additional half a furlong at Churchill Downs would clearly hold no fears for him; perhaps the strange dirt surface might. As it transpired, Arazi unleashed a display of which even 'Champion the Wonder Horse' would've been in awe.

Cauthen thus far had only enjoyed a rear view of Arazi in the Papin and Morny. At Churchill Downs he'd be a more-than-interested observer from the stands. He now had a vested interest in the colt. Paulson had sold 50 per cent of Arazi for a reputed $9m to Sheikh Mohammed. Arazi now became a Cauthen mount. But only in Europe. Paulson's long-term objective for Arazi was the Kentucky Derby (en route to the Triple Crown which carried a $5m bonus from one of Paulson's companies) in which he'd be partnered by his retained American rider, Pat Valenzuela. What Arazi proceeded to do at the eighth Breeders' Cup on 2 November 1991 would go down, rightly, in the annals of the Turf. After what he saw that day, Cauthen could not wait to get on board the colt – anywhere, any time.

Some racing folk aver juveniles cannot be regarded as great horses whatever they achieve because they are not the finished article. The two-word response to that opinion? The Tetrarch. The 'Spotted Wonder' was unable to run beyond the age of two yet is still regarded as one of the greatest thoroughbreds of all time. Age should not be allowed to harm a horse's eligibility for 'greatness'. More so if one considers the context of Arazi's mind-blowing display in the Juvenile Turf. At the time, European successes at the Breeders' Cup were less prolific than they would eventually become. After seven series, for example, just one juvenile had reached so much as a place. The transatlantic journey at the end of the European season, an alien dirt surface, its intimidating kickback and, in Arazi's case, a coffin-box draw on the outside of 14 runners with barely 250 yards to the first bend, threw up more than enough convenient excuses should the favourite's challenge fizzle out like a damp squib.

The occasional horse race makes even the most level-headed observer gasp in wonder. This race was one of those races. The third quarter was responsible. Arazi was languishing in rear, some 15 lengths behind Bertrando (his closest market rival, unbeaten and recent winner of a Grade One by nine lengths), who'd just posted the fastest half-mile of the day bar the Sprint with a split well below even-time at 46.60. Suddenly Arazi begins to pass one rival after another at breathtaking speed with no discernible effort or urgency from Valenzuela. If he couldn't set an air-speed record, it appeared he was determined to set one on land for the ensuing quarter mile; he crackled with so much relentless power one was left looking for his vapour trail. 'Whenever he saw an open spot, he went right through it,' reported the jockey. 'It was like playing a video game with one of those little cars in an arcade. He has the greatest turn of foot I've ever experienced.'

With two furlongs left, Arazi was upsides Bertrando without having turned a hair. This was no trick-of-the-eye scenario of a horse 'passing trees'. The official race chart told us Arazi had covered this mid-race quarter in something close to 22.20, a juvenile fraction not even Secretariat had beside his name. Then, afterburners no longer required, he strolls away from Bertrando to win by an officially judged five lengths as effortlessly as a pair of shires hauling an empty dray; three or more lengths further back trailed the winners of five other graded events, including Tri To Watch who'd just won the Grade One Champagne Stakes by seven and a half lengths. This was a performance for eternity; one to get the heads shaking. No Juvenile had been won by so great a margin – which could've been doubled. And we'd been privileged spectators to one of the greatest mid-race surges by a two-year-old that the clock had ever recorded. One can only guess what Steve Cauthen was thinking up in the stands at that precise moment. But calling on Lester Piggott for some 'jocking-off' tips wouldn't be far off the truth.

'Here indeed is a superstar!' cried race-caller Tom Durkin. Three hardened rail-birds thought they'd seen everything – until now. Messrs Lukas, McGaughey and Zito, three of America's most distinguished trainers, spoke as one: 'That was the greatest performance I've ever seen! That's a serious racehorse!' *The New York Times* was suitably thunderstruck: 'He passed through the crowd as if the other jockeys were riding bicycles.' Arazi scooped an Eclipse Award for the Outstanding Two-Year-Old Male; the Cartier Awards saluted him likewise – and also made him Horse of the Year; he was 8lb clear at the top of the International Classification and European Free Handicap; and *Timeform* rated him at 135, the Sixth-highest juvenile rating in its 44-year history (and two of those superior are highly questionable). But perhaps the supreme accolade came from Joe Hirsch, the dean of American Turf journalists, who stated in *Daily Racing Form*: 'Arazi is such an extraordinary animal that he makes other great horses look like hacks.'

'Arazimania' was born. And as America anticipated the little colt's return for the Kentucky Derby of 1992, the disease spread like a brush fire that eventually engulfed Europe as well.

That concluded the rise of Arazi. Now began his fall from grace. Before returning to France, Arazi underwent keyhole knee surgery to remove chip fractures from the top joint of both knees where bone spurs were forming and causing inflammation; he'd actually run at the Breeders' Cup with a shot of the painkiller Bute – legal in America but outlawed in Europe. Following six weeks recuperation, Arazi was back at Lamorlaye seemingly fully recovered. Nevertheless, he didn't resume work until 15 February. 'He had a long time off and I was a bit worried about him after his operation,' reported Boutin. 'Lately he has shown himself to be how he was before. He will improve another 30 per cent after his first race. If he wins the Kentucky Derby and the Epsom Derby he would have to be considered at least as good as, and perhaps superior to Ribot, Sea-Bird or Mill Reef. The first thing we have to do is win the Kentucky Derby. But the Triple Crown schedule is a lot to ask. It will be difficult to leave him in America for six weeks. It will be hard for him to retain his morale. The differences between here and there are so great. He may get fed up.'

Arazi was about to face a 1992 campaign that might conceivably encompass a Derby on both sides of the Atlantic. Corals offered odds of 4/1 against the historic Derby double. Steve Cauthen, for one, openly declared his preference for Epsom over Churchill Downs – which was entirely understandable given the geographical limits of his retainer to ride the horse. But first Arazi had to demonstrate he'd made it through an off-season of recuperation and inactivity without forfeiting any of that dazzling speed. It was a tall order. Little wonder Boutin selected the innocuous Prix Omnium over a mile at Saint-Cloud on 7 April for his star's comeback. The soft surface would certainly be kind to Arazi's knees and the seven opponents, none of them Group winners, were unlikely to pose any threat unless those knees gave up the ghost and Arazi wound up racing on two legs.

THE CADILLAC COLT

The favourite won like a 5/1-on shot should on ground described as 'heavy'. Settled in sixth early on, Cauthen eased him past horses down the back straight before turning left-handed and sweeping into the lead at the 300-metre pole to win on the bridle by five lengths. 'Arazi passes first test with flying colours,' insisted the headline in *The Times*; In truth, Arazi had completed little more than the kind of decent work-out he might've enjoyed back at Lamorlaye. Cauthen was pleased; it would pay him to be guarded and realistic. But it was hard.

> That was his first race and the first race is always one where something can go wrong. He was 75 per cent of what he needed at that time of year rather than for that type of race. I'd got to know him in the spring and regarded him as an exceptional horse. He settled well, would relax, and was suited to a good pace. I thought he could do most things.
>
> I thought Arazi would come back for the Derby at Epsom and I believed that was the right thing to do. The owners always said they were concerned about the horse's best interests and François Boutin felt it was in Arazi's best interests to be trained at Chantilly and to run on better surfaces and was worried about training him on a hard American track. I thought it was really frightening if he were to be trained on hard tracks.

Allen Paulson, however, was unmoved: 'I'm a Yankee and so I would like to see him go for the Kentucky Derby. American race-goers will crucify me if I don't go for it. And if he wins, he will have beaten the majority of the competition he would face in the Preakness and Belmont and we'd be in a grand position to do the Triple Crown. But if he was to win in Kentucky and go to Epsom, where racing is up a hill and the track has slants, and he loses, we have egg all over our faces. If we go to the Preakness and he doesn't win, he could come back for the Derby three weeks later.'

I thought he went to Kentucky in great form. He did a piece of work before leaving you don't see often. The last time I can remember one like it was with Slip Anchor before the Derby. He was so exciting. With most horses you know their limitations. This horse was unlimited at that time. He was freakish. You couldn't say how far he could go.

I was as sick as a pig not to ride him in the Kentucky Derby, but unfortunately that was the deal unless Pat Valenzuela took ill or was suspended. Bar bad luck, I believed he'd win. I am not saying the American horses were a bad bunch but I didn't know of anything that stood out. He showed that he could do it the previous year. I thought he'd run through them at Churchill Downs like he did before when it came to the important part of the race.

If he got to Epsom I was sure he'd handle the slopes and undulations. I'd seen all sorts of horses come round Epsom as long as they were travelling well.

Arazi left Lamorlaye having sparkled in a gallop over the Kentucky Derby distance around a tightly cornered replica of Churchill Downs and sauntering away from his two companions. He arrived in Kentucky with a recent headline in *Time* magazine to justify: 'Arazi races like the Second Coming of Secretariat.' Arazi was the horse the American public had been yearning for; 'Arazi could be the spark racing needs,' announced the front page of *USA Today*. And after he touched down at Butler Field a week before the Derby, his progress to Louisville Downs was followed by a convoy of disciples in the manner of, in the memorable words of Steve Haskin, 'Hebrews following Moses out of Egypt.' On race day the front page of *Daily Racing Form* was unequivocal: 'All eyes on Arazi.' Local residents to Churchill Downs were even hawking Arazi T-shirts from their front lawns.

The colt's jockey was dangerously confident: 'Arazi can do more than Sunday Silence!' said Valenzuela, who'd ridden the latter to success in the first two legs of the Triple Crown in 1988. 'This race is over! He is stronger than last year. He has got an unbelievable turn of foot, it's like pushing a button for a rocket. He goes off like Mr Paulson's GIV jet! He will win – I will guarantee you that.'

If that braggadocio wasn't enough to bring down the wrath of the gods upon Arazi, other portents suggested they were certainly considering it. First, a horse dropped dead in front of Arazi during a routine track canter and it was only the quick reactions of his work rider, Raymond Lamonorca, which prevented disaster. Then, on the Thursday, he dumped Valenzuela – just as he had when working before the Breeders' Cup. Students of English history were quick to put a 'spin' on the incident: when William of Normandy fell disembarking in Pevensey Bay in 1066 it didn't presage defeat at the Battle of Hastings. Arazi, they pronounced, would triumph like 'The Conqueror'. The chastened Valenzuela remounted for Arazi to work four furlongs with his lead horse, Akiko; he gave him two lengths start, and went by in two or three jumps to run out the half-mile in 49.20, easing up.

The Sporting Life entertained no caveats: 'If there is a third certainty after death and taxes, it is surely that Arazi will win today's Kentucky Derby. Arazi is the most exciting horse to emerge from Europe since Sea-Bird II in 1965 and appears the biggest steering job to have looked through a bridle.' Nor did *The Times*: 'Flying machine Arazi ready to sprout wings: Arazi to deliver Classic knockout.' Joe Hirsch mulled over Arazi's problematic draw but was equally emphatic: 'Arazi can overcome adversity.' The late defection of Arazi's principal danger, the Florida Derby winner AP Indy owing to bruising a foot overnight, merely seemed to seal the deal. Goodness only knows what the staff at *Daily Racing Form* had been ingesting but on Derby Day the paper didn't so much go over the top as over the moon: 'Arazi is faster than a speeding bullet, more powerful than a locomotive, able to leap tall buildings in a single bound … there's nothing he can't do. He doesn't appear to have any weaknesses. Vive la France! Arazi will give no quarter.'

This manner of premature adulation is seldom wise – it's frequently linked with egg flying in all directions. Nevertheless, for those of a superstitious bent, it hadn't gone unnoticed that 100 years previously the race had fallen to a horse called Azra! The gods had spoken. By post time at 5.32, over $1m had been bet on Arazi to win. The other 17 horses were running for second place.

Over 132,000, which included reporters and film crews from England, France, Germany and Japan, crammed Churchill Downs on a warm muggy day to watch Arazi (at 10/9-on) enter the stalls for the 118th 'Run for the Roses' aiming to become the first winning favourite since Spectacular Bid in 1979. He'd drawn another outside box: 18 of 18 – no horse had won from there in the 20th century; and only three drawn higher than 14 had won. But several other factors differed from Breeders' Cup day. Back in November he'd arrived in Louisville battle-hardened following eight races in six months; now he came having raced once in six months and that against mediocre opposition. Instead of a balmy Kentucky autumn afternoon he was now obliged to endure the debilitating humidity of a Kentucky early summer: indeed, one could slice the atmosphere, so thick was it with moisture; and minutes after the Derby runners had passed the wire an almighty thunderstorm crashed down on Churchill Downs.

At first, the race looked as if it would become a replay of the Breeders' Cup: Arazi came off the clubhouse turn with just Disposal behind him. Then once again he scythed his field down along the backstretch as if he were a corn-harvester in overdrive: 15th; tenth; eighth; fifth. He made up almost 13 lengths sailing past 14 horses to claim third spot rounding the crown of the last bend. How could we be sure our eyes weren't deceiving us? For the same reason we knew what Arazi had done in the Breeders' Cup Juvenile: the statistical bible, that is the race chart complete with its quarter times, positions and distances in running to which we may apply American track lore that states five lengths equals one second. On that basis, Arazi's supercharged progress from 17th to third between the six and the two poles down the backstretch saw him clock a half-mile two and a half seconds quicker than the leader's race split of 49.80, i.e. he made up 12½ lengths. The majority of that distance was clawed back in the first half of that blitz with a quarter between the six and four poles that we can calculate to have been a jaw-dropping 22.40. This amounted to speed almost impossible to maintain – let alone finding additional acceleration to settle the race.

'Arazi is flying. Arazi is gaining ground with every stride!' exclaimed race-caller Dave Johnson. 'When Arazi went by me,' said Chris McCarron, riding the English raider Dr Devious, 'I looked over at Pat and he had his feet on the dashboard.' Arazi came into the stretch three wide, poised to sprint away from his field. But when Valenzuela pushed the button the 'rocket' failed to fire. Arazi paddled and faltered. He was absolutely spent, punch drunk, out on his feet. The chasers swallowed Arazi as rapidly as he'd once consumed them. Suddenly he was back in fifth, jinking toward the rail ... then seventh ... and finally eighth under the wire, nine lengths behind long-shot Lil E. Tee – one of those swept aside so contemptuously on the backstretch. The winner's final quarter of 26.40 completed a slow Derby in 2:03.0. Any clocker would venture to say that the Arazi of the previous November would've found a sub-26 final quarter off this pace without batting an eye had he not run such a ferocious mid-race half-mile during a contest that was two furlongs further. As it was, Arazi finished with one close to 28.

Cauthen was in the safest place. The ensuing minutes, days and weeks were going to be uncomfortable for Paulson, Boutin and Valenzuela. Recriminations were instant. Under-trained and over-ridden was the general consensus of opinion in the American Press. He'd had a rushed preparation (the winner had four prep races to Arazi's one) – a view contrary to articles insisting 'Boutin will have him ready,' written beforehand. And his jockey left him with too much to do, pulling him back off a slow pace in the opening quarter and asking him to quicken when everyone else was also quickening. But Valenzuela wasn't about to shoulder the blame after riding Arazi in exactly the same way as in the Juvenile. His post-race comments covered all the bases: 'He felt 100 per cent sound. The outside post position didn't hinder us. He was moving well in himself. He just picked up horses left and right by himself like he was going to cruise home. With three furlongs to run, I thought the race was over. I got right to the leaders. I thought he was just going to inhale them. He didn't have the punch he had last time. He just didn't get home through the last eighth of a mile. Perhaps he just wasn't fit enough after only one prep race.'

Boutin took the blow and the brickbats as philosophically as he could but struggled to hide his desolation: 'Disappointed but not surprised. I was never in favour of coming. It was to do with preparation. It was too short and too quick, too much in a hurry. I made a mistake: I wanted to please the owners because they pushed me to do this. It was just impossible to get this horse prepared in two months. He needed another month. He had his operation – which I did not think necessary – and that stopped him for a month and a half. That just killed us.' Once back in France the trainer shared one more item of information with Anthony Stroud, Sheikh Mohammed's racing manager: Arazi had completed the Derby with his tongue down his throat. If the humidity, knee surgery, lack of match fitness and transatlantic journey weren't enough for Arazi to contend with, swallowing his tongue during the heat of battle was quite sufficient on its own to bring about a head-on collision with the reality of the task he'd been set.

The British media added another slant to the post mortem: would the outcome have differed with Cauthen in the saddle? Hindsight's gift of perfect 20/20 vision can often lure even the most wary into a bear trap. All one can say is that it would be wonderful to run the race again with Cauthen riding Arazi. Valenzuela was no mug. But he was no Cauthen either. One cannot envisage Cauthen keeping Arazi so far back off such a slow pace and burning his speed in the act of recovering forfeited ground mid-race. Cauthen, whether through the weighing room *omerta* of never criticising a fellow jockey or just his innate good manners, apportions blame elsewhere.

The fact was Arazi detested firm ground. He went on it the first time at Churchill Downs but he was hanging out into the centre down the stretch. You never know for sure whether a horse will go on hard ground until the second time of asking. His knee surgery wouldn't have helped; might have been stinging him in the Derby. And the humidity in Kentucky that time of year can wear anybody out: 85ºF there seems like 105 because of the humidity. Some horses adapt to it better than others. But I'd have to have been on him to know.

Arazi's participation at Epsom (the Derby went to his fellow Kentucky traveller Dr Devious) was ruled out before he even got back to Lamorlaye. The ten-furlong Grand Prix de Paris at the end of June was earmarked as his next run, but following Arazi's first piece of work since his return in the hands of Cauthen on 9 June, it was decided to send him to Royal Ascot for the St James's Palace Stakes over a mile one week later.

> He worked well at a good pace. He was more relaxed than usual because of the fog and dropped his bit during the gallop. But it wasn't possible to say whether he was back in the form he was before the Kentucky Derby when he was flying.

Arazi would meet the winner of the English and Irish Guineas in the Piggott-ridden Rodrigo de Triano, also on a retrieval mission having proved he was a non-stayer in the Derby. Neither horse shone. There was no fire in either horse's belly when Piggott and Cauthen applied pressure turning into the straight; Rodrigo beat Arazi for fourth place by three-quarters of a length as Brief Truce reversed Irish Guineas form to win. Cauthen was clearly dismayed and could offer no explanation after Arazi's challenge petered out just as it had over the extra two furlongs at Churchill Downs. On this occasion, Cauthen had got him covered up but no semblance of a 22 race-winning quarter ever looked forthcoming.

> Obviously there was some kind of problem because he was a brilliant horse. He was an excellent two-year-old and he worked like an exceptional horse in the spring. The trip to the Kentucky

Derby had a negative effect in the long term. He was found to be very dehydrated afterwards and his blood count wasn't right. I didn't know whether it was a physical or a mental thing. And after Ascot they found fluid on his lungs.

I was happy turning into the straight at Ascot. He was travelling sweetly but when I asked him for his effort he only ran for half a furlong before flattening out. He did not go through with his run. But that didn't mean he wouldn't find his form again.

But when would that be? Boutin decided he should have a two-month break; Paulson joked that his one-time 'world-beater' possibly needed an equine psychiatrist. An injured hock meant Arazi missed the Prix de Moulin (Group One) over a mile, and he was switched to the two-furlong longer and less competitive Prix du Prince d'Orange (Group Three) on 20 September. He'd now not had a race for 13 weeks. Only four opposed, one of them his pacemaker. The four-year-old Arcangues gave Arazi 4lb and beat him by over six lengths into third. Cauthen put on a brave face:

Arazi was over-fresh. We would have needed a couple of good gallops at home but that was just not possible. He ran well enough considering that he probably did not stay. I'd have preferred a slightly slower pace and I was not hard on him. He was bound to improve a lot for the run.

Boutin remained bullish; his colt was 'rusty' and he was still hopeful of 'rediscovering' his star of last year. Cauthen's final chance to conjure some of the old Arazi pizzazz would come in the Prix du Rond-Point (Group Two) on Arc day, a fortnight later. The going was invitingly soft (compared to good to firm at Ascot); and the opposition invitingly moderate. Unlike his rider, Arazi would not have to leave his homeland to gain redemption. But it was just as sweet.

THE CADILLAC COLT

'Arazi roars back to pay Boutin tribute,' blared the headline in *The Times*, after the colt had resumed winning ways with all his old flamboyance. 'The crowd cheered Steve Cauthen to the echo as he rode back in triumph to the winner's enclosure on their former idol.' Arazi shared the front page of *The Sporting Life* with the story of User Friendly's agonisingly close defeat in the Arc: 'Arazi zips back to the big time,' it proclaimed alongside a photograph of a smiling Cauthen patting his mount's head in the winner's enclosure.

Always travelling comfortably, as if he was thankful to be back on an easy surface, Arazi had stalked the leaders into the straight with Cauthen exhibiting the cold demeanour of a mafia hit-man waiting to 'ice' a rival. For a brief second Arazi seemed to go missing behind a wall of horses. But then Cauthen urged him into a gap between the two leaders and the crooked-blazed head shot out the other side like a jack-in-the-box. The Arazi who pounded down the Longchamp straight gave Europe a taste of his acceleration down the Churchill Downs' backstretch: only a hint because slow forgiving turf is not fast compacted dirt. He blasted the penultimate metric furlong in 11.90 and ran out the last quarter in 24.80 – over one and a half seconds faster than either of the other two Group One races over a mile that weekend. Cauthen was easing up when the post was reached; the official four-length margin of victory might've been multiplied to the factor of 'x' had he so desired.

> He was in good form and had worked brilliantly beforehand so I was hoping that had put him right for the race. It was the right distance and he'd no penalty to carry which meant meeting the others at favourable weights. He gave me a good 'feel' going to the start so I was hopeful. But given his series of setbacks I couldn't be more confident than that.
>
> He was fantastic. Before I asked him to go through a two-inch gap between Lucky Lindy and Calling Collect I felt I had plenty of horse – and hoped I was right. In two seconds he had

shot through and quickened away and clear. He ran straight and true, right to the line.

Arazi had shown Europe he was no back number. America would now get its opportunity to see the real Arazi of 1992 because he'd earned his ticket to the Breeders' Cup at Florida's Gulfstream Park on 31 October. But despite all the overtures from Sheikh Mohammed's camp on Cauthen's behalf, the mount stayed with Pat Valenzuela. After some prevarication, Arazi went for the Mile on grass rather than the ten-furlong Classic on dirt. The American public willed the genuine Arazi to appear. He entered the gate a 6/4 favourite; was third after a half-mile was covered in a white-hot 45.80; got buffeted into the hedge on the last turn; and went under the wire with just three of the 14 starters behind him.

One can detect the tinge of regret and sense of what might have been in Cauthen's voice and in his words when asked to sum-up one of his most enigmatic partners.

> I can honestly say Arazi was the greatest disappointment of my entire career as far as horses were concerned. I'd ridden a lot of good horses but this was the first horse I'd started to compare with Affirmed. He was only right three times that year. The week before the Kentucky Derby; before the Moulin, when he couldn't run; and then again for the Rond-Point. This was the day I became positive that the ground was the key to him. The horse loved the softer ground he got at Saint-Cloud and then in the Rond-Point. He was rolling like a freight train before he went to the Breeders' Cup and the hard ground at Gulfstream proved my gut feeling to be true. Clearly, after his knee problems, he appreciated some cut. He'd gone on the hard ground once but that was it.
>
> It had been a frustrating season. It was just unfortunate that he had so many problems and setbacks. He had such bad

luck. He could've done all sorts of things. Potentially, he had the scope to become a great horse. Riding Arazi was like riding in a Cadillac.

That was the last seen of a horse, at one point, Cauthen reckoned might, just might, put Affirmed in the shade. As it was, Arazi was rated equal third in the International Classifications in the seven furlongs-plus category, 4lb behind the filly Marling who'd won the Irish Guineas, Coronation Stakes and Sussex Stakes. His *Timeform* rating had dropped 11lb. Sheikh Mohammed acquired Paulson's 50 per cent and dispatched Arazi to the Dalham Hall Stud outside Newmarket at a fee of £20,000. In due course Arazi undertook stallion duties in Kentucky, Japan, Australia and even Switzerland before returning Down Under to spend his twilight years at Stockwell Stud in Digger's Rest near Melbourne. The best horse he fathered was probably Congaree, who won the Wood Memorial and Hollywood Gold Cup.

As Arazi's 31st birthday looms in 2020, the mail van still delivers requests for tail hair and shoes from the diminutive chestnut decorated with white that Steve Cauthen will forever remember as 'The Cadillac Colt'.

SEVEN

VALETE

CAUTHEN HAD by now won for himself the status of a respected 'elder statesman' in the weighing room alongside Lester Piggott, Pat Eddery, Willie Carson and Michael 'Muis' Roberts, the champion-elect for 1992 whose 206 winners would replicate the many double centuries he'd registered in his 11 South African championships. Furthermore, Cauthen's natural eloquence made him the logical spokesman on any issue causing concern to the jockey fraternity.

One such topic prone to ruffle feathers on a regular basis in 1992 as much as 2019 was the racing sin that dare not speak its name: use of the whip – or, to be more accurate, misuse of the whip. And when Cauthen was referred to the Jockey Club having been twice found guilty of its 'improper' use by the Goodwood stewards on 30 July 1992, it's fair to say the three-times champion, by his own impeccable standards of propriety, went ballistic at the perceived slur to his horsemanship.

The Goodwood watchdogs imposed a four-day ban for Cauthen misusing his whip 'down the shoulder in the forehand, and with unreasonable frequency' when riding Witness Box to finish second in the Goodwood Cup: the 'guideline' for the latter being ten hits. After Cauthen subsequently won the Levy Handicap on Daru, the stewards had him 'on the carpet' a second time for the same offence of striking down the shoulder – and referred him to Portman Square. Sussex gets pretty warm in mid-summer but the mercury in Cauthen's thermometer was threatening to break the glass. If not actually disgruntled by the attitude of the stewards, the former champion was, to steal a phrase from PG Wodehouse, 'far from being gruntled'.

When questioned on the BBC by Julian Wilson shortly afterwards, in what would be one of his last interviews on live television, Cauthen's eyes spoke as vehemently as his words: they were the kind of eyes one sees in a Kentucky beer-joint just before the first punch is thrown.

> The rule was brought in because of jump jockeys at the Cheltenham Festival overdoing it up the straight on tired horses. Hitting a horse in front of the saddle, down the shoulder, has never been an issue anywhere else in the world. I was taught to ride this way all my life. Using the whip in the forehand position as a corrective measure was the proper way we'd been taught to ride. Reg Hollinshead is one of the most respected tutors of young jockeys in England and he trains them to ride that way. And I've always done it in England, but only when necessary not as a practice. Some horses actually respond more to a slap down the shoulder than they do to one behind the saddle. Only a magician or an escapologist can do their jobs properly in a straitjacket. I tend to flick horses with the whip. I don't pulverise them. I'd never been considered a flogger of horses. Jockeys have been around horses all their lives and they love them. Why would you spit on your own supper?

Cauthen then commented over replays of the two races:

> I hit Witness Box 13 times, but the stewards were more worried about the fact I hit him down the shoulder five times with the whip in the upright position. I don't feel I abused Witness Box. He was lazy and every time I hit him he was responding. He was near the inside rail and I was trying to keep him straight and keep him running; if he'd brushed the rails it would've knocked

him off his stride and stopped his chance of winning. John Gosden was perfectly happy with the way I rode him. I'm the first to put the stick down when I know a horse has gone. Daru was coming down the outside of Muis Roberts's horse. He was a cagey old horse wearing blinkers for the first time. Muis's horse was coming out toward me and I was trying to avoid contact and any interference. I had to give Daru three taps down his right shoulder to stop him from bumping into Muis's horse. If we'd bumped I was afraid Daru might've stopped.

One can imagine the charged atmosphere as Cauthen was carpeted for the second time inside three hours for the same offence: that the American was 'taking the mickey' might not have been articulated aloud by the stewards, but it was certainly hanging in the air. To members of the English Establishment this kind of attitude toward authority amounted to insolence of the worst degree.

Cauthen concluded by saying:

I felt as soon as I walked into the stewards' room they thought I was just being bloody-minded in order to make the point I was going to carry on using the whip down the shoulder whatever they said. But that wasn't the case at all. I explained to them my reasons for doing it and I asked them what I should do – and they had no answer. And the idea, for example, that a jockey, locked in a tight finish with potentially millions of pounds at stake, can remember how many times he's hit a horse is the goofiest thing I've ever heard. You're so focused you don't even hear the roar of the crowd. You're wrong if you try too hard and wrong if you don't try hard enough.

To put Cauthen's reaction into context, one should state he'd never once drawn a ban for a whip offence in his entire English-based career; that ten hits was the number that triggered 'consideration' of an inquiry by the stewards and was not a hard and fast 'rule'; and that the rule relating to hitting down the shoulder was introduced in 1988 primarily with National Hunt jockeys in mind following a spate of incidents where a minority had taken to slashing their horses in front of the saddle.

Cauthen was accompanied to Portman Square for the hearing on 5 August by Eddery and Roberts, two men duelling for the jockeys' championship yet prepared to forego 14 valuable mounts between them to lend their support, plus the trainer of the two 'victims', John Gosden. They might've saved their travelling expenses. That Witness Box had responded to each stroke of encouragement and that both horses had been flicked down the shoulder as a corrective measure were arguments destined to fall on deaf ears. Cauthen was given an additional six days' suspension for his pains. Suffice to say, he didn't bother to lodge an appeal.

> I talked to most of the jockeys and they agreed that it was a bad rule and a difficult one for us to follow. It was a frustration to all jockeys. The whip is essential for encouraging horses and keeping them straight. The stewards needed to admit this rule was wrong. We tried to get the rule amended. But when we tried to explain our side of the story we seemed to be told that this is the rule, shut up and go and do what you are told. It was a case of having amateurs ruling over professionals. The rules were to appease animal rights people, who know virtually nothing about racehorses.
>
> Banning the whip is the craziest thing I've heard. Without it I'd never have won the Derby on Reference Point. Horses are like young children. It might not seem so but they're begging for guidance. The whip is a guide, telling him he's in a race and it's not time for sleep. Sending a jockey out minus a whip would be like sending someone down a hill in a car with no brakes. It's stupid.

In a manner of speaking, this unprecedented spat with authority and the eclipse of Arazi epitomised the waning of Cauthen's fortunes. The Sheikh Mohammed retainer brought mixed blessings. Quality struggled to keep pace with quantity. A 19 March victory on the Barry Hills-trained Touch Paper at Doncaster on his first ride of the 1992 season augured well enough and the numbers game peaked on 8 July with a six-timer the Sheikh (five trained by John Gosden) split evenly between Newmarket in the afternoon and Kempton in the evening. However, few wins came in races of any great consequence. During the two seasons as Sheikh Mohammed's retained rider, Cauthen supplied his boss with 188 wins, but there were only five Group Ones among them: Keen Hunter (Prix de l'Abbaye de Longchamp); Zieten (Middle Park Stakes); Rosefinch (Prix Saint-Alary); Kitwood (Prix Jean Prat); and Hailsham (Derby Italiano). These amounted to a poor crop by past harvests. In the bountiful seasons with Cecil between 1985 and 1990, Cauthen had presented the Sheikh with no fewer than 21 Group Ones. Cauthen's last group victory in the maroon-and-white jacket came courtesy of Lady Elizabeth in Saint-Cloud's Prix Eclipse (Group Three) on 5 October 1992.

> The Sheikh's operation had too many horses for one jockey to do the job properly. You're trying to ride the best out of 600 horses and at the same time keep all the trainers happy. Very often there would be four or five to choose from and each trainer thought they had the best horse for that particular race. Inevitably, that situation can lead to some conflict. My job was to get on the best horses and give the right advice. But it's not easy keeping tabs on so many horses from so many different yards.

Unbeknownst to the racing public, Cauthen had commenced a long goodbye with a number of poignant dues being paid. In June he flew to America for a New York swansong, riding the André Fabre-trained Cristofori in the Belmont Stakes for Sheikh Mohammed. The colt ran fourth behind AP Indy. It was Cauthen's first mount in an American Classic since that memorable Belmont afternoon 14 years earlier. Cauthen had ridden just 18 winners in his homeland after departing for England, but none since 1984; participation in three Breeders' Cups was fruitless; as was a trip to Santa Anita the previous November; and a fleeting visit to Canada's Woodbine on 18 October 1992 to partner Mashaallah in an abortive attempt on the Rothman's International proved to be his final mount in North America.

However, the Sheikh Mohammed retainer enabled Cauthen to repay his two principal English training allies. In April he rode a Group winner for Barry Hills on Sure Sharp in the Earl of Sefton Stakes (Group Three which turned out to be the 100th Pattern-race success of Hills's career; and five months later he supplied him with the Listed Macdonagh Boland Stakes at the Curragh on Norwich – his last win for his early English mentor and provider. There were also two Group victories for Henry Cecil: on Lord Howard de Walden's Rudimentary in the Gardner Merchant Mile (Group Two) and the Sheikh's Twist And Turn in the Chester Vase (Group Three). The last of the 418 winners he rode in total for Cecil came, fittingly, in the Sheikh's colours aboard Elkhart in a lowly Wolverhampton graduation race on 28 September. It was an afternoon for nostalgia. Later on, Cauthen rode the Sheikh's Iota to win a handicap for Julie Cecil. And, mindful of Cauthen's affection for his adopted home, there were a couple of successes in the Royal colours on Her Majesty's juvenile colt Sharp Prod at Epsom and Windsor.

Nor were students of the clock left out. In May of 1992, at his favourite York, Cauthen delivered yet one more masterclass in the art of winning a race from the front thanks to consummate pace judgement. Ever since Braulio Baeza had declared York's flat open spaces ideal for the successful application of even-time pace by engineering Roberto's victory over Brigadier Gerard, the Knavesmire had been waiting to host exhibitions of Cauthen's sleight of hand and mind. The vehicle in this latest renewal of the Dante was Alnasr Alwasheek.

Under the headline 'Classy Cauthen', my piece in the *Weekender* began as follows: 'Steve Cauthen's mount prevailed thanks to a ride from arguably the outstanding tactician currently performing in these islands. Comparison of the Dante's fractions with York's three other races over ten and a half furlongs shows how astutely Cauthen conserved the colt's speed for the decisive stages, even though he'd been obliged to set himself up as a target for other reputedly fast horses by making his own running.' I went on to point out how an hour earlier Shakela had covered the opening four and a half furlongs of the Middleton Graduation Stakes for fillies in 56.14, whereas Cauthen passed that point in 58.68. Thereafter, he began to increase the pressure via quarters of 23.90 and 22.74 in contrast to the 25.34 and 24.54 of the fillies. Nor, I stressed, was Alnasr Alwasheek noticeably stopping at the death despite being well clear: his furlong splits down the straight were a testament to sub even-time viz 11.59; 11.15; 11.36 and 11.80 – fractions neither Tuesday's Musidora Stakes nor Thursday's Glasgow Graduation Stakes could match.

Alnasr Alwasheek became Cauthen's final Derby ride. Starting third favourite, he looked as if he neither stayed nor acted on the track in coming a well-beaten seventh to Dr Devious. After further disappointing displays in the Juddmonte International and Prix Dollar, he was sent to race in America.

American racing, and American sports in general, are obsessed with 'numbers'. Status, greatness even, is measured by the 'numbers' accumulated in a career. Steve Cauthen's 'numbers' stack up. A total of 1,704 domestic winners marked his 14-year English Odyssey (easily surpassing Danny Maher's total); during the equivalent 14 years of their careers, Pat Eddery won 1,730, Lester Piggott 1,537 (that included 20 over hurdles) and Willie Carson 1,502. Cauthen's tally incorporated three jockeys' titles viz 1984 (130 wins); 1985 (195); and 1987 (197) – compatriots Maher and Lester Reiff only won two and one respectively. The last total was the closest any champion had got to a double hundred since Gordon Richards in 1952. In his homeland Cauthen rode 954 winners highlighted by that phenomenal 487 in 1977 (but just ten once based in England). Add another 136 wins garnered from across Europe (encompassing minor racing countries like Austria and Sweden besides Ireland, France, Italy and Germany) to far-flung Japan, Hong Kong, South Africa and Australia and his relatively brief 17 seasons in the saddle yielded 2,794 winners from 14,630 mounts – a ratio of one win every five rides. By comparison Eddery, Carson and Piggott fell short of the 2,000 mark in their initial 17 seasons; even the winner-hungry Richards amassed just 2,011. So, there's objectivity for you.

In terms of quality, Cauthen partnered 167 Group winners in Britain; a number easily increased by subsequent changes in Pattern-race designation. At the highest level, his tally reached 33. Adding 15 from France, seven from Italy, six from Ireland and four from Germany gives a European total of 65 Group Ones. Subsequent elevation of races then of lower status, such as the Lockinge, St James's Palace, Nassau and Sun Chariot to name just four, would inflate the figure by a further 17. The one that got away, and hurt the most, was beyond question: the Prix de l'Arc de Triomphe. Add 13 Grade Ones in three American seasons and Cauthen's global return at the elite level reaches 78.

The collection of European Classics ultimately reached 20 thanks to Possessive Dancer's Irish Oaks of 1991 and Mashaallah's Irish St Leger of 1992. It narrowly missed becoming 21 (notwithstanding voluntarily missing the Irish Oaks success on Alydaress owing to his brother's wedding) had Marling enjoyed a happier passage from the rear of the field in the One Thousand Guineas of 1992 and not failed by a head to catch Hatoof; the stewards held an inquiry lasting 30 minutes before confirming the result.

Possessive Dancer, on the other hand, gave Cauthen one of the smoothest rides he'd had in a Classic when beating the Epsom Oaks winner Jet Ski Lady by half a length at the Curragh on what was the jockey's very first ride for young Newmarket trainer Alex Scott. The Gosden-trained Mashaallah began the season winning a handicap off a mark of 96. His victory in an ultra-competitive all-aged Irish Classic featuring the 1990 Doncaster St Leger winner Snurge, the Ascot Gold Cup winner Drum Taps and the future Melbourne Cup winner Vintage Crop, proved markedly different to the filly's. The outcome had seemed plain sailing the moment Cauthen urged the four-year-old into the lead entering the straight; but the colt had to be rousted to hold off Snurge by a neck.

Cauthen's Classic haul comprised ten English (at least one in each Classic), five from Ireland, three from France and two from Italy (albeit one of them only rated Group Two). In both England and America he'd won a Triple Crown. And he's the single jockey to have won the Derby and the Kentucky Derby – with the Irish, French, Italian, Scottish and Ulster versions thrown in for good measure. In America his three Classic wins from four appearances still has a special ring to it.

The final winner of the 'English Odyssey' came on 30 October 1992 aboard the Michael Stoute-trained Shaiba in the Soham House Stakes at Newmarket. The two-year-old colt ran lazily and required all Cauthen's guile to get home by a neck. Cauthen took his final six mounts in England at Doncaster on 7 November. Four of them were for Sheikh Mohammed, all starting favourite, and included Refugio for Henry Cecil. But the closest to a farewell winner were the second spots earned by Daru in the November Handicap and Keen Hunter in the Listed sprint. Mount number 557 that brought down the curtain on his season and his love affair with England was Gone Savage, sent out by Toby Balding for the five-furlong Armistice Handicap. The four-year-old gelding, on whom Cauthen had won a Sandown handicap back in July, challenged the leaders below the distance but was swallowed up in a typically tight sprint finale to come seventh.

Accolades were duly bestowed. In 1994 Cauthen was inducted into America's National Museum Racing Hall of Fame; ten years earlier he'd been the recipient of the George Woolf Memorial Jockeys Award that recognises 'a career and conduct exemplifying the very best of participants'. Britain lacks anything of similar prestige. But a *Racing Post* assessment of the '50 Greatest Jockeys of the 20th Century' placed Cauthen at number eight in the list headed by Gordon Richards and Lester Piggott – but seven places above his great adversary Pat Eddery. Of his other contemporaries, Walter Swinburn was at 17, Willie Carson 19, Joe Mercer 24, Frankie Dettori 33 and Kieren Fallon 50.

Greatness, it's said, lies in the pages of history. And the aforementioned laurels and statistics ensure the name of Steve Cauthen will forever be found in those pages. But objectivity can't measure style and grace. Destined to tarry longer in the mind's eye is the thing of beauty that was the vision of Steve Cauthen finessing a thoroughbred racehorse in full cry, a marriage as harmonised and elegant as the satinwood veneer on a Sheraton table.

Cauthen knew the score. There was no need to scrutinise the wall for any writing. He was no longer 'The Kid' prepared to live on the oxygen of winners. That slip of a boy had grown up. He was now a family man with a child on the way. Here was an intelligent and articulate 32-year-old with any number of options other than dashing from one country to another on a diet a Spartan would complain about. The youth of 1979 who could make eight stone was long gone. The message of those large hands and feet had been delivered. By the time the pomp seasons commenced at Warren Place the minimum his five-feet-six-inch frame could manage was 8st 4lb; by the time he left in 1990 it was officially 8st 7lb – although it had not gone unnoticed that he'd persistent trouble making 8st 10lb. The debatable decision to 'flip' – gorge and regurgitate – as a means of satisfying the craving to eat but not gain the weight was an option long since abandoned for the danger to his health that it was. His summer diet now consisted of little more than black coffee, lettuce leaves and slivers of tomato. No way was he going to risk an early grave like Danny Maher.

> I never really had any intention of riding until I was 50 or 60 because I knew that in the long run there were too many other things I would get interested in. From the day I started racing, I knew my longevity would be limited. I always wished I'd been a lot smaller so I could've ridden longer. But I knew the biggest threat was my size. I wasn't 4ft 11in any more. I was 5ft 6in and my natural weight was 10st. If I wasn't I'd probably be riding now! I gave it my best shot and I quit because I was sick of fighting the battle. You end up with a monastic existence – and I enjoyed life. But I got 17 years, which was wonderful.
>
> Not even people who shed surplus fat by the ton can appreciate what it's like to stay one stone underweight. Basically, you just don't eat. Twenty-four hours a day I was thinking of eating. I was bulimic at times. That was no fun at all - and at some point you crack. Riding a Group One winner for someone who then treats

you to a fancy dinner you can't eat even though food is all you're thinking about is terrible. At Ascot one time someone spilled water over a tiny smoked salmon sandwich I was saving for my supper; I'd not eaten for three days - and I lost it completely! I'd come away from Royal Ascot later on wondering if I'd make it through the season with my weight. I was about ready to walk off a cliff.

I used to be able to put my fingers round my ankles, and that's how I measured my weight. If I couldn't get my fingers round my ankles I knew I was heavy. Although I could get down to nine stone without too much difficulty, everything after that was a real struggle. Very occasionally I could ride at 8st 8lb but generally 8st 10lb was my minimum. I preferred to diet rather than sweat because sweating is just a temporary thing. All you're doing is jerking the fluid out of your body, dehydrating yourself. You can go only so long before damaging your health. Nothing worth having comes easy. I wish I could've ridden at lower weights – it would've been terrific! Now eating isn't the focus of my day I don't think about it until I really do get hungry!

I never had any doubts that I would ride out my career in England. I was glad I came. I loved what I did, the good fortune, the excitement, the people. I fell in love with the country and felt accepted. I did everything I wanted to do, even though I could probably have gone on if it hadn't been for my weight. I feel I rode ten years longer than I would have because I came to Europe – that actually extended my career. I feel very fulfilled about my career and I left no stone unturned, except maybe that I didn't win a Prix de l'Arc de Triomphe.

Cauthen's future was settled over the Christmas of 1992.

I had a telephone call on Christmas Eve telling me Sheikh Mohammed wanted to reduce my retainer by 40 per cent. I'd had every intention of returning to Europe in 1993 but I wasn't happy accepting that reduced offer. At first I was annoyed. I knew they needed to reorganise but I was a legitimate expense. I was the one proven thing they had. The pay cut was not related to reality.

To be honest, it made me feel unappreciated. We'd had no proper Group One horses to race in 1992. We were running Group Two and Three horses in Group Ones, expecting them to win and getting beat. I stole two Group Ones on Kitwood and Rosefinch, they shouldn't have won. I never saw myself running around chasing a few bad mounts just to keep riding. I had nothing left to prove and I was still young enough to do something else.

I didn't think I'd be a public trainer. I was very fortunate to have been around a lot of good trainers and I didn't stand around like a bump on a log. I tried to learn as much as I could. I felt I'd the interest and ability to help bring horses on but, at the same time, when you set up a public racing stable you're taking an awful lot on and I wasn't sure I wanted all that. There were too many other ways I could be involved without becoming a trainer. I had the farm back home and I was also interested in TV work. And I'd have a wife stuck at home on her own while I'm running around Europe. It would be tough on her. So it was either accept the terms or quit. I quit. The wisdom of the decision was made plain when Muis Roberts took the job and they wanted him out after six months.

Sheikh Mohammed, and the other Arab owners, realised they had the best horses and so they didn't have to pay jockeys to ride for them. It was the perfect time to bow out. Sheikh Mohammed was just doing business. I don't hold anything against him. We didn't part on bad terms at all and that means a lot to me.

In January 1993 it was announced that Cauthen had rejected Sheikh Mohammed's terms for the coming season. No one else was capable of offering Cauthen a retainer matching the money and horse-power he'd turned down; and there clearly were insufficient 'spares' likely to satisfy his aspirations. It was time. Time to go home. Racing had bestowed 17 good years on Cauthen. And Cauthen had rewarded racing with 17 years of rich memories in return. 'Racing will never be the same without Steve Cauthen,' said the man who brought him to England, Robert Sangster. 'On a rainy day at Redcar or Leicester he would put 10 per cent on the gate.'

> If the right offer had come along, say in England or Hong Kong, where the weights were higher, I'd have taken it in two seconds. When I retired from riding I realised I would never be as good at anything else in my life. But for a lot of different reasons it was the right thing for me to do. I loved what I did but realised long before I retired that riding was not a long-term thing for me. I'd kill myself if I'd kept trying to race forever and ever.
>
> I found my wife; and realised there were many more things important to me than just riding. I began to put things in perspective. Money and success are great, but they're not everything.

The journey had ended; its work completed. The first *canto* was long preserved in the annals of the Turf. The anguish of the second relegated to a footnote. Redemption was attained. And the saga concluded with an acclamation that would echo down the hallways of history. To leave while the public cried for more was tough, yet sensible. Valete. The 'Odyssey' was over.

> I think I rode in one of the best eras. In America I was up against Willie Shoemaker, Ángel Cordero, Jorge Velásquez and Chris McCarron. In Europe I was taking on Lester Piggott, Pat Eddery, Willie Carson, Yves Saint-Martin and Freddy Head. They were the best around. Lester was probably in his heyday in the earlier 1970s, just before my time. That's when he was jocking everybody off! But he was still the toughest to come

up against. Lester always tried to make sure he was on the best horse and once he was he'd ride with lots of confidence, afraid of nothing. I consider myself lucky to have been riding against such a great bunch of jockeys.

The rewards in the game are not just financial. I was successful but success is overrated. I enjoyed winning. But when you get down to it, it's the people around you, the trainers and the stable staff, who stick with you and make it worthwhile.

And if I inspired any kids to do something with their lives than just sit around then that's got to be a start. That's what life is all about, striving to achieve something, and if I set a good example then I'll feel I've achieved something too.

Racing's a great sport, with beautiful animals and lots of really nice people, from the stable lads to the Queen. If I was a good ambassador for the sport, that's basically because I am what I am. It's as simple as that.

The 'English Odyssey' may have concluded but the dream of watching Cauthen race-ride again proved no flight of fancy. The front page of Louisville's *Courier-Journal* on 22 May 2000 announced: 'The Kid rides again! Cauthen's Crown still shines after 22 years.' The previous day Cauthen had competed in the Blood-Horse Sportsman's Challenge over two miles at the Kentucky Horse Park in aid of two charities, Central Kentucky Riding for the Handicapped and the Horse Park's own Foundation. Young Katelyn Cauthen had wanted to see her dad ride. Her wish was granted; aided, one suspects, by the yearning of every former sportsman to revisit past glories. 'The bug's still there,' Cauthen confessed to reporters. 'I guess I'll always have the bug. I just hope I don't come up empty in the final furlong!' An ecstatic Bob Elliston, president of Turfway Park where Cauthen is a vice president, invoked images of a legendary Boston Red Sox 'slugger': 'It's like Ted Williams coming out of retirement to take one more swing at Fenway Park.'

On this occasion, however, it was a case of 'venit, vidit, vincere non' as 'The Kid' could only persuade Flyfisher into eighth place.

> I was knackered at the end! It was like the Epsom Derby to the other jocks and it got a little testy toward the finish. I was okay for the first mile but then things got a bit chaotic and hectic!
> I did it for my girls. But when I dismounted Katelyn said to me: 'Dad! What happened? I thought you were meant to be good!'
> I think I'm really retired now!

The mantle of Sheikh Mohammed's retained rider and the go-to jockey for all and sundry passed to Frankie Dettori. The flamboyant Italian was a perfect fit for a brasher, flashier, age and during his 18-year tenure sporting the royal blue silks of the Sheikh's Godolphin operation he collected top-flight wins as if they were going out of fashion – including two successes in Cauthen's *bête noire*, the Prix de l'Arc de Triomphe. But fine jockey as he proved himself, Dettori's legacy will fall short of anything revolutionary in the manner of Cauthen, whose toe-in-the-iron style was aped by others anxious not to look old-fashioned and whose trademark victories from the front based on pitch-perfect pace judgement changed the attitude of our jockeys towards forcing tactics and sent jockey after jockey across the Atlantic during the off-season the better to develop a 'clock-in-the-head'. Consequently, mindful of that legacy, we are left echoing Mark Antony's words at the passing of Caesar: 'When comes such another?'

The wait continues. And with each passing season Cauthen's talents and exploits become more entrenched in the past as the nefarious tendency to salute the 'latest' as the 'greatest' tightens its grip. But for those interested in the genuine article the advice is the same as in the late 1970s. Just drive about 70 miles up the Interstate and look at the sky. There's a star in the East.

APPENDIX I:
WINNERS BY SEASON

	USA	GB (Position)
1976	240	DNR
1977	487*	DNR
1978	209	DNR
1979	8	52 (17)
1980	5	61 (10)
1981	1	87 (7)
1982	1	107 (3)
1983	0	102 (5)
1984	3	130*
1985	0	195*
1986	0	149 (2)
1987	0	197*
1988	DNR	104 (5)
1989	0	164 (2)
1990	0	142 (3)
1991	0	107 (4)
1992	0	107 (7)
TOTAL	**954**	**1,704**

Rest of World	136
GRAND TOTAL	**2,794**

* Champion Jockey

APPENDIX II:
ENGLISH CLASSICS

Two Thousand Guineas **(Group One)**
1979 **Won Tap On Wood (Barry Hills) 20/1; 20 ran**
1980 11th Saint Jonathon (Barry Hills) 9/1; 14 ran
1981 10th Motovato (Barry Hills) 5/1; 19 ran
1982 2nd Wind and Wuthering (Henry Candy) 8/1; 26 ran
1983 9th Wassl (John Dunlop) 9/2; 9 ran
1984 4th Rainbow Quest (Jeremy Tree) 11/2; 9 ran
1985 7th Lanfranco (Henry Cecil) 10/1; 14 ran
1986 8th Faustus (Henry Cecil) 12/1; 15 ran
1987 3rd Midyan (Henry Cecil) 12/1; 14 ran
1988 6th Intimidate (Clive Brittain) 16/1; 9 ran
1989 5th Monsagem (Henry Cecil) 20/1; 14 ran
1990 8th Sure Sharp (Barry Hills) 9/1; 14 ran
1991 2nd Lycius (André Fabre) 16/1; 14 ran
1992 9th Alnasr Alwasheek (Michael Stoute) 5/2 fav; 16 ran

One Thousand Guineas
1979 4th Topsy (Geoff Wragg) 10/1; 17 ran
1980 5th Rapids (Barry Hills) 25/1; 23 ran
1981 13th Auction Bridge (Barry Hills) 33/1; 14 ran
1982 5th Slightly Dangerous (Barry Hills) 4/1; 15 ran
1983 9th Ski Sailing (Barry Hills) 11/1; 18 ran
1984 3rd Desirable (Barry Hills) 8/1; 16 ran
1985 **Won Oh So Sharp (Henry Cecil) 2/1 fav; 17 ran**
1986 9th Lady Sophie (Henry Cecil) 9/1; 15 ran
1987 7th Invited Guest (Robert Armstrong) 12/1; 14 ran
1988 3rd Diminuendo (Henry Cecil) 6/1; 12 ran
1989 Did Not Ride
1990 8th In The Groove (David Elsworth) 11/1; 10 ran
1991 6th Dartrey (Michael Stoute) 9/1; 14 ran
1992 2nd Marling (Geoff Wragg) 5/1; 14 ran

Derby
1979 12th Tap On Wood (Barry Hills) 15/2; 23 ran
1980 13th Saint Jonathon (Barry Hills) 33/1; 24 ran
1981 16th Kind of Hush (Barry Hills) 25/1; 18 ran
1982 13th Father Rooney (Barry Hills) 28/1; 18 ran
1983 11th The Noble Player (Barry Hills) 16/1; 21 ran

1984 13th Claude Monet (Henry Cecil) 12/1; 17 ran
1985 **Won Slip Anchor (Henry Cecil) 9/4 fav; 14 ran**
1986 3rd Mashkour (Henry Cecil) 12/1; 17 ran
1987 **Won Reference Point (Henry Cecil) 6/4 fav; 19 ran**
1988 7th Unfuwain (Dick Hern) 9/2; 14 ran
1989 10th Prince of Dance (Dick Hern) 11/2; 12 ran
1990 14th Razeen (Henry Cecil) 9/2 fav; 18 ran
1991 8th Hailsham (Clive Brittain) 28/1; 13 ran
1992 7th Alnasr Alwasheek (Michael Stoute) 9/1; 18 ran

Oaks
1979 8th Rheinsparkle (Barry Hills) 20/1; 14 ran
1980 6th Pieces of Gold (Giles Besson) 100/1; 11 ran
1981 9th Canton Lightning (Barry Hills) 33/1; 12 ran
1982 3rd Last Feather (Barry Hills) 11/2; 13 ran
1983 5th Ski Sailing (Barry Hills) 7/2; 15 ran
1984 3rd Poquito Queen (Barry Hills) 7/1; 16 ran
1985 **Won Oh So Sharp (Henry Cecil) 6/4 fav; 12 ran**
1986 Did Not Ride
1987 PU Scimitarra (Henry Cecil) 5/2 fav; 11 ran
1988 **Won Diminuendo (Henry Cecil) 7/4 fav; 11 ran**
1989 **Won Snow Bride (Henry Cecil) 13/2; 9 ran**
1990 Did Not Ride
1991 6th Dartrey (Michael Stoute) 7/1; 9 ran
1992 Did Not Ride

St Leger
1979 12th Cracaval (Barry Hills) 4/1 jt fav; 17 ran
1980 Did Not Ride
1981 Did Not Ride
1982 Did Not Ride
1983 Did Not Ride
1982 2nd Baynoun (Fulke Johnson Houghton) 5/2; 11 ran
1985 **Won Oh So Sharp (Henry Cecil) 11/8 on fav; 6 ran**
1986 2nd Celestial Storm (Luca Cumani) 6/1; 8 ran
1987 **Won Reference Point (Henry Cecil) 11/4 on fav; 7 ran**
1988 Did Not Ride
1989 **Won Michelozzo (Henry Cecil) 6/4 fav; 8 ran**
1990 3rd River God (Henry Cecil) 100/30; 8 ran
1991 Did Not Ride
1992 2nd Sonus (John Gosden) 15/2; 7 ran

APPENDIX III:
OTHER CLASSICS WON

IRELAND (Group One)
One Thousand Guineas
1990 In The Groove (David Elsworth) 5/1; 12 ran
Derby
1989 Old Vic (Henry Cecil) 11/4-on fav; 8 ran
Oaks
1988 Diminuendo (Henry Cecil) 9/2-on fav; 9 ran
1991 Possessive Dancer (Alex Scott) 8/1; 10 ran
St Leger
1992 Mashaallah (John Gosden) 11/4 fav; 9 ran

FRANCE (Group One)
Prix du Jockey-Club
1989 Old Vic (Henry Cecil) 47/10; 12 ran
Prix de Diane
1987 Indian Skimmer (Henry Cecil) 10/9 on fav; 11 ran
Prix Royal-Oak
1986 El Cuite (Henry Cecil) 54/10; 10 ran

ITALY
Group One Derby Italiano
1991 Hailsham (Clive Brittain) 9/2; 20 ran
Group Two Premio Regina-Elena (One Thousand Guineas)
1989 Miss Secreto (John Dunlop) 11/2; 15 ran

UNITED STATES (Grade One)
Kentucky Derby
1978 Affirmed (Laz Barrera) 9/5; 11 ran
Preakness Stakes
1978 Affirmed (Laz Barrera) 2/1 on fav; 7 ran
Belmont Stakes
1978 Affirmed (Laz Barrera) 5/3 on fav; 5 ran

APPENDIX IV:
SELECTED OTHER MAJOR RACES WON

GREAT BRITAIN
G1 Coronation Cup: Time Charter (1984); Triptych (1988); In The Groove (1991)
G1 Gold Cup: Gildoran (1984): Paean (1987)
G1 St James's Palace Stakes: Shavian (1990)
G1 Coronation Stakes: Chimes of Freedom (1990)
G1 Eclipse Stakes: Pebbles (1985)
G1 King George VI and Queen Elizabeth Stakes: Reference Point (1987)
G1 July Cup: Never So Bold (1985)
G1 Benson and Hedges Gold Cup: Cormorant Wood (1984)
G1 Matchmaker International: Triptych (1987)
G1 Juddmonte International: In The Groove (1990)
G1 Yorkshire Oaks: Diminuendo (1988)
G1 William Hill Sprint Championship: Never So Bold (1985)
G1 Champion Stakes: Cormorant Wood (1983)
G1 Cheveley Park Stakes: Desirable (1983)
G1 Middle Park Stakes: Creag-An-Sgor (1983); Gallic League (1987); Balla Cove (1989); Zieten (1992)
G1 Racing Post Trophy: Be My Chief (1989); Peter Davies (1990)
G2 Prince of Wales's Stakes: Kind of Hush (1982); Stagecraft (1991)
G2 St James's Palace Stakes: Horage (1983)
G2 King's Stand Stakes: Indian Ridge (1989); Elbio (1991)
G2 King Edward VII Stakes: Lanfranco (1985); Bonhomie (1986); Private Tender (1990)
G2 Ribblesdale Stakes: Alydaress (1989)
G2 Hardwicke Stakes: Khaipour (1984); Orban (1987)
G2 Trusthouse Forte Mile: Pebbles (1985); Reprimand (1989); In The Groove (1991)
G2 Forte Mile: Rudimentary (1992)
G2 Temple Stakes: Never So Bold (1985)
G2 Dante Stakes: Claude Monet (1984); Reference Point (1987); Alnasr Alwasheek (1992)
G2 Yorkshire Cup: Mountain Kingdom (1989)
G2 Child Stakes: Meiss El Reem (1984); Chimes of Freedom (1990)
G2 Nassau Stakes: Nom de Plume (1987)
G2 Goodwood Cup: Heighlin (1982); Gildoran (1984)

G2 Geoffrey Freer Stakes: Baynoun (1984)
G2 Celebration Mile: Shavian (1990)
G2 Great Voltigeur Stakes: Reference Point (1987); Zalazl (1989); Belmez (1990)
G2 Gimcrack Stakes: Reprimand (1987)
G2 Lowther Stakes: Dead Certain (1989)
G2 William Hill Sprint Championship: Sharpo (1982)
G2 Park Hill Stakes: Lucky Song (1989); Madam Dubois (1990); Patricia (1991)
G2 Flying Childers Stakes: Abeer (1978); Gallic League (1987)
G2 Fillies Mile: Invited Guest (1986); Diminuendo (1987)
G2 Royal Lodge Stakes: Gold and Ivory (1983); Bonhomie (1985); Sanquirico (1987)
G2 Sun Chariot Stakes: Cormorant Wood (1983)
G3 Lockinge Stakes: Motovato (1982); Cormorant Wood (1984)
G3 Doncaster Cup: Spicy Story (1985)
Scottish Derby: Prince Roland (1980); Jalmood (1982)
Chester Cup: Arapahos (1980)
Cambridgeshire Handicap: Braughing (1981); Risen Moon (1990)
Extel Handicap: Indian Trail (1981)
Free Handicap: Motovato (1981)
Lincoln Handicap: Mighty Fly (1983)
Magnet Cup: Straight Man (1984)
Royal Hunt Cup: Mighty Fly (1983); Vague Shot (1987)

IRELAND
G1 Moyglare Stud Stakes: Chimes of Freedom (1989)
G2 Tattersalls Rogers Gold Cup: Opera House (1992)
G2 Beresford Stakes: Gulf King (1986)
G3 Larkspur Stakes: Storm Bird (1980)
Ulster Derby: Dowland (1991)

FRANCE
G1 Prix Saint-Alary: Indian Skimmer (1987); Rosefinch (1992)
G1 Prix d'Ispahan: Indian Skimmer (1989)
G1 Prix de l'Abbaye de Longchamp: Committed (1984); Keen Hunter (1991)
G1 Prix Jacques le Marois: Lirung (1986)
G1 Prix Jean Prat: Lapierre (1988); Kitwood (1992)
G1 Grand Prix de Saint-Cloud: Diamond Shoal (1983); Acatenango (1986)

APPENDIX FOUR: SELECTED OTHER MAJOR RACES WON

G1 Grand Prix de Paris: Risk Me (1987); Saumarez (1990)
G2 Prix Maurice de Gheest: Never So Bold (1984)
G2 Prix d'Harcourt: Panoramic (1992)
G2 Prix Hocquart: Nasr El Arab (1987)
G2 Prix Eugene Adam: Pollen Count (1992)
G2 Prix de Pomone: Patricia (1991)
G2 Prix du Rond-Point: Arazi (1992)
G2 Prix du Conseil de Paris: Village Star (1987)

ITALY
G1 Gran Criterium: Tanque Verde (1985)
G1 Premio Roma: Orban (1987)
G1 Gran Premio d'Italia: El Cuite (1986)
G1 Gran Premio di Milano: Diamond Shoal (1983); Mashaallah (1992)
G1 Gran Premio del Jockey Club: Gold and Ivory (1984)

GERMANY
G1 Aral-Pokal: Almaarad (1988)
G1 Preis von Europa: Gold and Ivory (1984)
G1 Grosser Preis von Baden: Diamond Shoal (1983); Gold and Ivory (1985)
G2 Bavarian Classic: Malmsey (1992)
G3 Hessen-Pokal: Hot Touch (1984)
G3 Bayerisches Zuchtrennen: Imperial Fling (1979)
G3 Oettingen Rennen: Miner's Lamp (1980); Enharmonic (1991)

UNITED STATES
G1 Californian Stakes: J.O. Tobin (1978)
G1 Futurity: Affirmed (1977)
G1 Hollywood Derby: Affirmed (1978)
G1 Hopeful Stakes: Affirmed (1977)
G1 Laurel Futurity: Affirmed (1977)
G1 San Luis Rey Stakes: Noble Dancer II (1978)
G1 Turf Classic: Johnny D. (1977)
G1 United Nations Handicap: Noble Dancer II (1978)
G1 Washington DC International: Johnny D. (1977)
G1 Whitney Handicap: Nearly On Time (1977)
G2 Excelsior Handicap: Turn And Count (1977)
G2 Jim Dandy Stakes: Affirmed (1978)
G2 Los Angeles Handicap: J.O. Tobin (1978)
G2 Malibu Stakes: J.O. Tobin (1978)

G2 Sanford Stakes: Affirmed (1977)
G2 San Felipe Handicap: Affirmed (1978)
G3 Affectionately Handicap: Illiterate (1977)
Busanda Stakes: Like Ducks (1977)
Gallant Fox Handicap: Frampton Delight (1976)
Premiere Handicap: J.O. Tobin (1978)
San Bernadino Handicap: J.O. Tobin (1978)
Toboggan Handicap: Great Above (1977)

APPENDIX V:
BEST HORSES (Timeform Highest Rating)

COLTS

139 Reference Point
136 Slip Anchor; Old Vic
135 Never So Bold
134 Rainbow Quest; Shardari
132 Wind and Wuthering; Teenoso; Saumarez
131 Celestial Storm; Unfuwain; Belmez; Opera House
130 Tap On Wood; Sharpo; Diamond Shoal; Cacoethes
129 Hawaiian Sound
128 Baynoun; Strawberry Road; Salse
127 Risk Me; Acatenango; Shady Heights; Glacial Storm; Michelozzo; Stagecraft
126 Shaadi; Hot Touch; Naheez; Village Star; Wolfhound
125 Last Fandango; Wassl; Drumalis; Bonhomie; Shavian; Mountain Kingdom; Elbio; Tel Quel; Brush Aside
124 Horage; Midyan; Lirung; Gold and Ivory; Most Welcome; Shining Finish; Lycius; Arazi
123 Gildoran; Lanfranco; Indian Ridge; Damister; Shining Steel; El Cuite; Paean; Orban; Mashaallah

2YO COLTS

134 Storm Bird
132 Reference Point
128 Gold and Ivory
127 High Estate
126 The Noble Player; Sanquirico
123 Be My Chief
122 Creag-An-Sgor
120 Peter Davies

FILLIES

135 Pebbles
133 Indian Skimmer; Miesque; Triptych
131 Oh So Sharp; Time Charter
130 Cormorant Wood; Sun Princess

128 Committed
127 In The Groove
126 Diminuendo
124 Meis El-Reem; Marling; Alydaress
123 Dead Certain; Rafha
122 Slightly Dangerous
121 Fatah Flare; Snow Bride; Chimes of Freedom; Madame Dubois
120 Last Feather; Gull Nook; Bluebook

2YO FILLIES

127 Forest Flower
115 Desirable; Bluebook
114 Dead Certain
112 Gwydion; Chimes of Freedom

ACKNOWLEDGEMENTS

FIRST, I'M indebted to Steve Cauthen for taking the time to speak with me and finding the patience to answer all my questions, several of which he must've fielded a hundredfold since his meteoric entry into the Turf firmament in 1976: without his co-operation and words the project would have been sorely lacking.

I'm also in debt to Robin Oakley for permission to quote from his own interviews conducted with Steve towards his biography of Barry Hills; these extracts are attributed in the text.

Thanks are also owed to Jimmy Lindley and John Hanmer for recalling times past; and to Allan Carter at America's National Museum of Racing for providing Steve's seasonal record of winners in the United States. I am especially grateful to George Selwyn for painstakingly searching his photographic archive to unearth bygone images that illustrate the peerless Cauthen style whilst demonstrating his own peerless ability with a camera.

The following secondary sources were consulted: Axthelm *The Kid* (Paddington Press 1978); Cecil *On the Level* (Harrap 1983); Hughes and Watson *My Greatest Training Triumph* (Michael Joseph 1982); Magee and Bayes *Champions* (Sidgwick & Jackson 1980); Miklowitz *Steve Cauthen* (Grosset and Dunlap 1978); Mitchell *Steve Cauthen* (Partridge Press 1987); Oakley *Frankincense and More: The Biography of Barry Hills* (Racing Post 2010); Oakley *Clive Brittain: The Smiling Pioneer* (Racing Post 2012); Raceform *Flat Annuals 1979 to 1992;* Reid *Emperors of the Turf* (Macmillan

1989); Rickman *Eight Flat-Racing Stables* (Heinemann 1979); Sahadi *Affirmed: The Last Triple Crown Winner* (Thomas Dunne Books 2011); Scott *Henry Cecil: Trainer of Genius* (Racing Post 2013); Tanner *Great Jockeys of the Flat* (Guinness 1991); Tanner *Great Racing Partnerships* (Sportsman's Press 1987); Tanner & Cranham *Great Jockeys of the Flat* (Guinness 1991); Timeform *Racehorses of 1979 to 1992;* Tuttle *Steve Cauthen: Boy Jockey* (Putnam's Sons 1978).

These magazines and periodicals proved fruitful: *Horse and Hound; Maclean's; Owner Breeder; Pacemaker; Paulick Report; People; Sports Illustrated; SportsWorld; Stars and Stripes; The Blood-Horse; The Badminton Magazine; The Cincinnati Magazine; Thoroughbred Daily News.* Among the many newspapers consulted were: *Daily Express; Daily Mail; Daily Mirror; Daily Racing Form; Irish Examiner; Los Angeles Times; Louisville Courier-Journal; New York Post; Racing Post; Sporting Life Weekender; Sunday Express; The Daily Telegraph; The Independent; The New York Times; The Observer; The Sporting Life; The Sunday Times; The Times; The Washington Post.*

To all those scribes whose words filled the pages and columns of the aforementioned goes my undying gratitude.

Finally: a raised glass in the direction of Brough Scott who championed the merits of sectional timing before me; advanced my involvement with *Channel 4 Racing*; and brought the value of this project to the attention of others; plus a sincere nod of appreciation to Michelle Grainger for exercising tolerance on a grand scale with an ageing author while steering this edition through production.